Number 7

Alexander Hamilton's Secret Attempts to Control American Foreign Policy

Number 7

Alexander Hamilton's Secret Attempts to Control American Foreign Policy

WITH SUPPORTING DOCUMENTS

———————————•~•———————————

by Julian P. Boyd

PRINCETON, NEW JERSEY

PRINCETON UNIVERSITY PRESS

1964

For one who fitly bears the name of Grace

Contents

Foreword

IN 1923 when Samuel Flagg Bemis published his path-breaking *Jay's Treaty, a Study in Commerce and Diplomacy*, he brought to the attention of the scholarly world the relationship between Alexander Hamilton, Secretary of the Treasury under George Washington, and Major George Beckwith, aide and emissary of Lord Dorchester, Governor General of Canada. The principal documents delineating that relationship—the reports made by Beckwith to Dorchester and to the British Secretary for Foreign Affairs—had been published earlier by Douglas Brymner, Archivist of the Dominion of Canada, as a part of his *Report* for 1890. But it was not until Bemis fitted these materials into his survey of the Anglo-American commercial and political background of Jay's Treaty that the use made by Hamilton of Dorchester's aide came into clearer focus. On the basis of these and a vast array of other sources Bemis demonstrated beyond question that the principal architect of the Treaty of 1794 was not John Jay, who negotiated it, but Alexander Hamilton, who laid the foundation for it by his indefatigable efforts to bend American foreign policy toward a closer connection with Great Britain, the first of these efforts after Hamilton entered office being addressed to the British ministry through Beckwith as early as 1789.

Indeed, so exhaustive were Bemis' researches and so penetrating was his analysis that *Jay's Treaty* still stands almost half a century later as the classic account of the first commercial treaty between Great Britain and the United States. A tribute to its formidable achievement lies in the simple fact that no historian has yet provided the amplification that Bemis himself would be among the first to acknowledge as an imperative need—a narrative account and systematic analysis at full length of the economic and political relations between the two countries in the first decade after the united colonies were formally recognized among the powers of the earth as having attained "the separate and equal station" to which they had declared themselves entitled. Bemis' background survey for the Treaty of 1794 will remain the trusted guide as it is the standard authority. But his canvas was perforce limited and the important supplementary task remains.

It has, in fact, become an urgent need in view of the almost total neglect of the impact of foreign influences on domestic institutions in this formative period. These influences were both cohesive and disruptive. It is scarcely too much to say that during these early years the gravest threats to the existence of the United States were external in origin, though historians have confined themselves largely to the internal divisiveness, the tendencies to separatism, and the turbulencies of the post-war period as being the primary dangers to the union. John Fiske's *The Critical Period of American History* is seventy-five years behind us, Charles A. Beard's *Economic Interpretation of the Constitution* is half a century away, and yet we are in the midst of a debate over the nature of the forces that led to the climactic stage of an evolving federalism rooted deep in colonial experience. Indeed the battle rages so furiously over the extent of the franchise, the distribution of real and personal property, the structure of society, and the diverse motives of debtors and creditors, farmers and merchants, back inhabitants and eastern townsmen, that the central issues seem hidden from all save specialists. It is in fact necessary at times even for those who are specialists to consult the guide to the battlefield that one scholar has had the humanity to compile for the benefit of contestants and bystanders alike. Such din and confusion seem not to have been echoed in the writings of Adams, Madison, Franklin, Jefferson, and other leaders, to say nothing of debtors and creditors, farmers and merchants, mechanics and artisans in stations of obscurity. The problems were many and grave on the domestic scene and the solutions were hotly debated from motives both high and low in origin. But to leaders and thoughtful people alike the step from a loose confederation to a stronger federal union, whether by extensive amendment or by total revision, was generally understood as a clear necessity and unified control over commerce equally regarded as the first essential.

Yet with agriculture the chief occupation of the people and its handmaiden commerce universally recognized as their principal reliance, it is strange that the search for the guiding impulses to union in this formative period seems to have stopped at the water's edge, as if the more perfect union with its commerce clause was formed in a domestic vacuum in which Shaysites, bankruptcy legislation, stay laws, paper money, and competitive tariffs among the states put—as John Marshall nervously expressed it—all sound principles of government afloat. In the writings of Bemis, Morison, Schlesinger, Graham, Setser, and others we do have some notable assessments of the impact of maritime factors and foreign influences upon domestic issues. But little if any attention has been given to the possibility that Lord Sheffield in his writings and Lord Hawkesbury in his stubborn adherence to mercantilist doctrine in its most orthodox form as the foundation of British policy may well have contributed more to the convoking and to the success of the Federal Convention of 1787 than many who sat in that august body.

There were to be sure other cohesive forces for union, most particularly the intangible power generated in the emotions of men by the mere fact of nationhood and by the transcendent ideals expressed in the Declaration of Independence. Men who chose the motto *Novus Ordo Seclorum* for the great seal of the union could not have been unaware of the potent force for nationality existing in the belief of many if not most Americans that this was in fact a new order of the ages in which they were destined for leadership. But the British Navigation Act of 1784 that excluded New Englanders from the West Indies, put the tobacco planters of Virginia at the mercy of London factors, and sent Nantucket whalemen petitioning for succor under British or French flags was a most powerful factor having a direct relationship to the commerce clause of the Constitution, as well as to the intangible spirit of nationality. The factor undergirding the formation of British policy in these years—the need to hold the empire together by preserving dominion on the high seas—is understandable. But to the historian if not to Sheffield and Hawkesbury the effect upon Americans of an increasingly rigorous mercantilist system is equally understandable. That effect was to prolong and to exacerbate during peace the role that Great Britain had occupied during war—that of a menacing hostility, however unintended, which quite naturally strengthened the bonds of union. The effect was in no wise diminished by the fact that, in keeping with the hope that a new era was dawning in the affairs of men, the United States had proffered to Europe a new system of commercial reciprocity and only the Netherlands, Sweden, Prussia, and Morocco had given their almost meaningless acceptances. Britain did not even deign to notice the offer made in 1786 by John Adams and Thomas Jefferson.

In these circumstances even *Publius* argued in *The Federalist* that the national government should be given power over commerce in order that it might be in a position to retaliate against restrictive measures taken by other nations. But that was the last time that Hamilton ever agreed with Madison and Jefferson on such a political use of the commerce power. Thenceforth, at least so far as England was concerned, whenever these two statesmen endeavored to advance the system of commercial reciprocity and its corollary exclusions against those not in treaty with the United States—an unprecedented system to which the nation had committed itself from the beginning and which Jefferson would even have extended so far as to make reciprocal all of the rights of citizenship among the contracting powers—Hamilton and the leading Federalists regarded their effort as being in effect a declaration of economic warfare against the country upon whose commerce, so their argument ran, the whole Hamiltonian system of finance and indeed the very existence of the nation depended. The argument has not been challenged by historians but it is unconvincing, if for no other reason than that its employment years earlier would have prevented the birth of the nation in the first place. But there are also other reasons, among them the willingness of Amsterdam bankers—a class of men not noted for either vacuity or recklessness—to underwrite loans to the United States long before the new system of national finance was established. John Adams saw this very clearly.

But if the commercial policy of England provided the most powerful of the external forces for cohesion, there were other factors threatening to pull the newest member of the family of nations apart. A young republic alone in a world of old monarchies, the United States was caught between the opposing aims of France and England and, like any neutral nation in the shadow of rival powers, was both a beneficiary and a victim. Each of these ancient enemies eyed the latest sovereign with cautious apprehension, fearing its revolutionary ideas, alert to use it as a makeweight in the balance of power, watchful not to commit an aggression but ready to take advantage of weakness or confusion, and all the while insinuating influences as far into its councils and affecting its decisions as much as possible. Spain blocked the trade of the western territories at the mouth of the Mississippi, the most important portal of the continent, and, using both bribes to leaders and lures to settlers, endeavored to loosen the bonds holding the trans-Allegheny inhabitants to their eastern countrymen. England looked on with close attention, if not encouragement, as the Allens in Vermont and their counterparts in Kentucky talked more and more of coming to terms with a nation that could protect their local interests. All up and down the great arc of the frontier from New Hampshire to Georgia there arose the specter of new and independent states seeking by intrigue to establish foreign connections. With two foreign powers holding possessions on her flanks to the north and south, with astute Indian leaders in both areas playing dangerous and unscrupulous games of international intrigue, with Spanish, French, and English agents roaming the country and conspiring among the settlements at her back, and with a wall of mercantilism blocking her in front and patrolled by the most powerful navy on earth, the youngest sovereign seemed not so much on the path to power and glory as on the way to a speedy disunion. In this predicament, in addition to the spirit and nature of her people, she possessed two obvious weapons. The first was a policy of neutrality that she feared, with good reason, could be violated at will by European powers. The second was the instrument of commercial retaliation that she had employed before the Revolution and would resort to again in 1807. What she did not need above all was to have either of these weapons blunted or destroyed by foreign influence penetrating her highest councils. But this is what she got.

"The worst Evil that can happen in any Government," wrote John Adams, "is a divided executive."[1] After the experience of his first term, Washington grimly declared that he would never knowingly bring into office any man whose tenets were adverse to those of the government—that, he said, "would be a sort of political Suicide."[2] Both men spoke from bitter experience. Alexander Hamilton voiced the same opinion before coming into office. "Energy in the executive," he wrote in *The Federalist*, "is a leading character in the definition of good government." He then placed first in importance among all of the elements requisite for an energetic executive that of "unity."[3] The principle of administration was elementary and no doubt the Secretary of the Treasury uttered the words with conviction. But the unity that he professed to place at the apex of his system of administrative theory was a principle that he himself —hailed as one of the greatest of administrators—was the first to violate, not as an isolated instance but as a consistent and characteristic pattern of behavior.

The present brief study is concerned with the manner in which the first Secretary of the Treasury through intrigue with Dorchester's agent endeavored to commit the government of the United States to a policy toward Great Britain at variance with that officially agreed upon. This intrigue began in the autumn of 1789

[1] Adams to Pickering, 31 Oct. 1797, MHi: AM; text in Adams, *Works*, ed. C. F. Adams, VIII, 560.
[2] Washington to Pickering, 27 Sep. 1795, MHi: Pickering Papers; text in Washington, *Writings*, ed. Fitzpatrick, XXXIV, 314-16.
[3] *The Federalist*, ed. Jacob E. Cooke, p. 471-2.

and was carried on with the strictest secrecy. It has been necessary to emphasize the clandestine nature of the relationship because it has been generally assumed that Major George Beckwith, in the absence of any formal diplomatic channels between the two countries, acted as a sort of *de facto* though unofficial minister and that he was regarded by the administration as such. This assumption has no basis in fact. Beckwith was a secret agent engaged in reporting upon American affairs. There is no evidence that either the President or the Secretary of State was aware of the true nature of his role until, in mid-summer of 1790, Hamilton felt obliged to make a momentary—and naturally a partial—disclosure of his connection with the intelligence agent. On that occasion, born of a threatened war between England and Spain, Hamilton not only did not disclose to Washington and Jefferson the extent or nature of the conversations between himself and Beckwith in the preceding months, but he went far beyond the mere act of violating his own cardinal principle of administrative unity—far indeed beyond the limits of honorable conduct in public office. For what the Secretary of the Treasury did on this occasion was to commit almost the gravest offense of which a cabinet officer can be guilty in his role of responsible advisor to the head of state. At a time when general war in Europe threatened and in the face of urgent decisions that this fact imposed upon the new republic, Hamilton misrepresented the attitude and intent of a foreign power and compounded this misrepresentation by fabricating rumors about the President's own official representative in London, Gouverneur Morris. There can be no doubt that the misrepresentation and the fabrication were deliberate and calculated.

They form, in fact, a part of the pattern of Hamilton's sustained effort to guide the conduct of American foreign policy that began in the autumn of 1789 and culminated in the Treaty of 1794. It was the Secretary of the Treasury who recommended the appointment of Gouverneur Morris as the President's accredited agent to London to sound the British ministry on its disposition to discuss the serious problems outstanding between the two countries. The ill-advised mission was doomed from the start to a predictable failure. When this was recognized to be so in the autumn of 1790, it was also Hamilton who placed the blame not where it belonged but upon the innocent and unsuspecting agent of the President. The act of misrepresentation by which he thus sought to salvage his own clandestine plans was based on such transparent inventions that Washington, though failing to guess then or ever the author of the deception, was not misled.

Such, in brief, is the episode in American foreign affairs in the first year of Thomas Jefferson's incumbency of the office of Secretary of State to which this short study is addressed. It is offered as a sort of footnote to Bemis' *Jay's Treaty*—almost literally so, for in substance it comprises the long introductory note to a group of documents appearing in Volume 17 of *The Papers of Thomas Jefferson*. The importance of the episode has long been recognized, but both its significance and the meaning of the pertinent documents must be reappraised in the light of the grave disclosures now made concerning the conduct of the Secretary of the Treasury. This is the principal justification for separate publication of the documents and their editorial comment, together with such additional explanation as is made necessary by their removal from the larger context of the edition for which they were first prepared.

In view of the gravity of the disclosures here set forth about one of the leading political figures in the history of the nation, it may not be inappropriate to suggest in this separate publication that the method of arriving at these disclosures is one that belongs primarily to editorial scholarship. Some have doubted the wisdom of comprehensive undertakings to edit and publish the total corpus of a statesman's papers, and there is no doubt that sense and discrimination must be rigorously applied in determining when such fullness is justified. But the editorial scholar who has assumed the responsibility for defining the central body of documentation belonging to a great man's recorded words and actions, for relating this to the larger body of the records of his age, for confronting every page of every variant text of each particle of this mass, for accounting for enclosures, memoranda, and every other ascertainable document that passed under his subject's eye and impinged upon his consciousness, and for presenting the result in systematic order with disciplined comment—such a scholar has assumed obligations of collation, comparison, and investigation that the biographer and the historian in their necessarily selective tasks are not normally called upon to meet in the same manner or in the same degree. The scholarly editor may not elect to employ any text of a document written or received by a statesman. He must employ all discoverable texts and to each of these he must address questions that the historian or the biographer usually does not have the need or the time to ask. What, for instance, called this particular text into being? What purpose did it serve? In what respects and why does it vary from other texts? What is the significance of these variations for the author or for the reader? It goes without saying that the editor like the historian must ask first of all: Is this document authentic? But even on this primary obligation there is a vital difference. The editor asks the question invariably, habitually, and searchingly of every document that he encounters and his ears must be attuned to the ring of a false note or he fails in the first test that justifies his existence, that of presenting a dependable body of authenticated documents. His first duty is to establish authenticity. His method is no more guaranteed to produce truth automatically than any other, but his systematic effort to meet this overriding obligation seems more likely to result in the isolation of unreliable texts than is the case with other means of historical investigation. His is a method with an old tradition, once esteemed as indispensable and now much misunderstood, that needs to be sustained for the results that it alone can achieve.

It was thus in facing my normal obligations as editor of the comprehensive edition of the papers of the first American Secretary of State that I encountered the memorandum of July 8, 1790 and the letter of September 30, 1790 that the Secretary of the Treasury addressed to the President of the United States. Neither of these documents that purported to be faithful communications of dependable facts could withstand the tests that an editor is obliged to apply. Both were palpable and demonstrable misrepresentations of a gross nature touching upon matters of the highest public import. For purposes of comparison, these two communications, together with Grenville's dispatch to Dorchester, Dorchester's instructions to Beckwith, and two of Beckwith's reports of conversations with Hamilton, have been added to the group of fifteen documents concerning the Anglo-Spanish war crisis of 1790 as printed in Volume 17 of *The Papers of Thomas Jefferson.*

With this act of deception there opened a decade of divisiveness in the highest councils of the state and among the people that might aptly be called the most critical period yet experienced by the young republic.

JULIAN P. BOYD

Princeton, New Jersey
July 5, 1964

Acknowledgment

THIS volume, as indicated in the Foreword, is an outgrowth of *The Papers of Thomas Jefferson*. Like the series from which it stems, it owes much to the interest, encouragement, and resourcefulness of three generous friends at the Princeton University Press, to whom my debt is greater than anyone save I can know: Herbert S. Bailey, Jr., Director and Editor; Miss R. Miriam Brokaw, Managing Editor; and P.J. Conkwright, Typographer. The task of seeing both the detached part and the whole through the press simultaneously created a number of complications and problems which they solved with their customary patience and ingenuity. Mrs. Dorothy S. Eaton of the Manuscripts Division of the Library of Congress; Dr. Oliver W. Holmes, Executive Director of the National Historical Publications Commission; and Miss F. Helen Beach, Archivist attached to the same useful public agency, are three other valued friends who have assisted this publication with the same zeal and generosity they have given to the *Papers* over the years. As always, L. H. Butterfield, colleague and friend in many editorial and other enterprises, has contributed his unfailing interest, expert knowledge, and criticism. I am especially indebted to him for his careful reading of the proofs. I acknowledge with much gratitude the benefaction of the Guggenheim Fellowship that enabled me to do research for this volume in England; the good offices extended by Ambassador David K. E. Bruce, Chairman of the Advisory Committee of *The Papers of Thomas Jefferson*; the kindness of G. G. Fortescue, Esq., Boconnoc, Lostwithiel, in granting me access to the papers of Lord Grenville; the assistance rendered by that remarkable agency, the National Register of Archives, through Miss W. D. Coates, Registrar, and her associates; and the civilities and aid extended by Mr. S. S. Wilson, Keeper of the Public Records, and Mr. Harold C. Johnson, Deputy Keeper, the Public Record Office. Unpublished Crown Copyright material in the Public Record Office has been reproduced by permission of the Controller of Her Majesty's Stationery Office. I am happy to have this opportunity of expressing my enduring gratitude to the New York Times Company and to the Ford Foundation for the generous grants that have sustained *The Papers of Thomas Jefferson*.   J.P.B.

Number 7

Alexander Hamilton's Secret Attempts
to Control American Foreign Policy

The Role of
Major George Beckwith

On 1 May 1790 Gouverneur Morris reported to Washington his most recent discussion with the British Secretary for Foreign Affairs. He was as unaware at the time as any Londoner that in the crucial cabinet meeting the night before William Pitt boldly took the risk of general war by seizing upon the Nootka Sound incident to deliver the first effective challenge to Spanish claims to exclusive rights of sovereignty and commerce in the Pacific since the origin of those claims in the forgotten Treaty of Tordesillas of 1494.[1] Morris' report, accompanied by private letters describing the excitement of the 6th of May when the issue was disclosed to a shocked nation, arrived in New York late in June. For the next four months war seemed inevitable, with the issue hanging on the question whether France would honor the Family Compact by supporting Spain. Despite debt and mounting taxes, England under Pitt's leadership seemed to embrace the danger eagerly: "a mad Credulity prevails here," one observer in London wrote as late

[1] Morris to Washington, 1 May 1790, Vol. 16: 532-5; a dramatic account of the beginning of the crisis is in Rutledge to TJ, 6 May 1790. For the general background, see W. R. Manning, "The Nootka Sound Controversy," Am. Hist. Assn., *Ann.Rept.*, 1904, p. 363-87; Bemis, *Jay's Treaty*, p. 70-85. Sparks, *Morris*, II, 4-56, contains the whole of Morris' correspondence with Leeds and of his reports to Washington. See also TJ's report on Morris' correspondence, 15 Dec. 1790.
Morris did guess that something was going on behind the scenes, possibly indicating war. He wrote Washington after his first conference with the Duke of Leeds: "from his Countenance and Manner on the Perusal of your Letter, he seemed to derive from it that Sort of Pleasure which a Man feels at the Removal of Something which every now and then brings to his Mind disagreeable Ideas. I do not exactly see from what Cause this Emotion was produced. By the Eagerness of his subsequent Expressions I conjectured that the critical Situation of Europe had excited some Disquietude respecting the Part which the United States might take in Case of a general War. What strengthened that Idea, and perhaps led me to form it was that in a Chamber to which I was introduced previous to the Audience there was a large Book of Maps open at that of Poland. But the Silence since observed leads to a suspicion that his Satisfaction was derived from another Source. I am told that in a late Debate the Ministers committed themselves by throwing out in pretty clear Terms the Idea that some sort of Treaty was on the Carpet with America; and if so, the Opening now given must have relieved them from the fear of future Contradiction" (Gouverneur Morris to George Washington, 13 Apr. 1790; RC in DLC: Washington Papers). The atlas in the antechamber open at the map of Poland may have been an intentional miscue for visitors to the Foreign Office, but there is no doubt that Washington's letter brought a sense of relief to the cabinet.

as November, "just as it did at the Commencement of the American War, we despise our Enemy, and dream of nought but Victory, and the capture of Spanish Wealth, the Mines of Mexico and Peru are already ideally in our Possession."[2] Simultaneously with the arrival of Morris' report in New York, the Governor General of Canada, Lord Dorchester, received important secret dispatches reflecting the concern of the ministry at the part the United States might play in a conflict between two powers possessing territories that encircled it.[3]

Dorchester at once sent his aide-de-camp, Major George Beckwith, hurrying down from Quebec on his fifth and final mission to the United States as confidential agent. In New York on the morning of the 8th of July Beckwith was closeted with the Secretary of the Treasury. At noon the latter reported to the President about the conversation with Dorchester's emissary, the Secretary of State also being present. Jefferson's preferences on commercial relations with England, on the unsettled issues of the Treaty of Peace, on preserving good neighborhood to the north and south, on binding the "men on the western waters" to the union, and on the paramount necessity of opening the navigation of the Mississippi were clear and had long been known. But the threat of a general European war brought into conjunction at mid-summer of his first year in office a complex set of forces that made it virtually impossible for the administration to speak with a coherent voice on foreign policy. All came to agree that this should be one of neutrality and Washington firmly supported Jefferson in defining that policy. But the extent to which the surface unity was undermined by the countervailing efforts of the Secretary of the Treasury was wholly unknown at the time to the President and the Secretary of State and has since been obscured by misconceptions of Beckwith's role in the United States between 1787 and 1792. This fact has unavoidably affected interpretations of matters of far greater moment than the missions of the able and respected officer whom Jefferson called, without derision, "the poor Major." That role must therefore be defined with some precision, particularly as it related to the initial appointment of Gouverneur Morris as the President's personal agent in London and also to the events set in motion by the war crisis of 1790. This becomes obligatory in view of the fact that the documents tracing the evolution of Jefferson's policy cannot be understood unless the validity of those to which in some degree they are a response is assessed.

When the Archivist of Canada, Douglas Brymner, first published some of Beckwith's reports in 1890, he stated that the agent was employed by Dorchester "in the absence of any resident recognized diplomatic agent from Great Britain" and that he was regarded by Washington's administration as "a real, although unofficial diplomatic agent, acting on behalf of the British government."[4] This estimate has been

---

[2] John Barker Church to Alexander Hamilton, 3 Nov. 1790, Syrett, *Hamilton*, VII, 136-7.

[3] Grenville to Dorchester, Dispatches Nos. 22-24, all dated 6 May 1790 and all marked "Secret"; PRO: CO 42/67, f. 87-9, 91-2, 93-102; texts printed in Brymner, *Report*, 1890, p. 131-3.

[4] Brymner, *Report*, 1890, p. xxxvi, xli.

accepted as accurate and indeed has been confirmed by emphasis and amplification.[5] Beckwith himself added to misconceptions of his role by stating three years after the event that in 1789 he bore a message from Grenville "to The Executive Government of the United States, on the subject of a discrimination of duties" and that this "led to certain overtures on the part of their Government . . . communicated by Lord Dorchester."[6] Both assertions are in error. Beckwith's mission was not to the government but to those individuals in and out of office known to support views friendly to Great Britain. While such persons expressed their opinions freely to Beckwith and these were promptly reported to Quebec and London, no overtures "on the part of their Government" were ever made in consequence of his missions. At no time from 1787 to 1792 was the agent clothed with public authority, informal or otherwise, either by Dorchester or by the British ministry, in such a way as to authorize him to speak for one government to another government. When Beckwith's agency was brought into the open in July 1790, Washington and Jefferson at once grasped the true status of the emissary without suspecting the full extent of his confidential role.[7] The subject of recognition or even of direct negotiation never arose because, as Hamilton himself said he told Beckwith, it was "out of question." Jefferson never held any conversation with the agent until his final mission had closed.[8] That Beckwith should have been

[5] For example, in "The United States and the Abortive Armed Neutrality of 1794," AHR, XXIV (Oct. 1918), 29, Bemis states: "Alexander Hamilton . . . had for five years been in confidential communication with the British Minister, George Hammond, and with Major George Beckwith, in an informal sense his predecessor." In 1940 Mayo stated that Beckwith "had been employed in the United States by Dorchester as confidential agent, and later by the Foreign Office itself as Great Britain's informal representative, from 1787 to the arrival of Hammond in October of 1791"; "Instructions to British Ministers, 1791-1812," ed. Bernard Mayo, Am. Hist. Assn., Ann.Rept., 1936, III, 21n. Bemis, Jay's Treaty, p. 57-9, 96-8, has the fullest and best account of Beckwith's role, but he goes so far as to suggest that Washington, after consulting members of the cabinet as well as Adams and Jay, made the "decision of the government not to extend any official recognition to Dorchester's aide, who carried no proper credentials." In this and in other respects Bemis' account differs from the interpretation set forth in the present analysis. See also Bemis, "Thomas Jefferson," in American Secretaries of State and Their Diplomacy, ed. Bemis, II, 27-9; Malone, Jefferson, II, 273, 309; Miller, Hamilton, p. 367-8; Freeman, Washington, VI, 269-70; Syrett, Hamilton, V, 482.

[6] George Beckwith to Henry Dundas, 20 June 1792, PRO: FO 4/12; text printed in Bemis, Jay's Treaty, p. 377-80.

[7] Washington, Diaries, ed. Fitzpatrick, IV, 139; TJ to Morris, 12 Aug. 1790, Document VIII below.

[8] Early in 1792 TJ wrote the following memorandum which he deposited in the files of the Department of State: "Colo. Beckwith called on me and informed me that tho' not publicly commissioned he had been sent here on the part of his government, that arriving before I came into office *he had been put into the hands of another department*, not indeed by the Chief Magistrate directly as he had never had any direct communications with him, but informally, and had never been transferred to my department: that on commencing his correspondence with the Secretary of State of Gr. Britain he had thought it his duty to make that circumstance known to us: that Mr. Hammond's arrival had now rendered his longer continuance here unnecessary, as his residence hitherto had been only preparatory to Mr. Hammond's reception, that he had received orders by the last packet from the Secretary of State to return to England by the next, and that

led to mistake the nature of his role is quite natural. He had access to men of influence in all branches of the government who at times spoke of themselves as the governing majority. It is particularly understandable that he should have regarded himself as dealing with the "Executive Government of the United States" when he held discussions with the Secretary of the Treasury. Hamilton said nothing at all to avoid creating such an impression, much to deepen it.

Major George Beckwith (1753-1823) came from a very distinguished military family of Yorkshire. His father was Major-General John Beckwith, who commanded the 20th regiment at Minden and who later served under Frederick II of Prussia. George Beckwith's rise in rank and his subsequent career prove him a man of talent and integrity. He was commissioned an ensign of the 37th regiment in 1771 and embarked the same year for America. He distinguished himself with that unit in active service throughout the war. He was made lieutenant of the 37th in 1775, captain in 1777, major in 1781, lieutenant-colonel in 1790, and colonel in 1795, the last two grades being partly in recognition of his missions in America between 1787 and 1792. In 1779 he served as aide to General Wilhelm von Knyphausen, perhaps because as a youth he had acquired a knowledge of the German language during his father's service in Prussia.[9] At the end of the Revolution he was appointed aide to Sir Guy Carleton. When the latter returned to Canada in 1786 as Lord Dorchester, young Beckwith—he was about two years older than the Secretary of the Treasury—went with him. In 1787 Dorchester sent him on the first of his missions to the United States.

The nature of Beckwith's role cannot be properly understood unless a distinction is made between the two periods into which his activities fall. The first period covered the four missions that he undertook between the spring of 1787 and the spring of 1790. The second covered

he should accordingly do so. He acknoleged the personal civility with which he had been treated generally, and his entire satisfaction. [Note this was the first conversation I ever had with him but merely as a private gentleman. I note it's purport because he was sent here by Ld. Dorchester from Quebec, which consequently authorises us to send such a character to Quebec]"; MS in TJ's hand, dated 12 Feb. 1792, in DNA: RG 59, MLR; not recorded in SJL or SJPL (brackets in MS, but emphasis supplied). It is possible that by 1792 Beckwith had persuaded himself that he had been sent to New York by his government and that this was done preparatory to the sending of a minister. It is also possible—such being the state of party animosities at the time—that he was urged by Hamilton to give such an account of his presence in New York and Philadelphia.

9 Beckwith achieved rank as a major-general in 1798 and as lieutenant-general in 1805. He served as governor of Bermuda (1797), St. Vincent (1804), and Barbadoes (1808), commanding the British forces in the West Indies and South America. For his conquest of Martinique in 1809 he was voted the thanks of both houses of Parliament and the same year he was created a knight of the Bath; DNB; MAH, X (1883), 330; Van Doren, *Secret History*, p. 260-3, 278-9, 321-2, 410-3; Bemis, *Jay's Treaty*, p. 58-9. Beckwith's father, after serving in the Prussian army, visited Paris in 1779 and offered his services to Franklin in the Continental army. Franklin declined on the ground that he had no authority to make such appointments (Beckwith to Franklin, undated, Franklin Papers, PPAP; Franklin to John Beckwith, 17 May 1779; Franklin, *Writings*, VII, 315). Franklin had known General John Beckwith in London (PMHB, LX [1936], 470-1).

his residence of nineteen months in New York and Philadelphia that began with the interview of the morning of the 8th of July with the Secretary of the Treasury.

In the three years from 1787 to 1790 Beckwith's role in the United States was that of secret agent serving under Lord Dorchester as Governor General of Canada. Like John Connolly whom Dorchester sent into the Northwest Territory early in 1788, Beckwith was part of an extended system of intelligence activity in America that was supplied with funds by the British government and received orders from it or from Dorchester. The object of that activity, of course, was the acquisition of information, the establishment of connections with influential Americans, and the cultivation of sentiments favorable to the interests of Great Britain. Its presence was manifested in such sensitive areas as Vermont, Kentucky, the borders of Florida and Louisiana, and the principal cities of the Atlantic seaboard. Those engaged in it operated covertly and often effectively, being aided by Tory refugees in London, by the United Empire Loyalists of Canada, and by their adherents in the United States who, in varying degrees of loyalty or disloyalty to the young republic, were friendly to or identified with "the British interest." The unifying bonds of friendship, family, and commerce, strengthened by preferences for monarchical over republican government, naturally did not terminate at the borders of the United States or cease with the Treaty of Peace. Their existence indeed provided the sinews of party division on the great issues that the nation faced in its formative years. As one of Beckwith's informants told him, there were at the beginning of the Revolution many Americans "who opposed Great Britain in certain points, who had no views of a separation and who were drawn on step by step into the measure of Independence; and many others much against their inclination, and without the power of looking back." There was not a gentleman from New Hampshire to Georgia, he added, "who does not view the present government [under the Articles of Confederation] with contempt, who is not convinced of its inefficiency, and who is not desirous of changing it for a Monarchy."[10]

Intelligence agents such as Beckwith found that these natural and powerful bonds of interest, consanguinity, and political principle opened up sources of information that in Europe would have required the outlay of vast sums of money. From 1790 to 1801 Lord Grenville in the Home and Foreign Offices disbursed the very considerable sum of £841,902 sterling for secret service operations in the diplomatic field alone, including £100,597 for the same period expended by George Hammond, who served as minister to the United States from 1791 to 1794.[11] No evidence is available to indicate what portion of this sum

10 Beckwith's report, enclosed in Dorchester to Sydney, 10 Apr. 1787, PRO: CO 42/50, f. 92, 94-9. William Samuel Johnson was almost certainly the person who made this statement.

11 Declaration of Account, 20 Feb. 1790 to 20 Feb. 1801, PRO: AO 1/ Bundle 2121; another account for the same period gives the total as £837,342, as stated "on protestation of honor" 31 Mch. 1801, PRO: AO 3/949. Neither of these accounts provides a detailed analysis of times, places, or purposes of disbursement; many letters between Hammond and Grenville in 1801 discuss secret service ac-

was devoted to intelligence activity in America, but it is very unlikely that more than a minute fraction, if any, could have been so employed. There was little need to purchase influence or information when friends, connections, and sympathizers, often in high place, made their services freely available as a quite natural consequence of the bitter divisions of civil war. Those who remained skeptical of the equalitarian principles of republicanism and who had not the power of looking back possessed nevertheless the means and the will to support those principles still claiming a residual allegiance. There were also the motives of ambition for position and power that prompted some not merely to serve Dorchester's emissary but also to make use of him.

Though the circumstances were as different as those of war and peace, Beckwith's role in this first period was in reality a resumption of the secret service operations he had carried on in the closing years of the war. As aide to Knyphausen while Sir Henry Clinton was absent on expeditions against Charleston and Newport in the spring and summer of 1780, Beckwith had handled the correspondence with Benedict Arnold as the treason plot unfolded, being addressed on one occasion as "G[eorge] B[eckwith] Ring [two rings were employed, one kept by Beckwith and one sent to Arnold to prove authenticity of messages] Executor to the late John Anderson, Esq. [Major John André] in care of James Osborne [the Rev. Jonathan Odell]." He was almost certainly the "officer in the department of the adjutant general" of the British commander-in-chief who made it possible for William Heron, the American double spy, "frequently to obtain important and very interesting intelligence" for General Samuel Holden Parsons, thus keeping this channel open for Clinton's intelligence service.[12] When Major Oliver DeLancey of the prominent Loyalist family of New York succeeded Major André in the office of adjutant general, Beckwith was his assistant along with Major Thomas MacKenzie.[13] These officers, aided also by Col. Beverley Robinson, a Loyalist, drew up in 1781 "Proposals for a Plan of Gaining Intelligence" that had for its object the opening of correspondence "with persons of consequence in different parts of the country." As one of the most experienced of these officers in intelligence work, Beckwith was probably the principal author of this scheme, as he was certainly the one most actively engaged in putting it into operation. All intelligence received was systematically recorded in a manuscript volume entitled "Private Intelligence . . . For Sir Henry Clinton," accompanied by another volume labelled "Information of Deserters and others not included in Private Intelligence," being almost entirely in Beckwith's hand.[14] These records of letters, conversations, and reports from deserters, Loyalists, and spies were continued until 19 July 1782

---

counts, but none in America; Grenville Papers, Boconnoc, bundle marked "Hammond."

[12] Parsons to Washington, 6 Apr. 1782, DLC: Washington Papers.

[13] MAH, X (1883), 330.

[14] Originals of both are in Emmett Collection, NN, and some extensive selections from the first are printed in MAH, X (1883)-XII (1884); Van Doren, *Secret History*, p. 406; texts of the André-Arnold correspondence in which Beckwith figures are conveniently accessible in same, p. 439-81.

when the volume called "Private Intelligence" was closed. The next day Beckwith alone assumed responsibility for secret service duties as aide to Sir Guy Carleton, who had succeeded Clinton as commander of the British forces. He continued to direct this intelligence activity up until the moment of Carleton's evacuation of New York late in 1783. If anything, his espionage work in this period of relative peace at the close of the war was heavier than during the period when the issue of the contest was still in doubt. For in the sixteen months between 20 July 1782 and 18 Nov. 1783 Beckwith's expenditures for secret service operations amounted almost to a fifth of the total spent by Sir Henry Clinton for such purposes during the critical years from 1778 to 1782, Beckwith's being £4,495 sterling and Clinton's £24,878 sterling.[15]

Thus for at least three years before the end of the war Beckwith had been stationed in New York with important responsibilities at the center of intelligence activities. He had become familiar with the leading Loyalist families of the city and with refugees of similar leanings from Pennsylvania, New Jersey, and New England. When he returned to Canada with Dorchester in 1786, therefore, he was the logical choice as a confidential agent to re-establish connections in the city where he had gained such an intimate knowledge of the attitudes of leading personages. Dorchester later made it clear that this, in fact, was the reason for his being chosen for the role—thus providing also the tribute of Beckwith's commanding officer to the competence with which he had discharged his secret service duties in wartime.[16] When he arrived in New York early in 1787, Beckwith was once again among friends, having ready access to homes and positions of influence.

This very fact has helped to obscure the true nature of his role as a secret agent. Such consular and commercial agents as Sir John Temple, Phineas Bond, George Miller, and John Hamilton regularly dispatched reports to Whitehall that duplicated some of the information sent by Beckwith. Indeed, in respect to commerce and economic conditions their reports, especially those of Bond, possessed much greater value than his. Dorchester was well aware of the fact that the ministry received intelligence from such sources and his initial purpose in sending his aide to New York was to satisfy himself about American affairs as these affected his own situation in Canada. But Beckwith opened up sources of information on matters of policy of such great importance as to give his reports a value in this respect greater than that of all intelligence gathered by others. Beckwith, Dorchester, and Grenville must have been astonished to find their recent enemies so fully and freely communicating their views and aims—even their cabinet secrets—to the confidential agent of a foreign power. The very success of the mission produced a natural and obvious change in the character of Beckwith's role, a change reflected even in the sums of money spent by him.

As a military intelligence officer in wartime, as noted above, Beck-

---

[15] Beckwith's Declaration of Account, 4 July 1785, PRO: AO 1/Bundle 2121; Account of Paymaster John Smith, 20 Dec. 1782, PRO: AO 3/118.

[16] Dorchester to Grenville, 7 July 1790, referring to his private letter to Sydney of 24 Oct. 1788 in which a similar view was expressed, PRO: CO 42/68, f. 252-3.

with had spent £4,495 sterling. In the three years from 1787 to 1790 his four missions cost a total of £224 5s. 11d. In the year and a half from 1790 to early 1792 his disbursements totalled £1,156 3s 4d.[17] The conclusion suggested by these figures is clear. During the war, Beckwith was obliged to employ informers, reward deserters, and pay for intelligence; in the first period of his peacetime services in New York he operated covertly and his expenses were such as a British army officer on his travels might have had; in the second period his activities were more open though still largely hidden from the government, his costs being amplified by the need to maintain a residence and to offer hospitality to friends and persons of influence; and in neither of these periods were the sums large enough to indicate that information or influence was procured by rewards in the classic European sense. Success of remarkable proportions transformed the secret agent into a means of communication, not between two powers in any diplomatic sense but between Great Britain and those friendly to her policy. Nor did the change wholly remove the element of secrecy.

Beckwith's changing role is further shown in the changing nature of his reports. The first report of March 1787 revealed how strong a monarchical sentiment prevailed in New York and showed what little expectations some Federalists had for the forthcoming Federal Convention except as a means of advancing further toward the English form of government. Dorchester was so impressed by this report that he at once sent it to the Secretary for Home Affairs, thinking it contained matters of importance that might "not all readily find their way into a more direct channel"—that is, by the reports of Bond, Temple, Miller, and others.[18] There were no further reports until Beckwith returned to New York in the autumn of 1788. He found the same monarchical attitudes prevalent there, though subdued. The adoption of the Constitution had forced some who held such views to conclude that "the re-union of the empire" was not then practicable.[19] He was also told that there was "a growing British interest in the United States" and that it would be "good policy to hold a friendly language to that Country, and to show a disposition to form a treaty of commerce with them." This report revealed such a range of important sources and contained such highly significant matter that it may have prompted Dorchester to suggest that Beckwith report his findings in person to the British cabinet. In any event, Beckwith did return to England and in the spring and summer of 1789 held various conversations with Lord Hawkesbury, Lord Sydney, and Lord Grenville. He was in London when reports of debates in the House of Representatives on the tariff and tonnage bills

[17] "Extraordinaries abroad from 1784 to 1791," Quebec, PRO: PMG 14/73, f. 170, 217, 274, 332, 338, 341; PMG 14/74, f. 1,2.
[18] Dorchester to Sydney, 10 Apr. 1787, PRO: CO 42/50, f. 92; Beckwith's report, same, f. 94-9. Reports of Bond, Temple, and Miller are in the FO 4 series in PRO; most of those of Bond, with important omissions of enclosures, are in Am. Hist. Assn., *Ann. Rept.*, 1896, I, 513-659; same, 1897, p. 454-568.
[19] Dorchester to Sydney, 14 Oct. 1788, PRO: CO 42/61, f. 104; Beckwith's report, same, f. 106-17. In this period of Beckwith's absence in England, Peter Allaire, who went to Quebec in the summer of 1788 to arrange a means of communication, kept Dorchester informed of events in New York. On Allaire, see below, note 121.

arrived from consular and secret agents. Grenville, who had succeeded Sydney as Secretary for Home Affairs, authorized Beckwith on his return to New York to sound warnings of commercial retaliation should Madison's "discriminating clauses" be adopted.[20]

The report of October 1789, which Beckwith delivered in person to Dorchester after having transmitted Grenville's message to those in New York for whom it was intended, was by far the most important intelligence gathered by the agent up to that point, for it was the first to be made after the successful launching of the new government. This fact gave new significance to Beckwith's role and, above all, to the meaning of the part played by those upon whom he relied. Some of the latter were now no longer private individuals free to voice their political preferences at will. They were clothed with public responsibility as members of the executive, legislative, and judicial branches of government, a fact that should have limited the freedom with which they could discuss the policy of government with the secret agent of a foreign power. It was also in the autumn of 1789 that the Secretary of the Treasury entered into these discussions, becoming thenceforth the most important public character upon whom Dorchester's agent depended. In this opening interview Hamilton manifested his aim to influence foreign policy, thereby initiating the long divisive struggle in the cabinet—a struggle culminating five years later in the settlement that, in the words of the leading authority, more "aptly . . . might be called Hamilton's Treaty."[21]

In brief, while the significance of Beckwith's role had been greatly augmented by the newly assumed public character of his sources of information and less so by the British ministry's use of him as a direct channel of influence with friends in positions of influence, its clandestine character had not been altered in any degree. He was still the covert agent of an alien power, a fact given fresh emphasis at this time by his beginning the use of a cipher to protect the names and rank of his informants while disclosing their identity to the ministry.[22] His presence

---

20 Bemis, *Jay's Treaty*, p. 56, 59. There is no other authority for the responsibility given Beckwith by Grenville than Beckwith's own statement (see note 6), but since this was an assertion easily verifiable by Henry Dundas to whom it was made, it must for this and other reasons be given full credit.

21 Bemis, *Jay's Treaty*, p. 373.

22 The cipher key for the discussions in the autumn of 1789 was transmitted in Dorchester to Grenville, 28 Oct. 1789, marked *"Private,"* PRO: CO 42/66, f. 245, 247. The most important individuals in this list, excepting Washington with whom Beckwith exchanged two unimportant remarks, were William Samuel Johnson (No. 1), Philip Schuyler (No. 2), "A Gentleman in Office of the United States," who can only have been Henry Knox (No. 4), and Alexander Hamilton (No. 7). The cipher key for seven additional names of persons consulted in the spring of 1790 was enclosed in Dorchester to Grenville, 7 June 1790, marked *"Private,"* PRO: CO 42/68, f. 229, 231. The principal persons in this group were William Paterson, Senator from New Jersey (No. 10), John Jay (No. 12), and Thomas Scott, "Member of House of Representatives from Counties West of Allegheny Mountains" (No. 14). The cipher key for six further names was transmitted in Dorchester to Grenville, 25 Sep. 1790, marked *"Private,"* PRO: CO 42/46, f. 384, 385. The principal informants of Beckwith in this group were Fisher Ames (No. 17), Richard Henry Lee (No. 18), and Isaac Sherman (No. 21). The entire list is printed in Brymner, *Report*, 1890, p. xli, xlii, consisting of twenty-three names. Of these David Humphreys (No. 20) and Gouverneur Mor-

in New York was known to Washington, of course, and doubtless to many others in government who were not aware of the nature of his mission. Washington had known Beckwith in 1783 as the officer who brought Carleton's dispatches when preparations were being made for the evacuation of New York.[23] When he saw Dorchester's aide there again in 1789 he may have considered him merely as an officer on his travels—such, for example, as Lieutenant John Enys, who had come down from Montreal in 1784, had met leading figures in New York and Philadelphia, and had been entertained by Washington at Mount Vernon.[24] More likely the President, wise in the ways of intelligence work, guessed that Beckwith had returned from England by way of New York in order to gather what information he could about American affairs.

But Washington certainly could not have known that his Secretary of the Treasury had requested an interview with the secret agent and had advanced the "certain overtures" that were to be transmitted to Dorchester and to the ministry. For the fact is that, while Hamilton was willing to give Dorchester blanket authority to use his communication "in whatever Manner" he should judge proper, he did not "chuse to have this go any further in America."[25] Hamilton and Beckwith might reassure themselves time and again, as each did, that theirs was only "a private conversation," and each might flatter the other's sense of delicacy in respecting divergent loyalties, but this was in truth nothing less than a penetration of the highest councils of the nation by the confidential agent of another power. Beckwith's astonishing success had indeed justified Dorchester's confidence that "the advantages which this gentleman derived from his employments [in secret service activities in

---

ris (No. 23) were alluded to in the reports but were not among Beckwith's informants.

[23] Washington to Carleton, 14 Nov. 1783, *Writings*, ed. Fitzpatrick, xxvii, 240. John Hamilton, British consul at Norfolk, saw Beckwith at Philadelphia early in 1791 and reported to Leeds: "He assumes no official Character, but attends all Levées, which occasions some uneasiness and suspicions, but he is generally very much respected" (Hamilton to Leeds, 10 Apr. 1791, PRO, FO 4/9, f. 225). Sir John Temple also reported to Leeds about the same time: "Lord Dorchester has had one of his aids de Camp here and at Philadelphia, for the year past! The status of this Person about Congress hath indeed disgusted not a few who heretofore leaned towards Great Britain. An Envoy, say they, from a Colony Governor, to a Sovereign power is a business heretofore unheard of! He can be considered in no other light than as a petty Spy! What the purposes of Major Beckwith's being sent here, or By What Authority he is here,—or, of what his Powers may be (if he has any in the Diplomatic line,) I am totally ignorant! I have however shown him all the Countenance and respect, due from me, to any Officers of His Majestys army, and heartily wish that his Mission, if any he has from Authority, may not turn out fruitless, or detrimental to His Majesty's General Service in the States" (Temple to Leeds, 23 May 1791, PRO, FO 4/10, f. 62). That Temple—vain, garrulous, indiscreet, and lavish with exclamation points—should have known so little of Beckwith's purpose or mission is itself an eloquent tribute to the prudence and trustworthiness of Dorchester's agent.

[24] MS journals of John Enys, 1783-1787, originals in possession of Miss E. D. Enys, The Cottage, Enys, Penryn, Cornwall; microfilm in NjP.

[25] Beckwith's report, enclosed in Dorchester to Grenville, 25 Oct. 1789, PRO: CO 42/66, f. 278, 280-310; that part of the report quoting the conversation with Hamilton is conveniently accessible in Syrett, *Hamilton*, v, 482-90.

New York] during the war . . . rendered his being employed on those occasions the more eligible."[26] This greatly understated the case, yet, able and experienced though he was, Beckwith could scarcely have accomplished this remarkable result had he not been so warmly embraced by men in office eager to share in the covert shaping of foreign policy. His timely appearance in the autumn of 1789 bearing Grenville's warning provided a convenient instrument that was immediately and boldly grasped by the Secretary of the Treasury. As the events of the summer of 1790 proved, this was a two-edged tool, for it involved the brilliant but unpredictable Gouverneur Morris and his appointment as Washington's informal but official agent in London. The fact that such an appointment was made at that precise moment is no less surprising than that the influences prompting it have never been examined.

[26] Dorchester to Sydney, 7 July 1790, reiterating an opinion stated in his private letter to Sydney of 24 Oct. 1788 (not found); PRO: CO 42/68, f. 252-3.

II

The Appointment
of Gouverneur Morris

The decision to appoint Morris as agent came just after Washington had signed Jefferson's commission as Secretary of State. Hamilton learned of the intention to name Jefferson only the day before the nomination was sent to the Senate, though Madison had known for some weeks that this would be done.[27] At this juncture in 1789 Congress was on the point of adjourning, Washington was preparing to set off on a tour of New England, the French minister and the Spanish *encargado de negocios* were about to depart for home, the debate over Madison's "discriminating clauses" and the residence question—the two most serious threats to legislative harmony—had been stilled for the time being, and relations with Canada were so tranquil that Dorchester had just asked leave to return to England on private affairs.[28] One ardent Federalist assured Beckwith after Congress adjourned that the session on the whole had been a smooth one and that a foundation had been laid "for much future good."[29] It was at this quiet moment, in fact, that Dorchester received the first official communication from the United States since his appointment as Governor General in 1786— a request that Andrew Ellicott be permitted to make astronomical observations at Niagara to define the limit of the New York cession of 1781. Dorchester was so impressed by American "assurances of a friendly disposition towards Great Britain" that he promptly sent the letter to Grenville so that the ministry might read these sentiments of the President as transmitted by John Jay, then acting as Secretary for Foreign Affairs: "It gives me Pleasure, my Lord, to be instructed, to assure you of the President's Disposition to promote an Interchange of friendly Offices between the two Nations, and particularly to protect and maintain between their bordering Territories, the Right of Hospitality and good Neighbourhood."[30] Dorchester, always remember-

[27] Brant, *Madison*, III, 285; Syrett, *Hamilton*, V, 409.
[28] Freeman, *Washington*, VI, 234-9; Dorchester to Sydney, 22 Aug. 1789, and to Grenville, 8 Feb. 1790, PRO: CO 42/65, f. 77; CO 42/67, f. 25.
[29] Beckwith's report, enclosed in Dorchester to Grenville, 25 Oct. 1789, PRO: CO 42/66, f. 278, 281.
[30] Dorchester to Grenville, 30 Sep. 1789, enclosing copies of Jay to Dorchester, 4 Sep. 1789, Henry Motz to Jay, 24 Sep. 1789, and related documents, PRO: CO 42/65, f. 199-207; Washington to Knox, 5 Sep. 1789, *Writings*, ed. Fitzpatrick, XXX, 394-5.

ing the "surprize . . . done at Tyconderoga" in 1775, keenly aware of the weakness of his own far-flung defenses, and disturbed by the steady march of the American line of frontier settlements, was by no means disposed to welcome visitors from the United States. But in this instance the friendly attitude of the American government won his consent, though the civility was accompanied by orders to the military escort for Ellicott's party to be on guard "to prevent the King's interest being injured . . . by any surveys or reconnoitering of the country foreign to the ostensible object."[31]

In brief, in the autumn of 1789 no domestic or foreign urgency existed that required the immediate appointment of an agent in London to manifest friendly dispositions or to ascertain the attitude of the British ministry on such questions as treaty obligations and commerce. Not only was the general situation of affairs tranquil—there were also powerful arguments that counseled delay in the making of such an appointment. The ablest and best informed American diplomat abroad, whose advice could presumably have been useful both as to the decision to make the appointment and as to the person to be chosen, was known to be on his way home and was expected to arrive in the United States at any moment. Indeed, under the circumstances Jefferson could have expected to be consulted on such an important move—his commission as Secretary of State had just been signed. Washington himself conceded as much both by his scrupulous regard for proper procedure on other occasions and by the instructions given to Morris. "This Communication," he wrote, "ought regularly to be made to you by the Secretary of State, but that Office not being at present filled, my Desire of avoiding Delays induces me to make it under my own Hand."[32] A few months earlier the President had expressed his general policy to De Moustier: "I have . . . been taught to believe, that there is, in most polished nations, a system established, with regard to the foreign as well as the other great Departments, which, from the utility, the necessity, and the reason of the thing, provides that business should be digested and prepared by the Heads of those departments."[33] On the matter of subsequent diplomatic and consular appointments the President usually consulted Jefferson and depended largely upon his recommendations—with the significant and notable exception of the appointment of Gouverneur Morris in 1791 as minister to France.

There were even more cogent reasons for delay, as Washington was soon reminded by the one who up to this point had been his principal adviser, James Madison. It was not Madison, however, but John Jay with whom Washington first discussed the propriety of taking "informal means of ascertaining the views of the British Court with respect to our Western Posts . . . and to a Commercial treaty." This was on the 7th of October and Jay had just given Washington the substance of the British ministry's inquiries about American trade, pro-

[31] The orders are among the related documents indicated in the preceding note; the weak condition of Canadian defenses is a constant theme in Dorchester's dispatches during this period; the allusion to Ticonderoga is in Dorchester to Gordon, 9 May 1791, PRO: CO 42/72, f. 155.

[32] Washington to Morris, 13 Oct. 1789, *Writings*, ed. Fitzpatrick, xxx, 440.

[33] Washington to De Moustier, 25 May 1789, same, xxx, 333-5.

ductions, tonnage duties, manufactures, population, debts to British merchants, and other matters—information that he had obtained from Sir John Temple. Jay thought the move advisable and recommended as agent Dr. Edward Bancroft, "a man in whom entire confidence might be placed."[34] That same day Washington consulted Hamilton, who "highly approved of the measure, but thought Gouv'r Morris well qualified."[35] The fact that Temple had seen fit to reveal to Jay, and the latter to the President, the important and comprehensive inquiries reflecting the ministry's interest in matters about which the informal agent in London would concern himself suggests that this may have been the means by which the question of an appointment was raised in Washington's mind. This may have occurred to Washington himself on reading the ministry's inquiries about comparative duties on imports, tonnage fees, and port charges as between English vessels and those of other countries—inquiries that were given added significance in light of the debate over Madison's "discriminating clauses."[36] Since Jay was acting as Secretary for Foreign Affairs, it would have been quite proper for him to have opened the subject in this manner and to have suggested the important step of appointing an informal agent in London. Washington on this day noted in his diary that he had consulted Jay on the propriety of taking the New England trip, but on the topic of the appointment of an agent stated only that he had "had conversation" with him. The difference in phraseology may or may not have significance, but the former suggests that Washington himself initiated the subject while the latter leaves the question open.

The next day Washington sought the opinion of Madison, who was just setting out for Virginia. The response was immediate, emphatic, and negative. The President carefully recorded in his diary the three cogent reasons advanced against making the appointment at that time— "if the necessity did not press." In the first place, Madison pointed out, it "would be better to wait the arrival of Mr. Jefferson, who might be able to give the information wanted on this head." Second, if Morris were appointed agent—a supposition indicating that Washington had already accepted Hamilton's recommendation as to the person to be named—it "would be a commitment for his appointment as Minister, if one should be sent to that Court, or wanted at Versailles in place of Mr. Jefferson." Finally, if Morris wished either of these diplomatic appointments, his reports on the views of the British ministry "might . . . be made with an eye to it."[37] Washington was undoubtedly given

[34] Washington, *Diaries*, ed. Fitzpatrick, IV, 16. Jay's recommendation is plausible and understandable. Bancroft was a native American, he was in London, he was respected in scientific circles as a member of the Royal Society, he was friendly with Lord Sydney and others in the ministry, and he enjoyed the esteem of Franklin, Jefferson, and other Americans. It was not until a century later that his remarkable role as a double-spy came to light. Arthur Lee and George III were among the few of his contemporaries who distrusted him; see articles by the Editor in WMQ, XVI (Apr., July, Oct. 1959), 166-87, 319-42, 515-50.

[35] Washington, *Diaries*, ed. Fitzpatrick, IV, 16.

[36] Washington made extensive notes of Jay's communication; same, IV, 15-16. On the general scope of the inquiries from the ministry, see note to TJ to Harison and others, 12 Aug. 1790.

[37] Madison had come to take leave of Washington when the subject of the

pause by these arguments. He passed over the first in silence, so far as the diary reveals, but conceded the force of the last two by agreeing with them. To the weight of all of these opposing factors he paid the tribute of delaying his decision almost a week.

A significant omission occurring in this interval must be noted. On important matters Washington was accustomed to ask the opinions of the Chief Justice and the Vice-President as well as the heads of departments. Under the circumstances it would seem that John Adams would have been the logical if not indeed the first person to be sought out for advice. He was the second officer in the administration, he had been American minister at London, he had proposed in 1785 an exchange of ministers as well as a commercial treaty, and the next year he and Jefferson had in fact submitted the projet of such a treaty to the British Secretary for Foreign Affairs. During this interval between the discussion with Madison and the appointment of Morris, Washington saw Adams at least twice. One of the occasions was at dinner and the other was on an all-day excursion by presidential barge to the gardens of William Prince at Flushing. On the return from that expedition the party stopped at the seat of Gouverneur Morris in order to see a barn of which Washington had often heard its owner speak. The question still unresolved surely could not have been far from the President's mind that October day in the barn at Morrisania. Yet it was not until the war crisis of the summer of 1790 that Washington placed in Adams' hands the correspondence between Morris and Leeds, informed him of the decision that had been taken months before, and asked for his opinion under the circumstances then existing. It is revealing that, though Adams naturally was not asked to approve the decision after the fact, Washington recorded in his diary that the Vice-President "expressed his approbation that this step had been taken."[38]

The conclusion suggested by this seems inescapable. Having already encountered Madison's forceful arguments, Washington must have intentionally avoided the risk of meeting with another negative vote—indeed less risk than certainty. Adams was not only firmly fixed in the opinion that Great Britain, having ignored American overtures, should make the first move toward an exchange of ministers. He also had no very high opinion of Gouverneur Morris, thinking him a man of wit who "made pretty verses—but of a Character trés legere."[39] The significant point is not that Adams in all probability would have agreed with Madison but that Washington seemed to avoid opposition to a decision toward which he was evidently inclined either for his own reasons or for others suggested to him.

There is no doubt that Washington felt strongly about the im-

appointment was broached; Washington, *Diaries*, ed. Fitzpatrick, IV, 17, under 8 Oct. 1790.

[38] Same, IV, 132, under 1 July 1790. It is worth noting, as possibly indicating the President's state of mind, that at Prince's famous gardens Washington found the "shrubs . . . trifling, and the flowers not numerous" and at Morrisania he thought the barn expensive and not of a construction to suit him. The Adamses were at dinner with the President on the day that the conversation with Madison took place; same, IV, 17, 18, 19.

[39] Butterfield, *Adams Diary*, II, 390, under 22 June 1779.

portance of executing the provisions of the Treaty of Peace and of re-
moving the source of friction in the continued British occupation of
the posts. Some Americans were already demanding removal by force
rather than by diplomacy.[40] There is also no doubt that he was equally
troubled by the closing of the West Indies to American trade and by the
long-standing threat of commercial retaliation most recently expressed
in the form of Madison's resolutions. Both of these concerns were given
emphasis in the instructions to Morris, which Washington evidently
drafted himself. On the first problem the agent was directed to note
that the establishment of the new government and a federal judiciary
removed the objections theretofore made by the ministry for retaining
the posts. Washington had no need to refer to the problem of debts
or to explain the implications of this bare statement to one who had also
sat in the Convention of 1787. He shared the general expectation that
the federal courts would uphold the treaty provisions over any state
laws tending to impede British merchants in the collection of debts owed
them by Americans.[41] On the second source of danger, Washington
pointed out that "a very respectable number of both houses were inclined to a discrimination of duties unfavorable to Britain, and that it
would have taken place but for conciliatory considerations, and the
probability that the late change in our government and circumstances
would lead to more satisfactory arrangements." Morris was therefore
to inquire whether the ministry contemplated a treaty of commerce with
the United States and on what general principles. Then came the point
of greatest emphasis: "In treating this subject, let it be strongly impressed on your mind, that the privilege of carrying our productions
in our vessels to their Islands, and of bringing in return the productions
of those Islands to our own ports and markets, is regarded here as of
the highest importance; and you will be careful not to countenance any
idea of our dispensing with it in a treaty."[42]

These were powerful motives but they provide no satisfactory answer to Madison's arguments. Both sources of friction had existed for
some years and the need to remove them at this moment did not press

[40] For example, a Connecticut friend of Dr. Edward Bancroft wrote in 1786
reporting a conversation with one of the latter's former friends in New England:
"You know his disposition, sanguine, turbulent, avaricious, and fond of troubled
waters. He has however considerable influence in our councils. From what he said
ought to be done I confess I have my fears of what is *intended* to be done. He
said that the Forts on the Frontiers held by G. Britain contrary to treaty should
be demanded at the head of an Army, and if refused to be delivered up, taken
by Force." The friend added: "It is not an acquisition of territory I want . . . it
is their Floating riches"—that is, the opportunity for privateering ("Extract from
Connecticut," 1 Apr. 1786, PRO: FO 4/4, f. 79-80). Bancroft at once sent the
extract of this letter to the Foreign Office.

[41] See note, TJ to Temple, 11 Aug. 1790.

[42] Washington to Morris, 13 Oct. 1789 (letter of instructions), of which there
is no retained file copy in the Washington Papers; Washington, *Writings*, ed.
Fitzpatrick, XXX, 440-2. Fitzpatrick printed the text "from Ford, who took it
from Sparks" (see Sparks, *Gouverneur Morris*, II, 4-5). The text is also printed
in Morris, *Diary*, ed. Davenport, I, 462-4. Washington wrote two other letters to
Morris on the same date: (1) a private letter (text in *Writings*, ed. Fitzpatrick,
XXX, 442-5); and (2) the letter of credence (same, XXX, 439-40; RC in Washington's hand in NNC: Gouverneur Morris Papers).

with any urgency. Washington explained to Morris that he made the decision in order to avoid delay—and had delayed the making of it for some days because of divided councils. Yet he was unwilling to postpone it longer to await the arrival, momentarily expected, of the man he had just appointed Secretary of State. This, Washington's first significant act in foreign affairs, had ramifications and results that affected many things, among them the ultimate designation of Morris as minister to France, the resultant disappointment of William Short, the silence that Jefferson was forced to maintain towards his mortified friend on this subject, the inability of the Secretary of State to press Short's appointment or to oppose that of Morris, and, most significant of all, the declining influence of Madison and the rising power of Hamilton in the administration. Why, then, was the decision made?

Madison obviously guessed at once that some influences in the background were at work. On the day Washington asked his advice, he wrote a letter to await Jefferson's arrival that was expressed in such urgency its relevance to the consultation cannot be doubted. He was about to depart for Philadelphia and would welcome the opportunity to make the journey to Virginia with Jefferson. He then added: "I wish on a public account to see you as soon as possible after you become informed of the new destination provided for you. It is of infinite importance that you should not disappoint the public wish on this subject. Be persuaded of this truth, with proper opportunity it can be demonstrated to you."[43] When he wrote this, Madison did not know what the ultimate decision would be. But he knew, as Jefferson did, that to press a matter too far with the President was to undo its effect. He could thus guess at the strength of the demand for Morris' appointment from the power of the argument he had dared mobilize against it. Like Jefferson, Madison preferred amicable to adversary relations in commerce, yet both dared to act on the belief that, as Jefferson expressed it in his outline of policy in 1790, "the latter would be infallible, and in our own power." From this Washington shrank back, preferring to see whether conciliation could be brought about. But even at the moment the President was making his troubled decision, a Federalist Senator was saying to Dorchester's secret agent: "To suppose Great Britain should in any shape sollicit our Commercial Friendship is idle, and absurd; there are individuals who profess such opinions, but the more enlighten'd part of the Senate hold them to be ridiculous."[44] In the long fight that was just beginning, Washington in this troubled week chose not to align himself with the views on commercial policy that Madison and Jefferson had long supported. The mission of Gouverneur Morris ended in failure, but this was of less importance than the fact that Washington's underlying purpose was thwarted in the very act in which it was stated. "It is in my opinion very important," he wrote Morris, "that we avoid errors in our system of policy respecting Great

43 Madison to TJ, 8 Oct. 1789.
44 William Samuel Johnson, as quoted in Beckwith's report of "Conversations with different persons," enclosed in Dorchester to Grenville, 25 Oct. 1789, PRO: CO 42/66, f. 278, 280-310; text in Brymner, *Report*, 1890, p. 121-9. Johnson added: "were this to be done I should be sorry for it."

Britain; and this can only be done by forming a right judgment of their disposition and views."[45]

In making the appointment Jay and Hamilton had recommended, Washington unwittingly committed his administration to a course in which, despite the fidelity Morris gave to the charge placed in his hands, the disposition and views of the British government were obscured by the worst fate that could befall the Chief Executive in his conduct of public affairs—that of deliberate misrepresentation on the part of a trusted member of his cabinet.

[45] Washington to Morris, 13 Oct. 1789 (see note 42 above).

III

Hamilton's Opening
Move, 1789

It has been generally assumed that Major George Beckwith arrived in New York only in October of 1789 and that this was after the appointment of Gouverneur Morris had been made. This assumption is based upon Beckwith's statement three years later that "in the month of August . . . he was the bearer of a message from" Grenville which he delivered "in the October following."[46] It is very likely that Beckwith left for America in the August packet that arrived late in September. Whether he came by that vessel or not, he was definitely in New York and in consultation with those upon whom he depended at least as early as the 30th of September, the day after Congress adjourned.[47] For on the 30th Beckwith was closeted with Dr. William Samuel Johnson, president of Columbia College and Senator from Connecticut. This eminent lawyer, who made no attempt to hide his distaste for republican principles or his disapproval of Jefferson, was evidently the first person to whom Beckwith addressed himself on this third mission. In the cipher key that he began at this time Beckwith assigned to Johnson the symbol Number 1—a designation well deserved until Alexander Hamilton entered the discussions a few days later as Number 7.

Johnson had long been useful to Beckwith and to Sir John Temple. "I have since my Residence here found him undeviating in his attachment to the interests of our nation," the latter had written in 1788, "and I have had some usefull information from him. Though much courted and solicited by the people, he would have nothing to do with public affairs during the late contest, nor until his Majesty had granted independence to the states. After that he took a seat in Congress and had a great share in framing the new Constitution, and would now probably be sent Minister to London if the states were not fearful of his being too much attached to the interests and government of Great Britain."[48] Johnson was almost certainly the man whom Beckwith had consulted

---

[46] George Beckwith to Henry Dundas, 20 June 1792, PRO: FO 4/12. On the basis of this statement, Bemis and others have assumed that "Beckwith reached New York . . . in October, 1789" and that when he arrived the decision to send a person to the British court had already been made; Bemis, *Jay's Treaty*, 61, 65.

[47] This is proved by the assertion made to him by William Samuel Johnson that Congress had "adjourned yesterday"—that is, on 29 Sep. 1789 (see note 44).

[48] Temple to Sneyd, 2 Oct. 1788, PRO: FO 4/6.

in the spring of 1787 and who informed him that even "the Presbyterian Clergy are become Advocates for Monarchy, the community in general finding from experience, that a Republican System however beautiful in theory, is not calculated for an extensive country."[49] He was beyond question the Senator who told Beckwith the day after Congress adjourned in 1789: "I am naturally well disposed to the Country, in which I live, and however I may lament and condemn the dismemberment of a great Empire, to the government and principles of which I have ever been strongly attached, in the present posture of affairs I certainly cannot have any views or motives unconnected with the general good, but I do think that, in the hands of able and dispassionate men, a system might be formed to the advantage of both countries." Johnson was very clear as to where the general good lay.

It was absurd, he said, to suppose Great Britain would solicit commercial friendship with America in any form. Madison, "an eleve of Mr. Jefferson's," had with great warmth and spirit pressed his "discriminating clauses" in the late session. But when the measure came before the Senate, the majority were too enlightened and too moderate to approve measures "they viewed . . . as a declaration of commercial war, which it was neither wise nor just to commence against a powerful nation." Johnson coupled this with a warning that Beckwith underscored in his report. The advocates of discrimination had brought in a quick report which had in view "the *not permitting your shipping to clear out from our ports, either for your West India Islands, or for your Provinces upon this Continent, but the Senate thought it prudent to let the matter lay over until next session.*" With this hint at the means that Jefferson a year later thought "infallible, and in our own power," Johnson underscored the point that Washington had emphasized so strongly. He could not tell whether the President was "perfectly free from a French bias or not, but the moderate and thinking party" wished greatly for a commercial treaty and "nothing would facilitate this more than the admission of small vessels" into the British West Indies under certain regulations. He could assure Beckwith that a majority of the Senate were disposed to enter upon the consideration of such a subject dispassionately, but he was not certain about the attitude of the House of Representatives. Further, no minister would be sent to London. Indeed, if one had gone "he would not have been a person of a disposition to promote those views of harmony and friendship between the two countries" that Johnson had at heart: he "would have been a second edition of Mr. Adams." The Senate, therefore, had struck from the appropriation bill clauses enabling the President to send ministers abroad if he should "judge it necessary to send any to Europe, prior to [Congress'] next meeting in January."[50]

Such was the reply that Johnson gave to the secret agent after the latter had delivered Grenville's unveiled warning: "I am authorized to acquaint you, and the gentlemen in public office here, that had the

49 Dorchester to Sydney, 10 Apr. 1787, enclosing "Certain Communications of a very interesting nature" received from Beckwith, PRO: CO 42/50, f. 92-9; text in Brymner, *Report*, 1890, p. 97-9.
50 Beckwith's report of "Conversations with different persons"; see note 44.

Bill in question passed as sent up from your House of Representatives with those discriminating clauses, which appeared in your public papers, we were prepared to meet it; a discretionary power is by an annual Act of Parliament, vested in the King and Council for such purposes, and the continuance of the indulgencies shewn to your shipping in our ports in Europe, depends upon your own Conduct."[51] This was blunt talk straight from Whitehall. Fisher Ames a few years later in denying the charge of British influence, defined such influence as "political power . . . exerted to modify or control, or prevent the public measures of the American nation."[52] Other powers pressed the young republic also by bringing similar influences to bear, but, by the definition of one of the highest of Federalists, the message brought by Beckwith was in fact an effort to prevent public measures. There can be no better proof than this of the secrecy of the interviews. Knowledge of foreign influence thus operating within the legislature would have given unity and strength to the system of commercial reciprocity of which Jefferson's "infallible means" was a last resort.

Beckwith next consulted Senator Philip Schuyler, father-in-law of Alexander Hamilton and one of those who, in the biting words of William Maclay, were "amazingly fond of the old leaven" of monarchism.[53] Again the agent sounded the warning to a Senator whose disposition of friendliness to Great Britain could not be doubted: "Whilst you were without an efficient Government, and some of the local Legislatures adopted such measures, we did not take any steps whatever, trusting that the formation of a strong government here would lead to their repeal, but if one of the first measures of the present government had such objects in view, the case was materially altered, and certainly, if the States chose to mark commercial hostility to us, we were to lose no time in changing our system."

Schuyler echoed in his reply the sentiments Johnson had expressed. He shared the general regret in the Senate that treaties with France did not permit the United States to give "a decided preference to Great Britain" in matters of trade, declared that he thought a firm connection with England "to be preferred to that of all the powers of Europe besides," and stated that "the President wishes well to this principle." He also said the funds for sending ministers abroad during the recess had been withheld because "the extent of those appointments ought to depend upon the character of the men employed, and the nature of the objects." Schuyler then asked Beckwith two blunt questions. Would England send a minister to the United States if one were sent there? Would Beckwith permit him to mention the conversation—that is, the warning from Grenville about commercial retaliation—to the Secretary of the Treasury? The agent could not answer the first, but to the second he gave an emphatic "by all means," indicating that Hamilton was the person whom he was most "pleased to communicate it to."

It was natural that he should have been pleased. Hamilton stood

---

[51] Same, text in Brymner, *Report*, 1890, p. 121.
[52] Essays of *Phocion* (Apr. 1801) in Fisher Ames, *Works*, ed. Seth Ames, II, 152.
[53] Maclay, *Journal*, ed. Maclay, p. 167.

high in "The Executive Government of the United States" and this was as far as Beckwith dared go with the ministry's warning. The agent could report only an exchange of two sentences with the President. Washington hoped the application for permission allowing Andrew Ellicott's surveying party to enter Canadian territory would be granted. "Sir," the agent replied, "I am persuaded of Lord Dorchester's general disposition to promote mutual harmony and the extension of science." That was all. The brief, formal, and polite exchange perhaps took place at a levée, certainly not in private. If any serious discussion of matters of public business had taken place, Beckwith would surely have reported it to his commanding officer. If conveyed at all, the message from the ministry had to reach the President by indirection.

Beckwith next gathered some gleanings of little consequence from a New York merchant and from John Trumbull. From "A Gentleman in Office of the United States" who can only have been the Secretary of War, Henry Knox, he learned something of Indian affairs and the situation of the army. He was also told that the "very favourite object" of obtaining the posts was obstructed solely by lack of resources in the hands of those "men in office in the States, who in their hearts aim at no less than the subversion of the British Power in North America." He was pointedly made aware of the fact that the activities of the secret agent John Connolly were well known to the government. "These things cause jealousy," Knox added.[54]

The seventh interview was with Hamilton. "I have requested to see you," the latter remarked at the opening of the talk, ". . . from a wish to explain certain points relative to our situation, and from a desire to suggest a measure, which I conceive to be both for the interest of Great Britain and of this Country to adopt. We have lately established a Government upon principles, that in my opinion render it safe for any nation to enter into Treaties with us, either Commercial or Political, which has not hitherto been the case; I have always preferred a connexion with you, to that of any other country, *we think in English,* and have a similarity of prejudices and of predilections. . . . We wish to form a commercial treaty with you to every extent, to which you may think it for your interest to go." The broad plan of this nature that Lansdowne had contemplated at the close of the war was not now attainable, *"considering the spirit of* [Great Britain's] *late navigation and regulating Acts, as well as from various publications by persons of considerable weight in England."* Yet a treaty might be formed *"upon terms advantageous to both countries."*

Specifically Hamilton suggested what William Samuel Johnson had urged: admission of small vessels into the British West Indies so as to enable Americans to carry their produce there "and to bring from thence the productions of those Islands to [American] ports" under such restrictions as to prevent the possibility of interference with the British carrying trade in Europe. This would be better, Hamilton told Beckwith, than "by *a rigid adherence to your present plan to produce a system of warfare in Commercial matters"* such as France had en-

[54] Beckwith's report of "Conversations with different persons"; see note 44.

couraged during the late session of Congress and such as he had always regretted "as being directly opposed to that system, which upon mature reflexion, I have thought it most eligible for us to pursue."[55] This was very close to saying that the rigid mercantilist policy advocated by Sheffield and Hawkesbury had initiated the chain of events productive of commercial warfare, though such was far from the language used to defeat Madison's system of reciprocity, so closely allied to that of Shelburne in principle.[56]

Again Hamilton echoed what Johnson had said: "The present moment I view as particularly favorable for a plan of this nature. We are now so circumstanced as to be free to enter into a discussion of this sort, from our condition with regard to the other maritime powers: this may not be the case hereafter." The navigation of the Mississippi was "a matter of great importance to settle with Spain." The western territories, he added, "must have that outlet" or be lost to the union. The United States had no interest in extending her territories to the northward. If the United States were forced to rely on the House of Bourbon, such a connection might "become important to [British] West India possessions." But this, Hamilton implied, was a necessity to which the United States could only be driven: "connected with you, by strong ties of commercial, perhaps of political, friendships, our naval exertions, in future wars, may in your scale be greatly important, and decisive. These are my opinions, they are the sentiments, which I have long entertained, on which I have acted, and I think them suited to the welfare of both countries. I am not sufficiently authorized to say so, it is not in my department, but I am inclined to think a *person will soon be sent to England to sound the disposition of your court upon it.*" Beckwith said in response that he had told Schuyler what would have resulted if the "discriminating clauses" of the tariff bill had been adopted and asked if the conversation arose from Schuyler's request for permission to communicate this to Hamilton. Hamilton replied: "It does." He went on to say—as each assured the other this was "merely a private conversation" —that the "ideas . . . thrown out, may be depended upon as the sentiments of the most enlightened men in this country." More pointedly, he added: "they are those of General Washington, I can confidently assure you, as well as of a majority in the Senate."

Thus with a single voice the close-knit majority of the Senate and the Secretary of the Treasury tried to commit the government to a policy through covert consultations of which, so far as the records and the plausibilities indicate, the President was wholly unaware. Even Hamilton with all of his daring could scarcely have done this had he not been confident that the pledge would be met. Beckwith thought he clearly understood the scope of Hamilton's communication, but the implications must have shaken him, for he asked bluntly: "Pray what use do you intend me to make of it? Is it with a view to my mentioning it to Lord Dorchester?" Hamilton replied: "Yes, and by Lord Dorchester

---

[55] Same; emphasis supplied in the last two of the italicized passages, the first being underscored in Beckwith's report.

[56] For a discussion of the liberal principles of Shelburne, see Gerald S. Graham, *British Policy and Canada 1774-1791* (London, 1930), p. 56-7.

to your Ministry, in whatever manner His Lordship shall judge proper; but I should not chuse to have this go any further in America." There was much else in this extraordinary consultation, but Hamilton reinforced his insistent emphasis on the idea that that moment was particularly favorable for a commercial treaty by stating two points. The first, again echoing William Samuel Johnson, was that the "advocates for discrimination . . . had in view *a much stronger measure*." Beckwith correctly interpreted this to mean an embargo on British shipping in American ports for the Canadian provinces or the West Indies—a recourse to the harsh measures of 1770 and a precursor to those of 1807. The second point concerned Washington's emissary, who Beckwith had feared might frustrate the object if "his mind should have any bias towards any other foreign power." On this Hamilton reassured him by saying that "these nominations originate with General Washington, who is a good judge of men, and the gentleman, to be employed in this business, is perfectly master of the subject, and if he leans in his bias towards any foreign country, it is decidedly to you."

These discussions offer the most plausible explanation for the puzzling fact that Washington rejected Madison's plea for a brief delay in the appointment of an agent to London when no apparent urgency existed calling for haste. The threat of renewal of Madison's proposals in the next session, the danger even of resort to the drastic weapon of an embargo, the desire for a lowering of barriers to trade with the West Indies, Beckwith's timely arrival, his repetitive warnings of more rather than less restrictions on commerce with England and her possessions, the withholding of authority from the President to send ministers abroad, the wish of the Senate to have a voice in the choosing of such a person as would promote harmony between the two countries—all of these factors revealed in the conversations could have prompted those who thought of themselves as the governing majority to believe that this was an auspicious moment for a bold stroke. If so, and if a single factor towering above all others was needed as a catalyzing force, it was provided by the President about the time of Beckwith's arrival late in September.

On 25 Sep. 1789 Washington asked Hamilton to consult with John Jay about the names of thirty-five persons he had culled from the mass of applicants for office and to advise him if one could be found who was, "under all circumstances . . . more eligable for the Post Office than Col O[sgood]." He then added: "And, that you may have the matter *fully* before you, I shall add that, it is my *present* intention to nominate Mr. Jefferson for Secretary of State, and Mr. Edmd. Randolph as Attorney Genl; though their acceptance is problematical, especially the latter."[57] The next day the Senate confirmed the nomination of Jefferson and forty-seven others with so perfunctory a voice that Senator William Maclay did not even bother to note the proceedings in his diary.[58] But

---

[57] Washington to Hamilton, 25 Sep. 1789; Syrett, *Hamilton*, v, 409; Washington, *Writings*, ed. Fitzpatrick, xxx, 413, contains the full list of names.

[58] JEP, I, 29-33. Most of the nominees were those of the Chief Justice, the Justices of the Supreme Court, and the judges, attorneys, and marshals of the Federal District Courts that had been submitted by Washington on 24 Sep. 1789.

there can scarcely be room for doubt as to the feelings of some as they cast their votes for the Secretary of State. William Samuel Johnson four days later told Beckwith plainly that he regretted Jay's removal from the Office of Foreign Affairs. And a few months later he said to him even more bluntly: "Mr. Jefferson . . . is greatly too democratic for us at present, *he left us in that way*, but we are infinitely changed, and he must alter his principles.—I think this Gentleman's ideas are not friendly to the formation of a commercial treaty with you. . . . Mr. Jefferson is a republican and a frenchman."[59] New Englanders in the Senate could be grateful for what Jefferson had done in France for the whale fishery and yet be far from sympathetic to Jefferson's use of it as a political institution to draw the United States closer to France by commercial ties that would aid "in maintaining the field against the common adversary." John Jay as Secretary for Foreign Affairs did not need to read between the lines of Jefferson's *Observations on the Whale-Fishery* to understand why he had been warned against letting such a document become public.[60] Neither Jay nor the Federalist majority in the Senate could be expected to look with enthusiasm upon a Secretary of State who, merely as a diplomat abroad, had devised such a retaliatory stroke of policy against the commercial and naval power of England. His advanced principles of commercial reciprocity were set forth in treaties of commerce that he had been sent abroad to negotiate with Adams and Franklin, and his disposition to use trade as an instrument of national policy was equally apparent, making it certain that during the ensuing session of Congress his sympathies would be on the side of Madison's hated proposals. A Secretary of State hostile to the idea of a commercial treaty with Great Britain—as one able and upright Senator genuinely believed Jefferson to be—could be expected to advise the President either that no minister be sent to London or that the one chosen should be only "a second edition of Mr. Adams." Those Federalists who could discern this possibility so clearly could also grasp the idea quite as readily as Washington and Madison did that a personal agent sent between sessions of Congress would involve something like a commitment to name him as minister should one be appointed. Viewing all the circumstances surrounding this surprising action taken by the President at so tranquil a moment, against Madison's strong argument, and at a time Jefferson was momentarily expected, it is difficult to avoid the conclusion that the designation of a Secretary of State so

---

The President's letter transmitting the names of TJ, Randolph, Osgood, and others was dated on the same day as his letter to Hamilton, 25 Sep. 1789.

[59] Beckwith's report of "Conversations with different persons" (italics supplied; see note 44). It is significant that Johnson was aware that TJ's principles were already formed and known before he departed for France in 1784. The two men could have had few opportunities to know each other before 1790, for Johnson had declined to serve in the Continental Congress before the Revolution and his service afterward began in 1785 when Jefferson was in Europe. But in the autumn of 1789 there were some among the Federalists in the Senate—Robert Morris, for example—who could have very easily acquainted Johnson with the general views of the new Secretary of State. Johnson's strong comments to Beckwith about a man he may not even have met up to that time must, therefore, reflect attitudes and comments prevalent among the governing majority of the Senate.

[60] See Documents Concerning the Whale Fishery, Vol. 14: 217-69.

unsympathetic to the views of the governing majority of the Senate produced in this situation a sense of urgency that was otherwise wholly lacking. Did the impetus for the appointment of an agent come out of such fears or originate with Washington? The answer must remain conjectural.

But Washington could not have shared the apprehensions about Jefferson that Johnson and others had. To suppose that he would have initiated Morris' appointment out of the same sort of distrust felt by the Federalists for the man he had just named Secretary of State is to suppose an act on his part that would have been not merely uncharacteristic but incredible. Nor could Washington have done this because of Beckwith's warnings of commercial retaliation, about which he had no knowledge. Had he known of these warnings there would undoubtedly have been aroused in him precisely those feelings of national honor and dignity that Beckwith had said Pitt and the ministry would feel should Madison's proposals be adopted. "Upon such minds," Beckwith said, "[the tendency of compulsory measures] must be diametrically opposite. The purposes of national glory are best attained by a close adherence to national honour, alike prepared to meet foreign friendships, and to repel foreign hostility."[61] Hamilton, engaged in a course that belied his words, told Beckwith that these sentiments did honor to any nation. Few could have known better than he that, however little the President might employ such declamatory expressions, Washington was the very embodiment of such concepts of national dignity.

Further, if direct disclosure of the hint of stern measures by the ministry was imprudent, means were readily available for the use of indirection. Sir John Temple had just received the ministry's extensive inquiries, reflecting among many interests a concern over possible discrimination in tariff and tonnage duties. If Temple required data and thus disclosed his circular for that purpose, presumably he would have turned first to the Treasury, where some of the information, if available, might be found. But why should he have made the inquiries known to Jay or Jay have given the substance of them to the President? The fact that Washington took pains to record the headings of the document suggests that the purpose for which these were disclosed to him was that of providing a hint of the attitudes of the ministry— a hint in which the connection with Madison's "discriminating clauses" was immediately apparent.[62] Jay and Hamilton a few days earlier had been consulted by the President on appointments to office. Then followed Jefferson's appointment and Beckwith's arrival. As acting Secretary for Foreign Affairs it was both proper and appropriate for Jay to have suggested—on the basis of the hint in Temple's circular of the

[61] Beckwith's report of "Conversations with different persons" (see note 44 above); text in Brymner, *Report*, 1890, p. 127-8.

[62] Under 7 Oct. 1789 Washington noted that "Mr. Jay communicated the purport of the Instructions received by Sir John Temple, British Consul, from the Duke of Leeds, Secretary for Foreign Affairs, viz. . . . What tonnage—whether any and what difference between *British* and others—what on *American*. What *Port charges* on foreign vessels—whether any and what difference etca. . . ."; Washington, *Diaries*, ed. Fitzpatrick, IV, 15-16.

ministry's disposition toward the United States—that an informal agent be appointed to ascertain this more precisely. The mere hint of a hardening attitude on the part of the ministry, coupled with the threatened revival of harsher measures of discrimination in the next session of Congress, would have been sufficient to indicate the need of prompt action. Hamilton's recommendation of Gouverneur Morris was as obvious and as natural a choice as that suggested by Jay on the same day. The supposition that the appointment was thus brought about by indirection and by the agency of such prompting influences must perhaps remain without the support of direct evidence. There is abundant proof, however, that such members of the Senate as Johnson, Schuyler, and Morris shared with the Secretary of the Treasury a confidence in Gouverneur Morris that they could not extend to the incoming Secretary of State. Hamilton had good reason to tell Washington that he "highly approved of the measure" and perhaps better reason to feel gratified that the person he thought leaning in his bias toward England had been chosen.

The question naturally arises whether Hamilton made his proposal to Beckwith before or after he recommended the appointment of Morris. It has been assumed that he did so afterwards, but the possibility that this assumption is unwarranted cannot be dismissed. Fully eight days intervened between Beckwith's opening interview with Johnson and Hamilton's recommendation of Morris. In view of Schuyler's intermediation and Hamilton's request—in neither of which can the note of urgency fail to be observed—it does not seem likely that Hamilton would have long delayed his solicitation of the interview. Hamilton's words to Beckwith—"I am not sufficiently authorized to say so, it is not in my department, but I am inclined to think *a person will soon be sent to England to sound the disposition of your Court*"—have been interpreted as if spoken even after the decision to appoint Morris had been made. But this interpretation was grounded on the assumption, now known to be untenable, that Beckwith had not arrived in New York at the time that decision was arrived at.[63] This would have placed the interview a full two weeks after Beckwith talked with William Samuel Johnson, an interval scarcely compatible with the sense of urgency that all participants save Madison seemed to feel. The words are equally applicable to the situation existing prior to Hamilton's suggestion of the name of Morris to Washington on the 7th of October.[64] For Hamilton to have disclosed the intent to Beckwith before that date would have represented an even less daring risk than the one he took the following spring in virtually identifying Washington with his own proposal of a closer

[63] See note 46 above.

[64] Two further points should be noted: (1) Hamilton advanced substantially the same observation to Beckwith that Washington made to Morris in his letter of instructions—that the establishment of the new government and its judiciary removed the objections theretofore advanced by the ministry for putting the United States in possession of the frontier posts; and (2) Beckwith referred to Hamilton's disclosure as "*its being your intention* to send a person to learn our disposition" (emphasis supplied), as if perhaps the object at this stage were no more than an intent. Both of these points seemed to lend strength to the assumption made above.

connection with Great Britain, for on this occasion he spoke tentatively, on the other with assurance. Such an interpretation gains force in view of Hamilton's confident statement to Beckwith in the autumn of 1789 that the ideas he threw out about "strong ties of commercial, perhaps of political, friendships" were "those of General Washington . . . as well as of a great majority in the Senate." It was Hamilton's nature to speak and act boldly, as if in fact he spoke for the administration. The supposition that the plan originated with him seems more plausible than that assumption which preceded it and which can no longer be given the status it once enjoyed. Since Beckwith first revealed his warning on the 30th, it is scarcely plausible to suppose that so bold an administrator as Hamilton would allow eight days to elapse before seeking an interview with the agent who brought the warning. As devious as he was bold, Hamilton could have seen at once the advantage of initiating such a move through John Jay as acting Secretary for Foreign Affairs, using as a reason for the manoeuver the circular that Sir John Temple had just received from the Secretary for Home Affairs. Such a move would have been far less disingenuous than that for which the Secretary of the Treasury was indubitably responsible during the war crisis of 1790. Both actions were characteristic of the man.

Beckwith returned to Quebec by way of Vermont presumably about the time that Washington left New York on his New England tour. When the latter departed on the morning of the 15th, Hamilton, Jay, and Knox rode a little way out of the city with him. The weather was cheerless, but the two Secretaries and the Chief Justice had cause for satisfaction. The government had been safely launched, all departments had been created, no urgent problems pressed, they were clearly of the majority in both cabinet and Congress, and two separate lines of communication with the British ministry had been established. The President, having left with Jay the letters of credence and instructions for Morris, could share all of these satisfactions save one. He could not have known two channels of communication with the ministry had been set up and that the one officially authorized by him as head of state was the one of lesser importance. The other, arranged in secret and now guided by the Secretary of the Treasury, was undoubtedly intended to prepare the way for a cordial reception of the President's agent.

But the report carried back by Beckwith nullified this intent by its evidence of an almost unanimous acquiescence under the warning brought by him from London. Dorchester at once forwarded the astonishing communication about those aligned with or friendly to the British interest—indeed so promptly that the ministry knew its contents a full month before Morris received Washington's instructions. The next spring, as the war crisis was developing behind the scenes, the Secretary for Foreign Affairs found it "necessary in the first instance . . . to hold a language of firmness" with Morris and to "point out the non execution of the Treaty on the part of America, and the inadequate return made for the liberal manner in which they [had] been treated in point of commerce."[65] This was a natural and logical position for Leeds to take. Morris could reply that he knew of no liberality save that the United States could easily dispense with—the impressment of seamen—but the attempted pleasantry fell flat. His position had been weakened by those most anxious to make it secure. In their anxiety to shape foreign policy, Hamilton, Schuyler, and Johnson had damaged their cause by placing themselves and their nation not in the posture of negotiators but in that of petitioners, the exact opposite of those principles that Hamilton told Beckwith reflected honor on any nation. The language held out to Morris was indeed less harsh than the admonition conveyed by Beckwith in 1789. But the two lines of communication, aside from becoming thus entangled in England, produced another unanticipated result in America in the summer of 1790. This arose from their differing auspices: being a public agent, Morris was obliged to report his discussions to the President.

Before this came about, another British secret agent in February 1790 sent an express to Dorchester from New York with alarming news of impending military preparations. "The pretence to the public," Dorchester reported in a secret dispatch to Grenville, "is to repel the Indians, but those, who must know better, and see that an Indian warfare does not require so great a force, nor that very large proportion of artillery, are given to understand, that part of these forces are to take possession of the frontier as settled by treaty, to seize the posts, and secure the fur trade; a more secret motive perhaps is to reduce the State Governments, and crush all internal opposition. . . . The United States should bring forward a frontier treaty, settling all past infractions, together with a treaty of commerce. This, as mentioned in [Hamilton's communication by Beckwith] is their true interest; their present politics I apprehend will lead to something less solid, but more brilliant; to what may captivate the people, and prepare their submission to new authorities, to what will strengthen that connection, which I think has great influence at present *as it may better answer personal views.* I send Major Beckwith to thank [Hamilton] for some complimentary declarations, and to inform him I have sent home his communications, that *I approve of the general idea, and think something might be formed on that plan to the advantage of both countries.*"[66]

Beckwith arrived in New York late in March and immediately consulted Hamilton. Jefferson had assumed office the day before, but Beckwith's informant already knew that the Secretary of State thought the struggle in France would be successful, that the outcome would mean great commercial benefits to the United States, and that this would be brought about, in Hamilton's words, by "the influence of the Marquis de la Fayette . . . as well as from that general bias, which

[65] Grenville to Dorchester, 6 May 1790, No. 24, "Secret," PRO: CO 42/67, f. 93-102; text in Brymner, *Report*, 1890, p. 89.

[66] Emphasis supplied in both passages. Dorchester to Grenville, 8 Mch. 1790, No. 18; PRO: CO 42/67, f. 116-23. The allusion to personal views, immediately followed by that to Hamilton, seems to make it clear that both Beckwith and Dorchester had formed a surmise that Hamilton was prompted in making his proposals by a desire to enhance his own power and influence in the administration.

those who guide that party" had always shown to America. Hamilton then revealed to the agent what effect this had had upon himself. "I am the more strongly disposed," he declared, "to view the present time as particularly favorable for the consideration of a Commercial Treaty." On the question of exchanging ministers, Hamilton, responding to a direct question as to whether he had "any further communications to Lord Dorchester," said: "I cannot at this moment determine whether it may be proper to communicate further with Lord Dorchester, or to carry it forward through a regular channel.—Mr. Jefferson arrived last night, and these matters are in his department." He thought it might be possible to say something on this head before Beckwith returned to Quebec. Later he assured the agent that nothing had happened to change the views expressed in the former conversation. A treaty of commerce was generally wished, the full consideration of the subject was desirable, the reciprocal appointment of ministers was also agreeable, and the particular rank was a matter of secondary consideration.

Beckwith had long conversations with William Samuel Johnson who spoke in almost identical terms about Jefferson's views and about the subject of a treaty and the matter of exchanging ministers. The astute politician put his finger on the heart of the matter. The great difficulty in the way of amicable commercial relationships, he said to Beckwith, is that "your Navigation Act is so very important to your naval greatness, that you will not be disposed to break through so essential a part of it, as to give us a share in your West India trade." In a late discussion of the problem in the Senate, he added, some had preferred to negotiate an amicable adjustment of differences "by a reciprocal appointment of Arbitrators, or in any other equitable manner, or if this [should] not be thought eligible, by the Appointment of Commissioners in Europe." Johnson, who had been one of the Connecticut counsel in the notable and impressively successful arbitration of the dispute between Pennsylvania and his native state, came nearer to an endorsement of republican principles than he may have realized in making this suggestion. But neither he nor the Senate had changed attitudes. In the Southern states, Beckwith was told by diminutive William Paterson, Senator from New Jersey, "peculiar as it may seem a more democratic opinion prevails . . . than in the middle and eastern States, where the science of government is better understood.—Mr. Jefferson is proof of this, he is a man of some acquirements . . . but his opinions upon Government are the result of fine spun theoretic systems, drawn from the ingenious writings of Locke, Sydney and others of their cast, which can never be realized."

Just before returning in mid-April, Beckwith sought another interview with Alexander Hamilton in order to ask what he felt to be a necessary but hoped was not an improper question. "I take it for granted," he said, "the different communications you have been pleased to make to me, flow from that source, which under your present Government, is alone competent to make them." A direct answer could scarcely have been avoided. The response proved how little Washington knew of these secret discussions that went so far towards committing his administration. "I am not authorized to say to you in so many words,"

Hamilton replied, "that such is the language of the President of the United States; to a gentleman, who has no public character such a declaration cannot be made, but my honor and character stand implicated in the fulfilment of these assurances."[67]

Early in April Beckwith reported to Grenville on the subject that had caused him to be sent to New York. The military plans on foot, he thought, had three objects: to meet the threat of an Indian war, to strengthen "the general government of the Union, by an increase in the military establishment," and to establish a force in the Northwest Territory that would be sufficient to overawe the Indian tribes and, ultimately, to undertake offensive war. The last he regarded as being no immediate aim: "on the contrary," he added, "I have ground to believe there is a wish to cultivate a connexion, infinitely important in my humble apprehension to the genuine interest and future prosperity of this country." On his way back to Quebec Beckwith was confirmed in this view by the sheriff of Clinton county, who saw something mysterious in the military preparations: at first a "very considerable body of Troops" had been proposed, then there was much secret discussion, and then a greater degree of moderation prevailed.[68] Grenville received the dispatch just four days after Leeds and Pitt, under the changed circumstances induced by the war crisis, had greatly softened the language held out to Gouverneur Morris. He concluded on the basis of that dispatch that there was "no probability of an immediate attack in the course of the present Year upon our posts from the United States."[69] There was no further softening of the language.

Beckwith arrived in Quebec just as the war crisis broke in London. This not only sent him hurrying back to New York in July but, through circumstances that compelled a removal of some of the secrecy shrouding his missions theretofore, brought to a close the first period of his activity as Dorchester's agent.

[67] Beckwith's report of conversations, Mch.-Apr. 1790, enclosed in Dorchester to Grenville, 27 May 1790, PRO: CO 42/67, f. 235, 237-63. The text of Beckwith's report is printed in Brymner, *Report*, 1890, p. 134-43, but with a very serious error. Brymner identified the first part of Beckwith's report of his conversations with the figure 1 (William Samuel Johnson) whereas the report itself as received by Grenville has the figure 7 (Hamilton) in the margin. Hamilton's remarks are those set forth by Brymner at p. 134-6, whereas Johnson's statements begin at the bottom of p. 136 where the figure 1 is repeated. The confusion of 1 and 7 was an easy error to make but it has had most unfortunate consequences, misleading even such thorough scholars as Bemis and Syrett (see Bemis, *Jay's Treaty*, p. 91).

[68] Beckwith to Grenville, 7 Apr. 1790, PRO: CO 42/72, f. 180-3; duplicate, f. 359-66, both endorsed as received 25 May 1790.

[69] Grenville to Dorchester, 5 June 1790, draft, Secret, PRO: CO 42/67, f. 160-2.

IV

The Threat of
War, 1790

If war "does happen," Gouverneur Morris reported to Washington after his conference with Leeds and Pitt on the 21st of May, "then they will give us a good Price for our Neutrality, and Spain I think will do so too, wherefore this appears to be a favorable Moment for treating with that Court about the Mississippi." The two ministers had assured him that he had misunderstood Leeds' letter respecting a treaty of commerce. "I answered coolly," Morris reported, "that it was easy to rectify the Mistake, but it appeared idle to form a new Treaty untill the Parties should be thoroughly satisfied with that already existing."[70] This brought on a discussion of violations of the Treaty of Peace by both nations. When Pitt stated that national honor required the retention of the posts as a guarantee of compliance by the United States, Morris replied with warmth: "the Conduct you have pursued naturally excites Resentment in every American Bosom. We do not think it worth while to go to War with you for these Posts, but *we know our Rights, and will avail ourselves of them when Time and Circumstances may suit.*" In response to Pitt's question as to whether he had powers to treat, Morris gave the answer that had already been hinted at more delicately to Beckwith in America—that since the United States had sent one minister to London, no other could be sent as long as England neglected to do the same. Pitt then asked Morris what Philip Schuyler had asked Beckwith nine months earlier. Would a minister be sent in return for one dispatched? Morris replied that he could "almost promise" that one would be sent, but had no authority to offer positive assurances. He proposed that a minister be appointed by England and offered himself to remain in London until informed of a similar appointment by the United States. The inconclusive exchange brought nothing save a promise that Leeds and Pitt would consult and inform Morris of the result.[71]

The language of the ministry had softened only to the extent of trying to avoid giving offense—not altogether successfully—at a time when the disposition of the American government was a matter of some con-

[70] Morris to Washington, 29 May 1790 (RC in DLC: Washington Papers).
[71] The whole of Morris' correspondence with Leeds and his reports to Washington is to be found in Sparks, *Gouverneur Morris*, II, 3-56; see also TJ's report to Washington, 15 Dec. 1790.

cern. That of Morris, however, offered a striking contrast to the position taken by his sponsor in the discussions with Beckwith. Hamilton's pledge of honor to the commitment he had assumed for the administration and Beckwith's reassuring news about developing military plans came to Grenville a few days after Morris' interview with Leeds and Pitt. But the ministry had not needed this reassurance to decide in what manner to counteract any inducements Spain might hold out to the United States as the price of alliance against England. Its decision was not to communicate directly with Washington's official agent. To have done that would have brought on all the risks of negotiation—offers, counter-offers, perhaps pledges—and it would not have enabled the ministry to pursue its growing interest in Vermont and Kentucky. The discussion would not be held with the agent of a sovereign power close at hand but rather with "the British interest" in America.

Two weeks before Morris' interview with Leeds and Pitt, Grenville sent three urgent and secret dispatches to Dorchester, all written the day Pitt disclosed the war crisis to the nation. The first announced the danger of conflict, expressed fear the Americans might seize the opportunity to demand the forts, and asked Dorchester to remain in Canada to direct defense preparations. The second was devoted to the importance of preserving friendly relations with Vermont. If it could be the means of "attaching the people of Vermont sincerely to the British interest," a concession to export flour into Quebec might be justified. The third dispatch, dealing directly with American relations, stands as a tribute to the strength of the British interest in the United States that Beckwith's reports had disclosed. In this Grenville admitted that Washington's letter of credence to Morris indicated "some disposition on the part of the United States to cultivate a closer connection." Even though the ministry had been obliged to hold out a firm language to Morris in the beginning, Grenville explained, "it will certainly be our object to establish, if possible, a greater degree of interest than we have hitherto had in that country." He thought it by no means impossible "to turn the tide of opinion and wishes of America" in favor of Great Britain by holding up to their view—particularly those in Kentucky and the western territories—the possibility of British aid in obtaining free navigation of the Mississippi, an "object . . . at least as important [to them] as the possession of the Forts." The instruments by which this desirable result might be achieved were precisely the same as those that had been employed in recent years. To cultivate the British interest in the United States and to increase it if possible, Dorchester was directed to "find the means of sending proper persons" to promote this object "and at the same time . . . to give . . . the earliest information of hostile designs, if any such should be meditated against the forts or against Canada itself." Such emissaries, Grenville explicitly stipulated, were *not* to be clothed with authority under any public commission. They would have no status equivalent to that of Gouverneur Morris.

Thus the ministry, holding Washington's agent at arm's length, appealed to its friends in America who could not know that the heart of its policy lay in a report just submitted by the Lords of the Committee of the Privy Council for Trade, presided over by the arch-mercantilist Lord Hawkesbury. Grenville's dispatches were grounded on that report: "The Lords are of opinion that, in a commercial view, it will be for the benefit of this country to prevent Vermont and Kentucky and all the other Settlements now forming in the interior parts of the great Continent of North America from becoming dependent on the Government of the United States, or on that of any other foreign country, and to preserve them on the contrary in a state of Independence and to induce them to form Treaties of Commerce and Friendship with Great Britain."[72] The British interest in America, unaware of the rising ascendancy of Hawkesbury's principles of exclusion, was also being held at arm's length. However much it might be courted through Dorchester and Beckwith, that interest had no ground to expect access to the West Indies or a commercial treaty such as the ministry was prepared to accord to independent settlements on the borders of the United States.

The moment he received Grenville's dispatches, Dorchester sent Beckwith off to New York on his fifth and final mission, hoping he would arrive there in time to take advantage of the July packet for England. He furnished the agent with two sets of instructions. The first restated the arguments set forth by Grenville and authorized him —as the occasion might require or his discretion direct—to express Dorchester's hope that the threat of war or even war itself would not "make any alterations in the good disposition of the United States to establish a firm friendship and Alliance with Great Britain to the Mutual advantage of both countries." Dorchester explained to Grenville that these instructions to Beckwith were intended to "clothe him with consequence, and authorize him to speak generally on certain public topics," but it is quite incorrect to speak of them as being public instructions or as being intended for the President of the United States.[73] They were merely, as Dorchester himself said, "of a less secret nature" than those accompanying them. They were in no sense comparable to the letter of credence that Washington as head of state had given to Morris, but were only instructions to a secret agent setting forth the hopes of the Governor General of Canada, to be disclosed to such persons as the occasion and Beckwith's discretion authorized.[74] If intended for anyone, they were presumably to be shown to the one to whom Beckwith actually disclosed them on arrival in New York, the Secretary of the Treasury.

The second letter of instructions was marked "*Secret*," thus to be hidden even from those who had proven themselves so friendly to Great Britain. These instructions directed Beckwith to try to discover the

[72] Report of the Committee, 17 Apr. 1790, PRO: Chatham Papers, 363; Grenville to Dorchester, Dispatches Nos. 22-24, all dated 6 May 1790 and all marked "*Secret*"; PRO: CO 42/67, f. 87-9, 91-2, 93-102; texts printed in Brymner, *Report*, 1890, p. 131-3.

[73] Fitzpatrick, for example, states that Beckwith "had presented a memorandum to the President"; Washington, *Writings*, ed. Fitzpatrick, XXXI, 102n.; see also, Syrett, *Hamilton*, VI, 486, note 8; Bemis, *Jay's Treaty*, p. 92.

[74] Dorchester to Beckwith, 27 June 1790, PRO: CO 42/68, f. 255, enclosed in Dorchester to Grenville, 7 July 1790, same, f. 252-3; both the covering letter and these "less secret" instructions are printed in Brymner, *Report*, 1890, p. 133, 143.

American attitude "towards peace or war, separately, and unconnected with the affairs of Spain . . . and whether they expect any assistance from France in her present situation"; to pay particular attention to the characters of military men and to all military arrangements; and, while being cautious in saying anything specific on the subject of the navigation of the Mississippi, to try to "ascertain the extent and importance of the adherents of each particular system." The agent was directed to remain in New York as long as he found his presence there to be "of advantage to the King's services."[75] It was the last instruction that altered the character of Beckwith's role and led to the unwarranted assumption that the emissary functioned as an unaccredited minister in residence. Neither the authority granted him nor the explanation made by Dorchester to Grenville justifies such an inference. Owing "to the shortness of his occasional visits to that country," Dorchester explained, "he can only procure such desultory information, as happens to fall in his way, without being able to follow the chain of events, or attend to the different changes, which that government is still liable to."[76] Beckwith's information on four previous missions had been far from desultory or accidentally come by, but it was natural for Dorchester to assume that, having achieved such extraordinary results on flying visits, Beckwith would be able to give added value both to his connections and his communications by a continuous residence. Far from interrupting or changing the nature of his role as a confidential agent, this order had the effect of strengthening it. The disclosure of that role to public view resulted from other factors than the instructions of the Governor General. The ministry, of course, had nothing to do with the choice of Beckwith. Grenville had only authorized Dorchester to "find the means of sending proper persons" to cultivate the British interest and to act as secret agents. Dorchester authorized Beckwith on occasion to communicate directly with Grenville only because the risk of delay by way of Quebec might be harmful to public affairs.

The journey from Quebec to New York normally required at least a fortnight. Since Beckwith's instructions were dated 27 June and since he disclosed these to Hamilton on the morning of 8 July, it is clear that the trip was uncommonly hurried and that the disclosure was made immediately on arrival.[77] At noon of that day Hamilton reported the conversation to Washington and Jefferson, thus for the first time bringing the role of the confidential agent into public view. There would

[75] Dorchester to Beckwith, 27 June 1790, "*Secret*," PRO: CO 42/68, f. 258-60, enclosed in Dorchester to Grenville, 7 July 1790 (see note 75); text of instructions in Brymner, *Report*, 1890, p. 144.

[76] Dorchester to Grenville, 7 July 1790, PRO: CO 42/68, f. 252-3.

[77] Beckwith's remarkable journey could not have taken more than ten days. In 1787 the secret agent Peter Allaire traversed the distance "in Twenty three days of Tedious Journey . . . riding 643 miles of Roads unknow[n] of in Europe," though on learning the route he stated that he could make the trip in fifteen days. Christopher Colles' *Survey of the Roads of the United States* that had appeared in 1789 extended only to Albany. Between that and Quebec lay great stretches of wilderness. This, Allaire stated, interposed such a barrier to communication that Canadians knew less of affairs in the United States than Englishmen knew of events in China (Peter Allaire to Sir George Yonge, 16 Aug. 1787, with enclosed report of "Occurrences," PRO: FO 4/5, f. 313, 323).

appear to have been less reason for this sudden revelation in 1790 than there had been in 1789. On the former occasion Beckwith had brought an authoritative message directly from Grenville, while on this he was only Dorchester's agent having private instructions that showed no discernible authority from Whitehall. He brought no offers or proposals, only Dorchester's hope that the threat of war had made no alteration in the disposition previously manifested by Hamilton. Further, the price attached to disclosure was the certainty of closer scrutiny, of aroused suspicions, and of diminished effectiveness—a price both Beckwith and Hamilton might have to pay. Both apparently had much to risk and little to gain by the ending of secrecy. Why, then, was Dorchester's vague and noncommittal expression of hope reported immediately to the President when Grenville's unequivocal warning of 1789 had not been? There is no doubt that it was Hamilton who, with characteristic boldness, chose disclosure and that he did so under the compulsion of untoward circumstances. This, as well as the motive that prompted it, is indicated by the manner in which the disclosure was made.

Under 8 July 1790 Washington made this entry in his diary: "About noon the Secretaries of State, and of the Treasury called upon me— the last of whom reported a communication made to him by Majr. Beckwith . . . which he reduced to writing." It has been assumed that Hamilton first reported the conversation to Jefferson and then to the President.[78] Other than the ambiguous allusion in Washington's diary, there is no evidence to support this assumption, though it is possible that it is well grounded and equally so that it is not. Nor is it clear from the entry whether Hamilton had already reduced the interview to writing or did so after first making an oral report to the President. Again either is possible, though the latter seems more plausible. The haste of Beckwith's journey from Quebec, the retrospective tone given to the title of Hamilton's memorandum, the "recollected" contents of Dorchester's letter, the delicate situation that brought about disclosure, the studied care with which the report was prepared—all tend to support this assumption.[79] Even so, Hamilton must have reduced the interview to writing with some haste, for Washington recorded the memorandum in full in his diary under the same date. That report can only be understood by a close comparison of Grenville's dispatch to Dorchester, the latter's instructions to Beckwith, and Hamilton's version of the conversation. Perhaps significantly, Beckwith made no report of what transpired that morning.

It is indicative but unimportant that Hamilton represented the agent's communication as having been made to him "by direction of Lord Dorchester," whereas Beckwith's instructions about disclosure were permissive and discretionary, not mandatory. But there are numerous discrepancies of substance between the instructions and the memorandum

[78] Washington, *Diaries*, ed. Fitzpatrick, IV, 137; Freeman, *Washington*, VI, 269-70.

[79] "Memorandum of a Communication made on Thursday the Eighth of July to the Subscriber by Major Beckwith *as by direction of Lord Dorchester*" (emphasis supplied); MS in Hamilton's hand in DLC: Washington Papers; text printed in Syrett, *Hamilton*, VI, 484-6. Washington transcribed the entire document in his diary under 8 July 1790; *Diaries*, ed. Fitzpatrick, IV, 137-8.

and two of these are of such importance that they must be particularly examined. The first concerns the mission of Gouverneur Morris. Grenville in his secret dispatch had sent Dorchester a copy of Washington's letter of credence to Morris of 13 Oct. 1789, together with a communication from Morris to Leeds and the latter's response. Grenville noted the good dispositions Washington's letter revealed, gave full value to the fact that it came from the President, and qualified this only by saying that it was "vague and inexplicit." Dorchester's instructions reflected Grenville's comments in this as in other respects. He had learned with satisfaction, Dorchester wrote, "that some steps towards an amicable System have been commenced at home, through the Agency of Mr. Morris, though not yet so explicit and formal as the case may require." He made no hint of any lack of cordiality on either side in such negotiations. This, however, is what Hamilton reported to Washington: "Major Beckwith . . . next proceeded to observe that Lord Dorchester had been informed of a negociation commenced on the other side of the water through the Agency of Mr. Morris; mentioning the Subscriber understood principally by way of proof of Ld. Dorchesters knowlege of the transaction that Mr. Morris had not produced any regular credentials, but merely a letter from the President directed to himself, that some delays had intervened partly on account of Mr. Morris's absence on a trip to Holland as was understood and that it was not improbable those delays and some other circumstances may have impressed Mr. Morris with an idea of backwardness on the part of the British ministry. That his Lordship however had directed him to say that an inference of this sort would not in his opinion be well founded as he had reason to believe that the Cabinet of Great Britain entertained a disposition not only towards a friendly intercourse but towards an alliance with the United States."

The first substantive discrepancy in the opening remarks of Hamilton's memorandum presents a puzzle. Why was it necessary to produce proof of Dorchester's knowledge of the negotiations? If proof were necessary and cordiality the aim, why the disparagement of Morris' credentials as "merely a letter from the President"? The British Secretary for Foreign Affairs had expressed himself as pleased with that letter, had given it due credit, and had proceeded to hold conversations with the agent it authorized. Nor had the Governor General of Canada made any such disparagement in his instructions to Beckwith. If proof were necessary in order to explain delays and to counter inferences, why was not that evidence used in which delay was mentioned and explained—that is, the letters between Morris and Leeds? These as well as a copy of Washington's letter of credence had been enclosed in Grenville's secret dispatch to Dorchester. If Dorchester had shown any of these secret documents to Beckwith—a supposition plausible enough but perhaps not provable—the agent could have known that Morris had mentioned his expectation "of hearing from his Grace at an early period" and that Leeds had explained the delay on the ground of Morris' absence in Holland, his own illness, and "a Multiplicity of Engagements."[80]

80 The texts of Leeds' letter to Morris of 28 [i.e. 29] Apr. 1790 and of Morris' reply of 30 Apr. 1790, together with Washington's letter of credence to Morris

Or, if these were not shown, Dorchester could have told Beckwith of these facts and prepared him against unwarranted inferences. But if this were to be done at all, why was it not done in the written instructions where the emphasis was upon cordiality rather than in an oral instruction where—according to Hamilton's memorandum—the emphasis was upon the untoward aspect of the negotiation and its purpose to dispose of ill-found inferences? The answer to such questions can only be deduced. But the fact is that Morris' first reports of his correspondence with Leeds had arrived in New York only a short while before Beckwith appeared. Hamilton knew well enough what inferences were being drawn from these reports by the President and particularly by the Secretary of State. Washington in fact had shown the correspondence to John Adams on the 1st of July and the Vice-President had immediately declared the result to be "of a piece with their conduct towards him whilst Minister at that Court" and "just what he expected."[81] These inferences, as the event proved, were essentially the same as those drawn by Morris himself—that the delays were evasive, that a commercial treaty was thought by the ministry to be unnecessary.

Was it Dorchester who instructed his agent to anticipate these inferences? It is quite implausible to suppose that he did, not only because his instructions carry no such allusions but also because of the simple fact that he had no reason to suppose anything untoward affected the negotiations. The exchange of letters between Morris and Leeds that Grenville sent him was polite, formal, and candid, but Dorchester on reading these letters alone can have had no such feeling for the tone of the negotiations as to have instructed his agent to counter its ill effect. Both the letters and the instructions convey at that point the impression that the discussions in London were proceeding amicably and normally. Grenville's secret dispatch had the effect of confirming this impression, containing nothing to offset it. Some months later Dorchester indeed stated that he had had no accounts of the progress of the negotiation and that he thought it natural enough the discussions with Spain "should have occasioned some delay."[82] But this was occasioned by Beckwith's

---

of 13 Oct. 1790, were enclosed in Grenville's secret dispatch No. 24 to Dorchester of 6 May 1790; texts of all are printed in Brymner, *Report*, 1890, p. 129-31, 133. See also Vol. 16: 531-6.

[81] Washington, *Diaries*, ed. Fitzpatrick, IV, 132, under 1 July 1790. It is obvious that Washington had shown Morris' report of the interview with Leeds and Pitt to Hamilton as well as to Adams and TJ (Beckwith's report, enclosed in Dorchester to Grenville, 10 Nov. 1790, PRO: CO 42/72, f. 61-8, 69-72; see Syrett, *Hamilton*, VII, 70).

[82] Henry Motz, secretary to Dorchester, to George Beckwith, 10 Feb. 1791, PRO: CO 42/73, f. 133-5; text in Brymner, *Report*, 1890, p. 168-9. This remark was in response to Beckwith's report that Hamilton seemed surprised at the reserve shown by the ministry toward Morris. In addition to the reason given, Motz added: "There is indeed another cause, from the influence of which it is to be hoped Mr. M[orris] is free, but which his Lordship is inclined to think has operated ever since the peace against a connexion between the two countries. No doubt many gentlemen, and some of high and distinguished character, in the states, see through the clouds, that have been raised with so much industry to mislead that people, but the general spirit and language for some years after the peace have been by no means of a conciliating nature. This disposition appears of late to have in a great measure abated, particularly on the shores of the

report of the surprise felt by Hamilton at a "certain reserve" exhibited by the ministry to Morris. Here Dorchester was responding to an inference in a very different manner from that attributed to him in the summer of 1790. All evidence points to the fact that when he drafted the instructions he gave Beckwith no authority to say more on the subject of the negotiations in London than these authorized.

But were the words attributed to him those of Beckwith? It is conceivable that he learned of Morris' report to Washington after he arrived in New York. If so, he could only have received the information from the person to whom he obviously addressed himself first, Alexander Hamilton. But it is scarcely in the realm of the possible that, having just learned of the inferences drawn from Morris' report, the agent would then have repeated this to his informant as his own; that he would have stated in the next breath that Dorchester had "directed him to say that an inference of this sort" was ill-founded; and that Hamilton, accepting such an absurd repetition at face value, would have solemnly passed the representation on to the President as coming from Dorchester through Beckwith. The implication is clear. Beckwith could not have said what Hamilton quoted him as saying about the London negotiations. These were words put in the mouth of the agent by Hamilton, who had every reason for doing so.

The second substantive discrepancy between Dorchester's instructions and Hamilton's memorandum involves a far graver matter, for it distorted the expressed intent of a foreign power and therefore was an act of deception on the administration in its conduct of foreign policy. According to Hamilton's memorandum, Beckwith quoted Dorchester as saying that "*he had reason to believe* that the Cabinet of Great Britain entertained a disposition not only towards a friendly intercourse but towards an alliance with the United States."[83] This is a gross misrepresentation of what Grenville had authorized and what Dorchester had actually said, committing both to a position neither had occupied. Dorchester's carefully drawn and less secret instructions to Beckwith said: "You will at the same time express my hope, that neither the appearance of a War with Spain nor its actually taking place, will make any alterations in the good disposition *of the United States* to establish a firm friendship and Alliance with Great Britain to the Mutual advantage of both Countries; I am persuaded it can make none on the part of Great Britain, whose liberal treatment of the United States in point of Commerce sufficiently evinces her friendly disposition, notwithstanding the non execution of the treaty on their part, which, and various misrepresentations, I have always attributed to an unsettled state of their government, and of the minds of the multitude, influenced per-

_____

Atlantic, though there are still some indications of it; but in the western territory it would seem great pains are still taken to keep it up at its original height. As this spirit operated, it would naturally produce a corresponding reserve on the part of our government. And perhaps the wisest plan, that could be followed by Great Britain, under such circumstances, was, to leave the states time to reflect, and by their own good sense to find out that course which is most consonant to their true interest."

[83] Italics supplied.

haps by a power not very cordial even to the United States.[84] The instructions and the memorandum could scarcely be more contradictory on the central point involved.

In drafting the instructions Dorchester no doubt intended only to follow the line adopted by Leeds of holding out a firm language to Morris. But there were at least three forceful reasons why the Secretary of the Treasury should not have wished these expressions to be transmitted undiluted to the President or the Secretary of State. First, the innuendo about the influence of France, the implied reflection on "the minds of the multitude," and the charges about various misrepresentations made presumably by the leaders of an unsettled government were little calculated to promote friendly dispositions, especially on the part of the Secretary of State. Second, Dorchester had in fact made no other assurances about British intent than that, despite the failure of the American government to live up to its treaty obligations, the threat of war would cause no alteration in her previous attitude of leniency in matters of commerce. This was to have been expected. It approximated the position taken by the ministry with Morris. It reflected also much of what Beckwith had said to Johnson, Schuyler, and Hamilton in 1789. The gist of the passage was that the threat of war would not cause any alteration in the previous "friendly disposition" of the ministry. Even this was set forth only as Dorchester's opinion, with much of its amicable intent being effaced by the claim of British liberality and the charges of American delinquency in which the opinion was imbedded. There was nothing in the passage conveying an authoritative expression of the ministry's intent. There could not have been, for Grenville expressly forbade Dorchester to clothe his agent with authority to speak under a public commission. The disposition of the British ministry was far more hidden in this passage than that of the President had been in the letter of credence to Morris that Grenville found so vague and inexplicit. Third, and most important of all, the Secretary of the Treasury could not have revealed the exact words of Dorchester's instructions without exposing himself to the President as having committed the administration on his own authority to a position it had not assumed and of having done this in secret negotiations, pledging in support of the commitment his own honor and character.

Far from manifesting a desire on the part of Great Britain to effect a "firm friendship and Alliance," Dorchester had merely authorized Beckwith to express his hope that the threat of war would not cause "any alterations in the good disposition *of the United States*" to establish such a connection.[85] The government of the United States had expressed no such desire for an alliance. But the Secretary of the Treasury had gone very far toward declaring this aim for the administration. In employing such an expression as "firm friendship and Alliance," Dorchester in effect was only paraphrasing Hamilton's proposed plan of 1789 for "strong ties of commercial, perhaps of political, friendships" between the two countries; his assurance that it was then safe for any nation to "enter into Treaties . . . either Commercial or Political" with

---

[84] Italics supplied.
[85] Italics supplied.

the United States; and his flat declaration to Beckwith: "We wish to form a commercial treaty with you to every extent, to which you may think it for your interest to go." The paraphrasing could not have gone to the President in Dorchester's own words without immediately raising delicate and searching questions. The risk of exposing to view the secret discussions of the preceding year and with it the commitment he had gone so far in making was one that Hamilton dared not take except on his own terms. In addition to the motives that had compelled secrecy up to that point, Thomas Jefferson was now a counterpoise in the administration.

The glaring discrepancy between what Beckwith was authorized to say and what Hamilton quoted him as saying forces the question of responsibility to be raised. Could Beckwith have so misrepresented his superior or Hamilton have so misunderstood the agent that this contradiction came about through mere mistake or defect in communication? Neither man theretofore or afterwards seems to have exhibited in their exchanges any lack of clarity or precision without taking pains at once to remove all ambiguity. Beckwith was especially careful to do this. The nature of the exchange placed this responsibility upon him particularly, for it was Hamilton's ideas about a closer connection that were being transmitted, not the reverse. There is no evidence to show that his reports in these five years ever failed to represent both his informants and his superior with fidelity and accuracy. He was an experienced intelligence officer, trusted by Dorchester on the basis of more than a decade of close association and knowledge of character. On a matter affecting the national interest so deeply, at so critical a juncture, it is implausible to suppose that either Beckwith or Hamilton could have permitted so gross a discrepancy between the agent's instructions and his alleged remarks to have occurred through mere inadvertence. Clearly the contradiction can only have resulted from deliberate choice, not from accident or failure of communication. Was this deliberate choice made by Beckwith or by Hamilton, the only two in the chain of communication who could have created the contradiction?

The effect of Hamilton's memorandum is to place the responsibility squarely upon Beckwith. According to this, Beckwith at the conclusion of his lengthy statement produced a letter signed by Dorchester containing "ideas similar to those he had expressed though in more guarded terms and without any allusion to instructions from the British Cabinet." Hamilton added: "This letter *it is now recollected* hints at the non execution of the treaty of peace on our part." The memorandum concluded with the statement that, on Hamilton's noting that the letter seemed to speak only the sentiments of Dorchester, Beckwith replied: "it was to be presumed . . . his Lordship knew too well the consequence of such a step to have taken it without a previous knowledge of the intentions of the Cabinet."[86] Thus, according to this memorandum, full responsibility for committing Dorchester to a step he had not taken rests upon his agent. But this cannot be made to accord with the facts or with reason.

[86] Italics supplied.

The letter supposedly introduced at the conclusion of the interview can only have been Dorchester's less secret instructions. The first point to be noted is that, assuming so experienced an officer as Beckwith actually had quoted his superior as saying he "had reason to believe that the Cabinet of Great Britain entertained a disposition" toward a friendly intercourse and even an alliance, it is scarcely conceivable that he would thereupon have been so imprudent as to bring forth the instructions and thus wholly discredit what he had just said. Further, this was the first time in all of his missions that, so far as the documents reveal, Beckwith carried written instructions with him. The critical situation justified this. Dorchester, carrying out Grenville's instructions to cultivate and strengthen the "growing British interest," must have intended the letter to be presented to Hamilton—as in fact it was, immediately on Beckwith's arrival. The agent thus could have disclosed the instructions at the beginning of the interview, permitting Dorchester to speak for himself and saving himself from the charge of going far beyond what his instructions authorized. Even if Beckwith had failed to follow this prudent course, Hamilton still had at hand infallible means of measuring the exact dimensions of the discrepancy between what the agent—according to his account—had attributed to Dorchester and what the latter had expressed for himself. In so important a matter it was his duty to do this with some precision in order to provide his own government with the most reliable representation possible of Dorchester's statements. Beckwith was authorized to reveal the instructions as the occasion and his discretion suggested. Hamilton could have insisted, in fact, upon transmitting the letter itself or a careful précis of its contents, just as Gouverneur Morris had done for his correspondence with Leeds. Beckwith in April had not hesitated to pin the Secretary of the Treasury down with a very blunt though politely-phrased question about his authority to speak for the government on the measure he had proposed the preceding autumn. But Hamilton, to judge from his own memorandum, did not insist upon defining Beckwith's spoken and written communications in a way that would have truly reflected their conflict. On the contrary, his report tended to erase all evidence of that conflict that could be removed. More than four-fifths of the memorandum focused on Beckwith's alleged words, while the contents of Dorchester's letter were noted in an almost off-hand manner. In effect, Hamilton asked the administration to attend the oral testimony of the agent rather than the written message of the principal. Dorchester's language was much firmer than that Leeds had held out to Morris, but no trace of this remained in Hamilton's memorandum save the vague recollection about neglect of treaty obligations. All stern admonitions, all innuendoes about the influence of France on the minds of the multitude, all charges of misrepresentation by the leaders of an unsettled government, all claims of British indulgence in matters of trade, all reference to the declared disposition of the government of the United States for a closer connection—indeed all offensive statements of whatever sort were screened from Dorchester's instructions by Hamilton's memorandum.

This much was only negative, a failure to report Dorchester in a full and accurate manner. But Hamilton went further. He declared unequivocally that the letter contained ideas similar to those expressed by Beckwith. Yet on the central question—the declaration that the British ministry desired friendly intercourse *and an alliance*—there was no similarity, only irreconcilable contradiction. Asserting the similarity, Hamilton compounded the misrepresentation by his supposed comment to Beckwith that the letter contained no evidence of instructions from the cabinet but only Dorchester's opinion. So far as the memorandum indicates, he thereupon accepted without comment Beckwith's reply that Dorchester knew the consequences of such a step too well to have taken it without a previous knowledge of the disposition of the ministry. But, having read the letter, Hamilton knew that Dorchester had *not* taken any step beyond the noncommittal response Leeds had given to Morris, that in fact there was nothing in the letter to warrant in any degree the asserted similarity on this central point. Neither the ministry nor Dorchester had given any evidence whatever of wishing to seek an alliance so far as the letter from Grenville or the letter of instructions to Beckwith revealed. Thus in asserting a similarity where none existed, Hamilton destroyed the credibility of his memorandum. On the basis of this single statement he exposed himself to two charges. Either he failed to detect the glaring discrepancy or he made a deliberate effort to conceal that discrepancy. There can be no doubt that Hamilton deliberately chose concealment. It seems likely that he had Dorchester's letter before him while preparing his own memorandum, and the nature of the latter certainly cannot have been revealed to Beckwith.[87] Hamilton alone must bear responsibility for the words that he attributed both to the agent and to the Governor General. The memorandum cannot be accepted as other than a deliberate and gross distortion. The question indeed is not whether Hamilton did this but what purposes moved him.

Beckwith could have had no apparent reason for wishing to misrepresent his superior, while Hamilton had every inducement to soften the impact of Dorchester's words. If he had disclosed the exact terms or even the substance of Dorchester's instructions, several results would have been certain to follow. The President and the Secretary of State would have been affronted by a language even harsher than that exhibited by Leeds to Morris. Questions of responsibility for creating in the mind of Dorchester any impression of the government's disposition for an alliance would have arisen, and with them the risk of exposing the secret discussions and Hamilton as the one who had made proposals leading to such an impression. Gouverneur Morris would have been

[87] Hamilton might also have shown his account of the conversation to Beckwith for verification if he had wished to report an accurate précis, but he only told the agent later that he had made the proper use of what was communicated. The supposition that he had Dorchester's letter before him as he wrote is supported not only by the circumstances that make it most plausible but also by the fact that (1) both Dorchester's instructions and his own memorandum parallel each other in the order in which the topics are taken up and that (2) Hamilton was able to remember the names and spelling of such obscure persons as Hart and Wemble, yet on the direct charge of delinquency as to treaty obligations he could only present this as a vague hint not categorically set forth but "as . . . now recollected."

confirmed in his belief that the ministry intended to retain possession of the posts and considered "a Treaty of Commerce with America as being absolutely unnecessary."[88] Advocates of Madison's "discriminating clauses" would have been given renewed strength. The *rapprochement* toward which Hamilton had labored so long and for which he had risked so much would have been correspondingly endangered. Madison, in fact, had revived his plan for commercial reciprocity immediately after news had arrived of the threat of war.[89] Simultaneously General Irvine's report that Benedict Arnold was in Detroit training the Canadian militia inflamed old passions and instilled in Washington the fear that a descent on Louisiana across American territory was being planned.[90] There was the possibility that other influences would drive the administration toward Spain. John Adams, agreeing with Morris' analysis of the ministry's attitude and believing war almost inevitable, went so far as to tell the President that he thought it good policy and to the interest of the United States to take sides against England in the conflict.[91] Hamilton could assume with certainty that the Secretary of State, aided by James Madison, John Brown, and other members of Congress from the South, would set about doing what he had so long been concerned about and what in fact he was about to do—to seize the war crisis as a means of bargaining with Spain over the opening of the Mississippi. The situation was indeed a critical one, threatening with defeat the carefully developed plans of the Secretary of the Treasury. Its urgency is reflected in the note that Hamilton sent on the day after his interview with Beckwith to John Jay, who was then in attendance on his dying father-in-law, William Livingston: "Certain circumstances of a delicate nature have occurred, concerning which the President would wish to consult you. *They press.* Can you consistently with the Governor's situation afford us your presence here? I cannot say the President directly asks it, lest you should be embarrassed; but he has expressed a strong wish for it."[92]

In this critical situation when war was considered almost inevitable, it is understandable that Hamilton should have made use of Dorchester's communication both to conceal its import and to offset the damaging effect of Morris' report. A measure of Hamilton's concern is to be seen in the fact that the price attached to a disclosure of Beckwith's role was a high one. Nor could his anxiety for his policy and his acute discomfort in the hard-pressing circumstances have been lessened by his own knowledge of the delicate circumstances. Placing Leeds' letter to Morris beside that of Dorchester to Beckwith, he alone in the administration knew that neither contradicted the other.

The two documents spoke the same noncommittal tones. Nowhere in them could be found a trace of a British proposal for "an alliance

---

[88] Morris to Washington, 1 May 1790; Vol. 16: 533.

[89] See Documents on American Commercial Policy, 1790, Vol. 16: 513-34.

[90] This report was brought to Washington by Irvine on Sunday, 4 July 1790; Washington, *Diaries*, IV, 136.

[91] This was on 1 July 1790; same, IV, 132.

[92] Hamilton to Jay, 9 July 1790; Syrett, *Hamilton*, VI, 488. Livingston died on 25 July 1790.

with the United States" or even for a commercial treaty. Hamilton was aware, too, that the responsibility could not be placed upon Gouverneur Morris. Only Dorchester had expressed approval of the "general idea" advanced by the Secretary of the Treasury, while the British cabinet had revealed its coolness to the suggested *rapprochement* by ignoring it.[93] Having done as much as possible to pave the way for a cordial reception of Morris, Hamilton might have been justified in feeling that he had been betrayed in the house of friends. If so, he gave no further expression of this than the pained surprise he expressed to Beckwith over "a certain reserve" shown by Leeds to Morris.[94] His response to the critical situation was not one of dismay or bitterness but of bold and characteristic action. In reshaping and concealing the true meaning of Dorchester's message, Hamilton measured his devotion to the policy he had promoted by these secret and circuitous means. While the treaty that should have been called Hamilton's was still years in the future, this first step towards it closed with an act of deception on the President and the Secretary of State in their conduct of foreign policy. This desperate act to salvage the policy at a critical moment was indeed one in which, as Hamilton had said to Beckwith in April, his own honor and character were implicated.

Desperate as the gamble was, it failed to convince. Jefferson saw at once—though he was obliged to accept Hamilton's version at face value—that no change had occurred to invalidate Morris' reports. He wrote to Morris a statement of policy in words of simple dignity: an honorable neutrality to be given in exchange for a pledge to execute the Treaty of Peace and to attempt no territorial conquests adjacent to the United States. As for the communications through Dorchester, these were mere "tamperings" by the ministry. "Besides what they are saying to you," Jefferson wrote Morris, "they are talking to us through Quebec; but so informally that they may disavow it when they please; it would only oblige them to make the fortune of the poor Major whom they would pretend to sacrifice; through him they talk of a Minister, a treaty of commerce, *and alliance*. If the object of the latter be honorable, it is useless; if dishonorable, inadmissible."[95] The emphasis given and the comment made on the words "*and alliance*" reflect Jefferson's disbelief of the ministry's intent as communicated by Hamilton. But in suspecting a dishonorable and deceptive act, the Secretary of State clearly focused his gaze in the wrong direction.

Nor was the President misled, though he, too, evidently accepted without question Hamilton's assertion that Beckwith had spoken of the ministry's desire for an alliance. Contrary to his usual caution in such matters and without waiting for advice,[96] Washington grasped the

93 Dorchester to Grenville, 8 Mch. 1790, "*Secret*," PRO: CO 42/67, f. 116-23.
94 See note 82 above. On 6 May 1791 Motz wrote Beckwith in further explanation: "The contexture of [Morris'] communications is easily accounted for from his personal views. It is rather surprising that this effect should have escaped the discernment of those, who were acquainted with the nature and extent of his private pursuits in France. Such channels naturally tinge whatever they convey"; Brymner, *Report*, 1890, p. 169-70.
95 Jefferson to Morris, 12 Aug. 1790, Document VIII below.
96 Freeman, *Washington*, VI, 369.

true nature of "this business in the moment of its communication," as he expressed it in his diary that day. Accepting the memorandum at face value, he thought the purported declaration from the ministry "appears simply, and no other than this;—We did not incline to give any satisfactory answer to Mr. Morris, who was *officially* commissioned to ascertain our intentions with respect to the evacuation of the Western Posts within the territory of the United States and other matters into which he was empowered to enquire until by this unauthenticated mode we can discover whether you will enter into an alliance with us and make Common cause against Spain. In that case we will enter into a Commercial Treaty with you and *promise perhaps* to fulfil what [we] already stand engaged to perform." The President decided, nevertheless, to ask Jefferson and Hamilton, as well as Adams, Jay, and Knox to "resolve this matter in all its relations in their minds" that they might be prepared to give their opinions in two or three days.[97]

Jefferson's opinion, delivered two days after it was requested, went further than anyone in the administration was prepared to go in stating the position of the government with precision and in tones both friendly and admonitory. He would have authorized Hamilton to say to Beckwith that nothing could be done about the supposed offer of alliance "till it's object be shewn" and even then unacceptable if inconsistent with existing engagements; that the United States had never desired a commercial treaty except on terms of "perfect reciprocity" and these provided its own price; that in matters of commerce the government preferred "amicable to adversary arrangements, *tho the latter would be infallible*" *and in the nation's power*—an ominous allusion to Madison's "discriminating clauses" and to the stronger threat of an embargo against British ships in American ports carrying produce to and from the West Indies; and that, in the event of war, the government was disposed to be neutral but would view with extreme uneasiness any attempts of either power to seize the possessions of the other" on the American frontiers.[98]

Two days after this opinion was submitted Washington conferred with Hamilton and Jay. There is no evidence that Jefferson was present at this conference and presumably he was not. The Chief Justice and the Secretary of the Treasury apparently did not prepare written opinions and Washington made no record of the discussion except to summarize its result. This stated the attitude of the government toward Beckwith and the message Hamilton said he had brought from Dorchester: "Had some further conversations . . . with respect to the business on which Majr. Beckwith was come on. The result—To treat his communications very civilly—to intimate, delicately, that they carried no marks official or authentic, nor in speaking of Alliance, did they

[97] This comment appears in Washington's *Diaries*, ed. Fitzpatrick, IV, 139, under 8 July 1790 immediately following the transcription of Hamilton's memorandum. Washington apparently made the request of TJ and Hamilton for their opinions on that day. He probably informed them also of his intention to ask similar advice of Adams, Jay, and Knox, for in his urgent letter to Jay on the next day Hamilton intimated as much; see note 92.

[98] See Document I below, enclosure (italics supplied).

convey any definite meaning by which the precise object of the British Cabinet could be discovered. In a word, that the Secretary of the Treasury was to extract as much as he could from Major Beckwith and *to report to me*, without committing, by any assurances whatever, the Government of the U. States, leaving it entirely free to pursue, unreproached, such a line of conduct in the dispute as her interest (and honour) shall dictate."[99] From this it is clear that the recommendations of the Secretary of State—which must have been shown by the President to Hamilton and Jay—were unacceptable. There was no question of extending recognition to Beckwith or even of carrying on formal conversations with him, for he had no status comparable to that of Gouverneur Morris. Possibly it was this obvious fact that enabled the President's advisers to persuade him that the policy suggested by the Secretary of State should not be stated to the agent. Even so, it is surprising that Washington did not insist on an expression of the concern voiced in that statement about attempts of conquest on American borders. For his alarm over the possibility that the British had a design on the Spanish settlements, "and of course to surround these United States," grew so vigorously that by the end of summer it had become a certainty in his mind—despite the fact that Dorchester on his part had fears just as strong about the danger of American aggression and, so far as the evidence discloses, neither he nor the ministry contemplated any attack on Louisiana by land.[100] Hamilton was aware of the President's concern, a fact that may have affected one aspect of his report of the next interview.

Thus the course to which Hamilton had pledged his honor collided with that Washington was determined to follow in maintaining the dignity of the nation. But this embarrassing dilemma gave him no pause. Having proved himself a faulty channel of communication from Beckwith to the administration, Hamilton now demonstrated equal unreliability in the reverse direction. Whatever the arguments employed in the consultation with Washington, the conversations with Beckwith were precisely on the ground on which Hamilton could have most desired them to be. All warnings of commercial retaliation and admonitory tones against aggression had been eliminated from the message he was to take back. He could not produce administrative proposals for a commercial treaty, much less for an alliance, but for the moment danger to the coveted *rapprochement* had been averted. Most important of all, the conversations were in his hands. The crisis had presented a serious threat to his plan, but this had been momentary. Hamilton moved boldly forward.

According to his version of what took place at the second interview, the Secretary of the Treasury told Beckwith that he had made "proper use" of what had been communicated at the first meeting. "As to what regards the objects of a general nature mentioned by you," Hamilton

[99] Washington, *Diaries*, ed. Fitzpatrick, IV, 143, under 14 July 1790 (italics supplied).
[100] Bemis, *Jay's Treaty*, 98. As indicated below, however, suggestions for such an overland attack were advanced by Americans and these were given close attention by the British government.

told Washington he said to Beckwith, "though your authority for the purpose from Lord Dorchester is out of question, and though I presume from his Lordship's station and character and the knowlege he appears to have of what is passing on the other side of the water with regard to Mr. Morris, that the Step he has taken through you is conformable to the views of your Cabinet and not without its sanction; yet you are no doubt sensible that the business presents itself in a shape, which does not give the proper authenticity to that fact, and is wholly without formality. You must also be sensible that there is a material difference between your situation and that of Mr. Morris. His Credentials though not formal proceed from the proper source. Your's are neither formal nor authoritative."[101]

There is nothing in this that conflicts with Hamilton's first memorandum. On the contrary, its polite tone suggests that only formal credentials were needed to support the fact that the step taken by Dorchester was indeed sanctioned by the ministry. Dorchester had taken no such step, but Beckwith did not know that this had been asserted in Hamilton's first memorandum. Thus the actual words Hamilton said he used would have meant far less to him than they did to Washington or to anyone who had read the memorandum. Even so, these are not the words Hamilton expressed to Beckwith—if we may judge from the latter's testimony. This, according to Beckwith, is what Hamilton said to him: "however authoritative [the subjects communicated] may be on your part, in so far as respects Lord Dorchester, and however evident it is to me that His Lordship is apprized by your Cabinet of Mr. Morris's Agency, yet you must be sensible, that official formality is wanting, but it is conceived that his Lordship would not have gone the lengths he has, without being acquainted with the general views of your administration, as they respect this Country."[102] The two reports, understandably different in phraseology, had a subtle difference of substance that could have been detected only by one standing in Hamilton's position. Fortunately for the Secretary of the Treasury, no one else was able to do this. As Hamilton struggled to move the administration toward the position that he and the ruling majority of the Senate had already assumed, and at the same time to conceal the embarrassing conflict from Beckwith, he seemed as little conscious of the danger of destruction as Washington had been at

[101] Undated memorandum in Hamilton's hand, DLC: Washington Papers; text in Syrett, *Hamilton*, VI, 493-5. In the memorandum itself Hamilton indicated that this interview took place on "Thursday the 22d. instant"; Beckwith early in August referred to the same interview as taking place "on the 15th. of last month," that is, on the day after Washington had consulted with Jay and Hamilton and had directed the latter what to say to the agent. Syrett points out the impossibility of proving which of the two men is in error, but concludes that Hamilton would not likely have waited eight days before carrying out Washington's instructions. This plausible conjecture is supported by the fact that Beckwith's report arrived in Quebec on 5 Aug. 1790, that the interview with Hamilton occupied first place in it, and that subsequent conversations with other persons took place just after Alexander McGillivrary had arrived in New York, which was on 20 July, N.Y. *Daily Advertiser*, 22 July 1790; see two following notes.
[102] Beckwith's report, undated, enclosed in Dorchester to Grenville, 25 Sep. 1790, in which he stated that he had received the communication on 5 Aug.; PRO: CO 42/69, f. 14, 16-25; text in Brymner, *Report*, 1890, 145-9.

Long Island in 1776. On the central question his performance—as he himself reported it to Washington—even had a touch of the dramatic:

> As to Alliance [he said he told Beckwith] this opens a wide field. The thing is susceptible of a vast variety of forms. 'Tis not possible to judge what would be proper or what could be done unless points were brought into view. If you are in condition to mention particulars, it may afford better ground of conversation.
>
> I stopped here for an answer.
>
> Major Beckwith replied that he could say nothing more particular than he had already done.
>
> That being the case (continued I) I can only say that the thing is in too general a form to admit of a judgment of what may be eventually admissible or practicable. If the subject shall hereafter present itself to discussion in an authentic and proper shape, I have no doubt we shall be ready to converse freely upon it: And you will naturally conclude that we shall be disposed to pursue whatever shall appear under all circumstances to be our interest as far as may consist with our honor. At present I would not mean either to raise or repress expectation.
>
> Major Beckwith seemed to admit that as things were circumstanced nothing explicit could be expected.

The pause for an answer was an imaginative touch, but the conversation could not have occurred in the sense in which Hamilton wished it to be understood by Washington. Since Beckwith had brought no general proposition about alliance, or indeed any proposal, he naturally was in no "condition to mention particulars." Beckwith's account of the conversation was much more prosaic. This, according to his usually reliable reporting, is what Hamilton said to him on the central point: "In the present stage of this business it is difficult to say much on the subject of a Treaty of Alliance; Your rupture with Spain, if it shall take place, opens a very wide political field; thus much I can say, we are perfectly unconnected with Spain, have even some points unadjusted with that Court, and are prepared to go into the consideration of the subject."[103] In his own account, Hamilton had placed Beckwith on the defensive as the messenger proffering alliance. In Beckwith's report, the roles were reversed, naturally enough, since the idea had been initiated by the Secretary of the Treasury.

On the draft of the memorandum reporting this second interview, Hamilton noted: "Mr. Jefferson was privy to this transaction." But the Secretary of State, like the President, was privy only to what Hamilton said of it. This concealed far more than it revealed and, most important of all, gave the false impression that the proposal of an alliance had come from the ministry by way of Dorchester. The bold deception was maintained with skill. At this second interview Hamilton even held the door open for future discussion should "the thing" thereafter "*pre-*

103 The last statement also tends to support the date of the interview as taking place on the 15th of July, for it was on the 12th that TJ submitted his outline of policy to the President; see Document I below.

sent itself to discussion in an authentic and proper shape."[104] He could have had no expectation that this would come about of itself or be initiated by the ministry. The Governor General had indeed authorized Beckwith to say for him: "I think the interests of the United States, in case of a war, may be more effectually served by a junction with Great Britain, than otherwise."[105] But this was very far from suggesting or proposing an alliance. Hamilton's reports of the interviews thus left him free in the widening field of the war crisis to continue pursuit of the object he had sought so perseveringly thus far. Beckwith and Dorchester understood him to mean this, however little they knew of the misrepresentations made of them to the President. Thus the course of secret intrigue could be pursued as before. The previous discussions between Beckwith and the Secretary of the Treasury evidently had not been suspected and certainly had not been disclosed. The secret line of communication nevertheless had failed to bring the desired object on for "discussion in an authentic and proper shape." This could be done only through an exchange of ministers and Hamilton at once turned his attention to this aspect of the problem. He did so at the same interview at which he was required to state the attitude of the government and to report back to Washington what had transpired.

"The rest of our conversation," Hamilton said in his memorandum to Washington, "consisted chiefly of assurance on my part" that the threats against the posts were unauthorized by the government and of a repetition by Beckwith of the assurances he had given of Dorchester's disposition to discourage Indian outrages.[106] He thus led the President mistakenly to believe that the conversation had ended at this point. In requiring his Secretary of the Treasury to report what was said at the interview, Washington naturally expected both an accurate and a full account. He received neither, but the significant omission in Hamilton's

---

[104] Italics supplied. In his note on the draft (DLC: Hamilton Papers) Hamilton also stated: "The views of the Government were to discard suspicion that any engagements with Spain or intentions hostile to Great Britain existed—to leave the ground in other respects vague and open, so as that in case of Rupture between G B and S—the U States might be in the best situation to turn it to account in reference to the Disputes between them and G B on the one hand and Spain on the other." This attributes to the administration views which, so far as the record discloses, Washington had not expressed. If the President had wished Hamilton to say—as Beckwith was led to understand was the case—that the United States was "perfectly unconnected" with Spain, it is strange that he failed to record so important an instruction in his otherwise explicit directions. The manner in which Hamilton explained the occasion for his own version of a milder assurance confirms the silence in the documents: it is a justification for a communication to Beckwith that Hamilton made on his own initiative, not one executed under orders. The conclusion suggested by this is clear: that the endorsement on the draft was made at a later date and that its purpose, like that of the explanation in the memorandum, was to justify. Washington certainly could not have authorized Hamilton to state to Beckwith that the administration was "prepared to go into the consideration" of matters unadjusted with Spain. This was a subject just unfolded in TJ's memorandum of 12 July 1790 (Document I, below) which inaugurated discussion of a plan surrounded from the beginning in the utmost secrecy.

[105] Dorchester to Beckwith, 27 June 1790, "*Secret*," PRO: CO 42/68, f. 258-60; text in Brymner, *Report*, 1890, p. 144.

[106] Memorandum in DLC: Washington Papers; text printed in Syrett, *Hamilton*, VI, 494-5.

report was set forth in detail in the report by Beckwith to his principal. "It appears to me," Beckwith quoted Hamilton as saying, "that, from the nature of our Government, it would be mutually advantageous if this negociation could be carried on at our seat of government, as it would produce dispatch and obviate misconception."[107] This hint was supported by Beckwith's later conversation with William Samuel Johnson, who told the agent that Madison continued indefatigable in his pursuit of commercial discrimination; that in fact the advocates of discrimination were gaining ground because of what they considered "as the commencement of a commercial warfare" on the part of Great Britain; that Jefferson, "a decided republican and perfectly devoted to a French interest," had been greatly instrumental "in promoting the removal of the Legislature from a city which he considers as being perfectly in an English interest"; that indeed his occupying the office of Secretary of State was "unfortunate in the idea of forming any close connection with [Great Britain] as he [could not] be confided in"; that Jefferson was thought to be "in great favor with the President"; but that the Secretary of the Treasury had more favorable sentiments, possessed "a solid understanding, great candor and sincerity in his dealings, and a manly mind, which [would] not be restrained from a free declaration of its principles." This from a distinguished lawyer, president of Columbia College, framer of the Constitution, and United States Senator could have been intended to allay any doubts about the pledge of honor given by Hamilton in April, a pledge that had resulted thus far only in a vague and noncommittal response.

Hamilton, who began the conversation with Beckwith "as from one gentleman to an other" because he thought he might not have the possibility of making such an explanation thereafter, moved on to the next step as if no shadow had been cast over the pledge:

If it shall be judged proper to proceed in this business by the sending or appointing a proper person to come to this country to negotiate on the spot, [he told Beckwith] whoever shall then be our Secretary of State, will be the person in whose department such negotiation must originate, and he will be the channel of communication with the President; in the turn of such affairs the most minute circumstances, mere trifles, give a favorable bias or otherwise to the whole. The President's mind I can declare to be perfectly dispassionate on this subject. Mr. Jefferson our present Secretary of State is I am persuaded a gentleman of honor, and zealously desirous of promoting those objects, which the nature of his duty calls for, and the interests of his country may require, but from some opinions which he has given respecting Your government, and possible predilections elsewhere, there may be difficulties which may possibly frustrate the whole, and which might be readily explained away. I shall certainly know the progress of the negotiation from the president from day to day, but what I come to the present explanation for is this, that in case any such difficulties should occur, I should wish to know

107 Beckwith's report, enclosed in Dorchester to Grenville, 25 Sep. 1790, PRO: CO 42/69, f. 14, 16-25.

them, in order that I may be sure they are clearly understood, and candidly examined, if none takes place the business will of course go on in the regular official channel.

Beckwith replied that he could not say what his government might do about this, that—"You may depend on it"—he would make proper use of what had been said, and that this would never be revealed by him in a way to create "an impression different from the causes which occasioned it."[108] None of this, of course, was reported to Washington.

Thus the pledge from one gentleman to another, meeting on the middle ground between their respective obligations. The meaning of this extraordinary exchange between a high official of one nation and the secret envoy of another has been assessed by one of the most sympathetic biographers of Alexander Hamilton, quite accurately, in these words: "In effect, Hamilton was proposing to aid the representative of a foreign power in counteracting the policies of the Secretary of State."[109] This was no new or sudden proposal. It was implicit in every move that the Secretary of the Treasury had made since he entered the discussions with Beckwith in the autumn of 1789. It was also far from being the last of such efforts.

[108] Beckwith's report, marked "Secret," undated, enclosed in Dorchester to Grenville, 25 Sep. 1789, PRO: CO 42/69, f. 14, 27-8. While this is a separate enclosure added to the longer report of conversations with Hamilton and others as described in notes 102, 104, and 107, there is no reason to suppose that it took place at a date other than that on which Hamilton had suggested the transfer of negotiations to America. Syrett, *Hamilton*, VI, 497, assigns the date 15 July 1790 to this separate memorandum and there can be little doubt that, as the opening sentence indicates, this was a continuation of the remarks that Hamilton failed to report to Washington. Beckwith's separating this part of the interview from that in the main body of his report can be explained on three grounds. First, its great importance: as a means of protecting British interests in case formal negotiations took place, this would have given the British minister to the United States a powerful advantage over the Secretary of State. Second, the substance was entirely confidential, hence the designation "Secret," not ordinarily given to other dispatches. Third, in assuring Hamilton he might depend upon proper use being made of this astonishing request, Beckwith may have meant he would make a separate report so that Grenville in the Home Office might at once forward it to Leeds in the Foreign Office, within whose jurisdiction such a matter lay.

[109] Miller, *Hamilton*, p. 368.

V

Division and Deception
in the Cabinet

The first and most essential requirement of a foreign policy is that it be coherent and consistent. For in discourse between one nation and and another, that speaking with a forked tongue—to employ the metaphor arising out of the simple wisdom of the American Indians in their forest diplomacy—inevitably discounts its own credibility. The cabinet of England, though marked differences of opinion existed within it, nevertheless spoke with a single voice in its relations with the United States. The American Secretary of State in his conduct of foreign policy stood on wholly different ground. He possessed no such system of intelligence as that available to the British ministry, had no funds available for the procurement of information or influence, and was unsustained by any trans-Atlantic bonds of interest, consanguinity, and loyalty reaching into the executive and legislative branches of the British government. Worse, he suffered the crippling handicap of the secret discussions that would continue long beyond that one forced momentarily into the open by the threat of war. It was not until the appointment of George Hammond as minister that Jefferson, through formal negotiation, possessed the means of verification and thus could begin to guess with some accuracy—but never with full knowledge—at the extent to which cabinet councils were placed at the disposal of those with whom it was his duty to negotiate. He could not even guess at the degree to which his own policies were in similar manner discounted by his colleague. The British minister, who promptly became the confidant that Hamilton desired him to be, felt some annoyance because the Secretary of State insisted on conducting the discussions in writing. But the betrayal of secrets began long before Jefferson suspected that written diplomatic discourse—for him a natural mode of doing any business— was also a necessary precaution. The most profound secret of the administration and the first to be violated was that involving Jefferson's overture to Spain.

If, as Jefferson and many others believed at the time, war was almost inevitable, there was no question but that neutrality was to be the policy of the United States. Jefferson himself was the first to hint at such a policy, doing so in a manner to insure its being communicated to the British ministry.[110] But this was far from being a mere passive

110 TJ to Benjamin Vaughan, 27 June 1790, note.

position as he conceived it. In his formal proposal of the policy he looked to the possible independence of Louisiana and the Floridas, suggested the approach to Madrid, and gave an intimation of how close to war he was prepared to go in order to achieve two paramount objectives, the preservation of a balance of power among neighbors and the opening of the Mississippi to navigation—an intimation that Jefferson thought prudent to make much softer in the final than in the first draft.[111] By the beginning of August it was clear that the President had given full support to the course suggested by Jefferson. Washington's letters to Rochambeau, La Luzerne, and others that David Humphreys carried with him when he departed on the mission to Spain made no allusion to that purpose, but the one to Lafayette was a perfect reflection of sentiments Jefferson had expressed long before the war crisis arose:[112]

> It seems to be our policy to keep in the situation in which nature has placed us, to observe a strict neutrality, and to furnish others with those good things of subsistence, which they may want, and which our fertile land abundantly produces, if circumstances and events will permit us to do so. This letter is committed to Colonel Humphreys to carry to London, whither he is going. Should he, by any accident be in France, he will be able to give you a full state of our affairs and prospects. Gradually recovering from the distresses in which the war left us, patiently advancing in our task of civil government, unentangled in the crooked politics of Europe, wanting scarcely any thing but the free navigation of the Mississipi (which we must have and as certainly shall have as we remain a Nation) I have supposed, that, with the undeviating exercise of a just, steady, and prudent national policy, we shall be the gainers, whether the powers of the old world may be in peace or war, but more especially in the latter case. In that case our importance will certainly increase, and our friendship be courted. Our dispositions would not be indifferent to Britain or Spain. Why will not Spain be wise and liberal at once? It would be easy to annihilate all causes of quarrels between that Nation and the United States at this time. At a future period that may be far from being a fact. Should a war take place between Great Britain and Spain, I conceive from a great variety of concurring circumstances there is the highest probability that the Floridas will soon be in the possession of the former. . . . P.S. Not for the value of the thing, my dear Marquis, but as a memorial and because they are the manufacture of the City, I send you herewith a pair of shoe buckles.

There can be no doubt that on all essential points Washington and Jefferson were in firm agreement. Even the language, the use of Lafayette as a channel of communication, the hint at the progress of local manufactures—all reflect views and methods of the Secretary of State. William Samuel Johnson told Beckwith about this time that Jefferson was "thought to be in great favor with the President," but neither he

111 See Document I, below.
112 Washington to Lafayette, 11 Aug. 1790; *Writings*, ed. Fitzpatrick, XXXI, 85-8. On the letters carried by Humphreys, see notes to Document VII below.

nor Hamilton could have looked with enthusiasm upon Jefferson's approach to Spain. The annihilation of all quarrels with that power would have been a serious blow to Hamilton's efforts of the preceding year.

This aspect of the policy was shrouded in profound secrecy. The selection of Humphreys was clearly that of the President, who had a confidence in the young aide that the Secretary of State could not have fully shared. Only five persons in the government were supposed to be privy to the mission to Madrid aside from the envoy himself—the President, the Secretary of State, the Secretary of the Treasury, and two members of Congress long active in the Mississippi problem: James Madison of Virginia and John Brown of Kentucky. Even Gouverneur Morris and William Short, the two representatives abroad, were not informed of it in the instructions given them. Humphreys' letter to Jefferson late in July shows that the need for keeping this secrecy inviolate had been impressed upon him:[113]

> Upon finding that the Packet would sail sooner than I had expected, I hastened to make the necessary arrangements for my departure. Apprehensive, however, that I may be too much pressed for time, to have opportunities of acquiring, in conversation, as much information as could have been desired on the different subjects which will claim attention, I shall be extremely happy to have the deficiency supplied by such written Notes as Mr. Madison, Mr. Brown and yourself may think proper to give. The best possible care will be taken of all secret papers, as well as of the Cyphers which shall be committed to me for my use, and for the Consul or Agent who may be employed in London.—I beg leave to suggest whether a Copy of the Treaty as signed on our part with Portugal, together with any observations which may have since occurred, will not be requisite for me.—It is my intention to be in New York on Tuesday night if practicable.

The language of this letter suggests that Humphreys must have regarded himself as the personal representative of the President, somewhat in the capacity of aide-de-camp in which he had so long served, and that he therefore considered himself free to discuss the mission with all who knew of it. But Humphreys' instructions, which ignored the suggestions while urging secrecy, came from the Secretary of State, as was proper. While Jefferson had directed him to depart by the first convenient vessel, the knowledge that he intended to go in the English packet must have raised some doubts about security. Whether this was the cause or not, passage was engaged for him on another vessel, said to be a swift sailer but "not . . . a very safe one." That vessel was also British-owned, and before embarking Humphreys consulted both "the Secretaries of the States and the Treasury in order to learn what they would wish to have done" with their secret papers in case of war and

[113] Humphreys to TJ, dated at "Mrs. Haviland's Tavern," Rye, 31 July 1790; RC in DNA: RG 59, DD, endorsed by TJ as received 1 Aug. 1790 and so recorded in SJL; on the treaty with Portugal, signed but not ratified, see Vol. 9: 410-33.

capture.[114] Benjamin Walker, another close friend and former aide of the President, was the person consulted about the vessel and the fact that he also embarked at this time suggests that Washington—who was well experienced in the methods of secret intelligence—may have urged him to make the trip as protective cover for Humphreys' mission. For it is remarkable that Walker suddenly chose this moment to ask his superior, the Secretary of the Treasury, for leave of absence from his post as naval officer of the district of New York in order that he might go to England. Whether intended or not, this move and the personal reason advanced for its being undertaken became known at once to Beckwith and were promptly reported to Dorchester: "Colonel Walker who was an Aid de Camp to General Washington during the war, has lately sailed from hence to London; this gentleman . . . is by birth an Englishman, although he has been many years here, and his father, who is a brewer near Knight's bridge has pressed him greatly for some years to pay him a visit, to which he has at length consented; whether Mr. Walker has any thing in charge of a public nature I do not know, but he has always been on the best terms with the President."[115] There is no evidence to show how Beckwith became possessed of these details, but Walker had stated his reasons to his superior in asking leave, Hamilton had referred them to the President for his decision, knowing that such absences were contrary to general policy, and Washington had referred them back to the Secretary of the Treasury.

The extraordinary precautions taken to protect the secrecy of Humphreys' mission are also reflected in the arrangements for the necessary funds. On 14 Aug. 1790 Jefferson wrote Hamilton:[116]

> Colonel Humphreys will be entitled to draw from the Treasury of the United States from about this date till further order, at the rate of two thousand two hundred and fifty dollars, a year, and in addition to this a sum for postage of letters, the amount of which cannot be known beforehand, and will not be considerable. This is to be charged to the fund of the foreign department. I must ask the favour of you to let him know in what manner he can receive this money in the several situations he will be in. I think he ought to receive the full sum, and to have nothing to do with the loss or gain of exchange, charges of negociating &c.

Hamilton replied the same day:[117]

[114] Humphreys to Washington, 1 Sep. 1790, Humphreys, *Humphreys*, II, 25-7.
[115] Beckwith's reports, received at Quebec 27 and 30 Oct. 1790, enclosed in Dorchester to Grenville, 10 Nov. 1790, PRO: CO 42/72, f. 59-60, 61-8, 69-72; Hamilton to Washington, 28 Aug. 1790, and Lear's response, same date, Syrett, *Hamilton*, VI, 575, 577-8. It later developed that, in addition to the personal reasons of the nature stated, Walker was engaged by William Duer to look into the affairs of the Scioto Company in England; Walker to Hamilton, 28 Dec. 1790, same, VII, 388-9.
[116] FC in DNA: RG 59, PCC No. 120.
[117] RC in DLC, endorsed as received 14 Aug. 1790 and so recorded in SJL. The warrant was actually received by Remsen in TJ's name and converted into money, which Remsen gave to TJ and he in turn issued a receipt for it; MS in TJ's hand, DLC: TJ Papers, 57: 9707, dated 14 Aug. 1790; the letter of credit

I enclose you a warrant for 500 Dollars for Col. Humphreys use; and shall for the present take arrangements for paying his salary or allowance by a Credit on our Commissioners in Holland. Hereafter we will endeavour to put this matter upon some more convenient footing.—I draw in your favour to avoid introducing Col. Humphreys into the books of the Treasury, which would excite more conjecture than is perhaps desireable in the outset considering the nature of his mission. I hope this will be agreeable to you.

On obtaining this sum, Jefferson made the following note in his personal Account Book: "received by warrant from the Treasury 500 Dollars, which I paid immediately to Colo. Humphreys for a public purpose known to the President, Colo. Hamilton, Mr. Madison and Mr. Brown, not to be entered in my private account as it no ways concerns me but as minister for the foreign department."[118]

Such precautions are understandable and Hamilton's expressed desire to avoid public conjecture could be accepted as genuine were it not belied by an extraordinary move that he made just before Humphreys departed. That move, unknown to the President and the Secretary of State, would have had the effect almost of a guarantee that the public character if not the nature of Humphrey's mission would become known to the British ministry. It was, however, only one more characteristic step in the studied invasion of the domain of the Secretary of State that had begun with Jefferson's appointment. It can best be understood against the background of public attitudes which seemed to make Jefferson's proposed policy of neutrality virtually impossible of fulfillment in the event of war between England and Spain.

Beckwith, other secret agents, and the British consuls in America were almost unanimous in their reports of the national mood. "In as far as I can judge at present of the general disposition of this country," Beckwith reported, "it is by no means favorable to a Spanish interest. The bias of mercantile and seafaring men, both here and to the eastward, appears to me to be evidently in our scale, and there are symptoms of a privateering spirit, which may be readily brought forward in the event of a Spanish war." From a member of Congress Beckwith learned that many in the West looked to the "probable dismemberment of the Spanish Monarchy" as hastening forward an event theretofore considered as remote. "Your possessing New Orleans," this representative from Western Pennsylvania declared, "we think an object of great consequence both to You and to Us, and we feel deeply interested in the event. . . . We think the present moment peculiarly favorable for you, and we are capable of great exertions at this time, from the military spirit, which every country possesses at the close of a civil war, and from the number of officers, who, having acquired military habits, are anxiously desirous of service; of these there are some of high rank, and

---

for $2,500 per year drawn on Wilhem & Jan Willink, N. & J. Van Staphorst & Hubbard was sent by Hamilton to Humphreys the same day; Syrett, *Hamilton*, VI, 557-8.

[118] Account Book under 14 Aug. 1790, MHi.

I am strongly inclined to think, that General Knox, our Secretary at War, would be eager to promote any system of national friendship with you, both from his general turn of thinking, and from his passion for military command. If such a plan should be followed up he would be a proper man to command a body of troops to clear away the Spanish Posts on the upper part of the Mississippi, whilst you should attack New Orleans, and this effected, to conduct an Army, to be formed in the Western country, by land from thence into Spanish America; we think such an undertaking very practicable."[119]

This remarkable language was similar to what had been coming to Dorchester from Kentucky for the past year or two, coupled with reports of a growing inclination among the people of that region "to declare Independence of the Federal Union, take possession at New Orleans, and look to Great Britain for such assistance as might enable them to accomplish these designs."[120] Such language had made a deep impression on Grenville and now during the summer and fall of 1790 a succession of dispatches came from the secret agent Peter Allaire, portraying Louisiana and the Floridas as a vast granary filled with resources that would make it a new and greater East Indies, ripe for the harvest. From five to seven thousand men on the Western waters, he declared, "would assist any nation" to dispossess the Spaniards on condition of being given free navigation of the Mississippi. "It is now in your power," Allaire wrote to the ministry at the height of the war crisis, ". . . to bind us in Adamantine Chains of Friendship and Alliance with you. Take the Floridas, Open a free Navigation of the Mississippi for the Western Inhabitants, and you bind that Country and its inhabitants for Ever in spite of Congress and all the world."[121] The men from the West

---

[119] Beckwith's report, enclosed in Dorchester to Grenville, 25 Sep. 1790, PRO: CO 42/69, f. 14, 16-25. The member of Congress is identified in Beckwith's cipher key as "14. Mr. Scott, Member of House of Representatives from Counties West of Allegheny Mountains." This was Thomas Scott (1739-1796) of Washington county, a lawyer and member of the Pennsylvania ratifying convention of 1787 (*Biog. Dir. Cong.*).

[120] Dorchester to Sydney, 11 Apr. 1789, PRO: CO 42/64, f. 152-5; same to same, 7 June 1789, CO 42/65, f. 10-13, "Secret"; Grenville to Dorchester, 20 Oct. 1789, CO 42/65, f. 193-6, "Secret."

[121] "Occurrences" (the form in which Allaire sent his reports) from 5 July to 3 Aug. 1790, PRO: FO 4/8, f. 284. In this dispatch Allaire also reported: "You may Rest Assured nothing can be done with this Government at present. No Offer would tempt them at present to Enter into a War."

The identity of Peter Allaire has been confused even by such able scholars as Frederick Jackson Turner and Samuel Flagg Bemis, both of whom regarded the name as a pseudonym for an unknown secret agent and the former thought that the initials "R.D." were also pseudonymous (Turner, AHR, VII, 716; Bemis, *Jay's Treaty*, p. 98, n. 20). The fact is that Peter Allaire (1740-1820) was a respected New York merchant who belonged to the well-known Huguenot family of that name and whose ancestor, Alexander Allaire, had settled at New Rochelle late in the 17th century. Allaire was employed by the British secret intelligence during the Revolution but, while he was known to Franklin in Paris, he failed to gain Franklin's confidence in the way that Edward Bancroft had. After the war he engaged in trade in New York City, and on occasion accepted members of Congress as boarders —among them David Ramsay and Richard Henry Lee. He was also involved in trade with the West Indies. He was a friend of Sir George Yonge and it was through Yonge's influence that Allaire was engaged to report American intelligence, for which he was paid £200 sterling per annum. There is no mystery about the

would join in the enterprise to recover the Floridas, he wrote in another dispatch, "not by Order consent or Approbation of the United States, but by those who Acknowledge Allegiance to NONE. Men hardy, inured to fatigue and danger, expert woodsmen, who live by hunting and who . . . Above all . . . Want Employ being most of them destitute of Clothes and Money."[122] The prospect was a tempting one, for by this one stroke the ministry could look to the encirclement of the Atlantic states by unbroken possessions running from the Gulf of St. Lawrence to the tip of Florida and could behold the promise of lumber and provisions for the British West Indies, that source of clamorous cries to Parliament and the ultimate target of American statesmen who spoke of infallible instruments of commercial retaliation.[123] Pitt, like Grenville the year before, was deeply impressed and gave orders that Allaire be encouraged to continue his reports on the possibility of repossessing the *"Southern Farms."*

It is not surprising, therefore, that when the member of Congress from western Pennsylvania unfolded the object of great consequence both for Britain and the United States, Beckwith should have decided that the time had come to make use of the discretionary power given him in Dorchester's secret instructions. "In case of a war with Spain," he replied, "I see no reason, why we should not assist in forwarding whatever your interests may require."[124] In this climate Jefferson's policy seemed all but reversed. He had urged that Beckwith be given

---

manner in which his reports of "Occurrences" came to the attention of Grenville and Pitt. All save a few reports to Dorchester were sent to the Foreign Office through Yonge, with whom Allaire was engaged in land speculation in the Champlain valley, and were delivered by the agent himself to the captain of the British packet boats. Communications to him were received in the same manner and were addressed to "P. Arlington"—the only pseudonym Allaire is known to have used (the initials that Turner read as "R. D." were Allaire's monogram "PA"). The agent's best guarantee of security was his own respected name. He knew, and often commented upon, Sir John Temple, Phineas Bond, and Beckwith, but he did not disclose himself as an intelligence agent to any of these. The identity of Allaire is derived from the following sources and from a comparison of the distinctive handwriting in the dispatches with his own authentic letters, though most of the facts about him are to be drawn from his own reports: Robert Bolton, *History . . . of the County of Westchester* (New York, 1905), I, 677-9; "The Narrative of Peter Allaire written in the Bastile," George G. Wood, ed., *Now and Then* (Muncy, Pennsylvania), VIII (April, 1948), p. 297-305; letters to Franklin concerning the imprisonment in the Bastile are in the Franklin Papers in the American Philosophical Society.

A more extended account of Allaire, to be published in a volume containing the texts of his important dispatches as well as those of Edward Bancroft and George Beckwith, is in preparation by the Editor.

122 "Occurrences" from 6 Aug. to 1 Sep. 1790, PRO: FO 4/8, f. 307; same 4 Sep. to 7 Oct. 1790, FO 4/8, f. 409; same 1 Dec. 1790 to 6 Jan. 1791, FO 4/9, f. 50-3. Some of the principal people in North Carolina later authorized John Hamilton, British consul at Norfolk and formerly a wealthy Loyalist of that state, to say to Leeds "that if Hostilities had, or should commence between Great Britain and Spain . . . Twenty thousand men could be easily raised in the service of Great Britain to act against the Spaniards, under proper Authority and encouragement from the Court of Great Britain"; Hamilton to Leeds, 25 May 1791, PRO: FO 4/10, f. 63-6.

123 See enclosure, Document I, concluding section.

124 Dorchester to Beckwith, 27 June 1790, "*Secret,*" PRO: CO 42/68, f. 258-60; text in Brymner, *Report,* 1890, p. 144.

a warning on the supposition that, if British councils were divided as to whether to mount an attack against Spanish territory adjacent to the United States, this might tip the scales by the "prospect of having an enemy the more or less, according to the object" the ministry should select. This was an essential element of the policy of making an overture to Spain, but it was almost cancelled out by the western Congressman who in effect altered it to mean "an ally the more or less"; by men in shipping and trade in the eastern states who caught visions of commerce opening up with South America; and by the continuing efforts on the part of Hamilton and members of the Senate to achieve a closer connection with England. With Washington's support and in the total absence of a Spanish interest except for purposes of bargaining, the policy of neutrality was not difficult to endorse by those who leaned toward Great Britain. Even William Samuel Johnson told Beckwith that he thought the United States should remain neutral, but, he added, "whether this will be our conduct I really do not know."[125]

Hamilton did not openly oppose the approach to Madrid, but he used the opportunity to allay Washington's fears of a British overland expedition against Spanish possessions—and also to reassure Beckwith. In the report that Washington required him to make of the second interview with the British agent, Hamilton stated that "Something was said respecting the probable course of military operations in case of war between Britain and Spain" and that "Major Beckwith supposed [these] would be directed towards South America alleging however that this was mere conjecture on his part." There are valid reasons for concluding that Beckwith did not make this conjecture, quite aside from the fact that, having proved himself an unreliable reporter on the central object of the discussions, Hamilton thereby drew a veil of doubt over all unverifiable matters in his account. First, he knew that Beckwith's opinion about strategy could not be discounted as the supposition of a junior officer: it would be assessed by Washington as the view of one who had served through years of confidential relationship with the commander-in-chief of the British forces in America—of a commander who, on the authority of Hamilton's own reports, was assumed to be privy to the aims of the ministry as these had been shaped by the crisis. Second, Beckwith scarcely needed the ideas advanced by the member of Congress from western Pennsylvania to be aware that, whatever else might be contemplated, an overland expedition was assuredly in the realm of probability. Third, it is scarcely plausible to assume that so seasoned an officer of military intelligence would have volunteered his opinion of future military objectives to an official of a recent and potential enemy of his nation—unless to mislead. Finally, there is no mention in Beckwith's reports of his discussion of military strategy with Hamilton. It seems safe to conclude that, knowing how deeply the President feared a British attack on New Orleans, Hamilton could not have been unaware that a supposition of operations directed at South America, coming from a source so close to Dorchester, was one

[125] Beckwith's report, enclosed in Dorchester to Grenville, 25 Sep. 1790, PRO: CO 42/69, f. 14, 16-25.

calculated to allay apprehensions and that he included it in the report for that reason.

In the same vein Hamilton said that he "hinted cautiously our dislike of an enterprise on New Orleans." This assertion is also suspect. If uttered at all, it was very far indeed from being the grave warning suggested by Jefferson that England might have an enemy the more or less according to the object chosen for attack. If expressed at all, the hint found its place in the following summation made by Beckwith of American attitudes:[126]

> In case of a rupture with Spain the probable effect, which such an event may produce upon the navigation of the Mississippi attracts the very particular attention of this government, and excites the notice of all orders of people; our power to take possession of New Orleans, and to retain it, is not doubted, but the consequences of this measure are considered to be of the first importance. If the fate of war should give us possession of New Orleans, its vicinity to the West India Islands, the immense resources of the countries on the Western waters in lumber, naval stores, hemp, flour, tobacco, and other exports are contemplated as forming a competition with the Atlantic States, as having a direct tendency to accelerate the population and wealth of the former at the expense of the latter, and as the laying an immediate foundation for a rivalship.

The "consequences . . . of the first importance" comport with the ideas of the western member of Congress and with the plan of Allaire for repossessing the *"Southern Farms"* quite as well as they do with a supposed hint of dislike conveyed by Hamilton. It is possible, however, that Hamilton did hint at the danger of dismemberment of the union for fear a hostile move against Spanish possessions would drive the administration closer to an accommodation with Spain and thus endanger his long-laid plans for a commercial treaty with England. But this was far more than a cautious softening of the position advocated by the Secretary of State.

It must be noted in this passage that someone in office had informed Beckwith of the "very particular attention" being given by government to the Mississippi Question. This, in the context, could scarcely relate to the interest excited in "all orders of people" or to the expressions of the member of Congress: it must have alluded to the concern of the administration, not of the Congress that was about to adjourn. If so, the statement could only refer to the cabinet discussions late in July leading up to the decision to send Humphreys to Spain, and in that case the information must have come from one of the five persons who were privy to the profound secret. Four of these—Washington, Jefferson, Madison, and Brown—may be dismissed at once as the probable source of Beckwith's information. None had ever had an interview with the agent except for the President's brief exchange of pleasantries with him. Even so, it is implausible to suppose that the Secretary of State who originated the plan, or the President and the two members of Congress who supported it, would have unveiled the discussions to that nation

[126] Same.

against which it had been thought necessary to erect a barrier of utmost secrecy and of which Beckwith was a known agent. The supposition that it was Hamilton who must have revealed the direction in which the attention of the administration was being focused is supported by Hamilton's later conversations with Beckwith and by the latter's comment on the attitude of the administration.

In July Hamilton had assured the British agent that the United States was "perfectly unconnected with Spain," had some points unadjusted with that nation, and was "prepared to go into the consideration of the subject."[127] By late September, after Humphreys had departed, Beckwith again summarized American attitudes and found his previous report confirmed:[128]

> The inhabitants of the Western country wish New Orleans to be in our possession, as the best means of getting a good price for their productions.—The Atlantic people in general wish the navigation to remain closed, from the dread of a rivalship, especially in the West India market.—The Executive Government are anxious to possess it themselves, in order to connect and consolidate both sides of the Allegany Mountains, knowing that although the western exports must issue from the Mississippi, their imports will to a certainty be conveyed through the Atlantic States. The free navigation of this river, whether to have been secured by the possession of New Orleans, or by the erection of a post in a preferable situation, was I am convinced the boon of all others the most likely to have induced the States to have taken an active part against Spain. They do not wish for a West India island at this time, sensible that they have no marine to protect it; these remarks apply to the executive government.

There can be no doubt that these remarks about administration views came from Hamilton. In the same memorandum in which they are recorded Beckwith quoted the Secretary of the Treasury as saying:[129]

> *We look forward to procuring the means of an export for our western country, and we must have it.* We cannot suffer the navigation of the Mississippi to remain long in its present state. That country is at this moment ready to open it if they met with the smallest encouragement, and undoubtedly we look forward to the possession of New Orleans.

This was said after Hamilton had assured Beckwith the United States had no desire for a West India island and had no wish to extend its territories in the north beyond the existing boundaries, *"with an exception to the Forts."* In an interview taking place presumably soon thereafter, Hamilton returned to the theme:[130]

> You have considerable American and West India possessions, our friendship or enmity may soon become important with respect to their security, and I cannot foresee any solid grounds of national difference,

[127] Same.
[128] Beckwith's report, before 30 Sep. 1790, enclosed in Dorchester to Grenville, 10 Nov. 1790, PRO: CO 42/72, f. 61-8, 69-72.
[129] Italics supplied.
[130] Italics supplied.

between us; I do not think the posts are to be considered in this light, and we have no desire to possess any thing to the northward of our present boundaries as regulated by the peace; but the navigation of the river Mississippi we must have, and shortly, and I do not think the bare navigation will be sufficient, we must be able to secure it by having a post at the mouth of the river, either at New Orleans, or some where near it; there are reports, that the Spanish Government are disposed to change their system, but this I doubt, for it is so different from their national character.

You know we have two parties with us; there are gentlemen, who think we ought to be connected with France in the most intimate terms, and that the Bourbon compact furnishes an example for us to follow; there are others who are at least as numerous, and influential, who decidedly prefer an English connexion, but *the present condition of Great Britain and the States is favorable to the former party*, and they are zealous to improve it; the present therefore is the moment to take up the matter seriously and dispassionately, and I wish it done without loss of time.

We consider ourselves perfectly at liberty to act with respect to Spain in any way most conducive to our interests, even to the going to war with that power, if we shall think it advisable to join You.

Thus did Hamilton seize upon Jefferson's idea, including that of having a post at the mouth of the Mississippi to keep navigation open, in order to move as expeditiously as the Secretary of State was moving —but in the opposite direction and for different purposes, offering not an honorable neutrality in exchange for a pledge against aggression but a hint of alliance in order to achieve this great national interest. This was more delicately phrased than the language held out by the member of Congress from western Pennsylvania but its substance was the same. Accompanied by a glowing picture of the way in which English commercial capital and American agricultural production could operate in a harmonious and mutually advantageous exchange of produce and manufactures, this suggestion of a policy that would counterbalance conditions favorable to those who wished to move the United States to a closer connection with France was also accompanied by a subtle intimation: the nation was perfectly free to come to any arrangement with Spain that its interests—the sole guide for the intercourse of nations, Hamilton had told Beckwith—might suggest. In brief, the example furnished by the Bourbon compact might be followed. Outwardly identical with the effort of the administration to obtain free navigation of the Mississippi, Hamilton's clandestine manoeuver was in fact aimed at the defeat of the Spanish mission. None of this was disclosed, naturally enough, in a letter written by Hamilton to the President about this interview. That letter, besides misrepresenting the conversation, was intended to discredit the man whom Hamilton had recommended as the President's envoy to London.

VI

Libel on an Honorable
Public Servant

According to Beckwith, Hamilton opened their interview late in September with an expression of disapproval of Gouverneur Morris' conduct. He confessed that the Duke of Leeds' reply to Morris' first application had not led him to think favorably of the prospect. But the June packet had brought news of the interview with Pitt. "From [Morris'] own detail of what passed," Hamilton said, "there was something in his conduct on that occasion, which I confess I do not altogether approve." Beckwith then asked if Morris had been out of England, perhaps to France. To this Hamilton replied:[131]

> Not that I know of, and if [Morris] has cultivated an intimacy with the Ministers of any other power in Europe, or has caused suspicion on that ground with respect to France, or elsewhere, he has had no authority, for so doing; it occurs to me, that he was very intimate with Monsr. de La Luzerne the Ambassador of France now in London, when he was Minister in this country, possibly from that circumstance he may have been more frequently there, than prudence ought to have dictated, and the knowledge of this circumstance may have produced a greater reserve on the part of Your administration; *these ideas strike me, although I have no grounds to go upon.*

The conversation then turned to the navigation of the Mississippi, after which Beckwith, pointing out that he had always preserved the strictest silence respecting Morris, said that he had heard it said among Morris' relations and others that he had been frequently with La Luzerne and with Charles James Fox. Hamilton admitted that this had been reported and that he believed it in some measure to be true, the more so from extracts he had seen of Morris' letters. He added: "I do not question this gentleman's sincerity in following up those objects committed to his charge, but to deal frankly with You, I have some doubts of his prudence; this is the point in which he is deficient, for in other respects he is a man of great genius, liable however to be occasionally influenced by his fancy, which sometimes outruns his discretion." Beckwith then reported himself as paying tribute to La Luzerne and Fox, after which he added: "it is for Your consideration,

131 Italics supplied. Beckwith's report, ca. 25-30 Sep. 1790, enclosed in Dorchester to Grenville, 10 Nov. 1790, PRO: CO 42/72, f. 61-8, 69-72; see Syrett, *Hamilton*, VII, 70.

how far a gentleman in [Morris'] situation ought to form intimacies with persons in public political situations, excepting they are in administration." Far from taking umbrage at a suggestion about a relationship much less improper than the one in which he and Beckwith were engaged, Hamilton responded: "I am quite of Your opinion, and this amongst other causes led me to remark, that it is greatly desirable, that this negotiation should be transferred to our seat of Government."

Hamilton's letter to Washington about this interview stands in flat contradiction to what Beckwith reported, both as to the nature of the conversation and as to its object. He had lately had a visit "from a *certain Gentleman*," Hamilton wrote, "the sole object of which was to make some observations of a delicate nature, concerning *another Gentleman* employed on a *particular errand*; which, as they were doubtless intended for your ear, and (such as they are) ought to be known to you, it is of course my duty to communicate."[132] Hamilton added:

> He began (in a manner somewhat embarrassed which betrayed rather more than he seemed to intend to discover) by telling me that in *different companies* where he had happened to be, *in this City* (a circumstance by the way very unlikely) he had heared it mentioned that that *other Gentleman* was upon terms of very great intimacy with the representative of a certain Court at the one where *he* was employed and with the head of the party opposed to the Minister; and he proceeded to say, that if there were any symptoms of backwardness or coolness in the Minister, it had occurred to him that they might possibly be occasioned by such *an intimacy*; that he had no intimation however of this being the case, and that the idea suggested by him was mere matter of conjecture; that he did not even know it as a fact that the intimacy subsisted. But if this should be the case (said he) you will readily imagine that it cannot be calculated to inspire confidence or facilitate free communication. It would not be surprising, if a very close connection with the representative of another power should beget doubts and reserves; or if a very familiar intercourse with the head of the opposition should occasion prejudice and distance. Man, after all, is but man; and though the Minister has a great mind, and is as little likely as most men to entertain distrusts or jealousies; yet there is no saying what might be the effect of such conduct upon him. It is hardly possible not to have some diffidence of those, who seem to be very closely united with our political or personal enemies or rivals. At any rate, such an intimacy, if it exists, can do no good, may do some harm.

Such, Hamilton reported to the President, was the substance of what Beckwith had laid before him as "the sole object" of the visit. To this he told Washington that he had replied: "I have never heared a syllable, Sir, about the matter you mention. It appears to me however very possible that an intimacy with both persons you mention may exist." He explained, he said, that Morris and La Luzerne had been drawn by their

---

[132] Hamilton to Washington, 30 Sep. 1790, Syrett, *Hamilton*, VII, 84-5.

situations into an intimacy while both were in America. To have avoided this in London "would not have been without difficulty, on the score of politeness, and would have worn an extraordinary and mysterious aspect." As for Morris' association with Charles James Fox, this was equally natural, arising "from a similarity of dispositions and characters; both brilliant men, men of wit and genius; both fond of the pleasures of society." According to his report, Hamilton then added: "It is to be hoped that appearances, which admit of so easy a solution will not prove an obstacle to any thing which mutual interest dictates. It is impossible that there can be any thing wrong.—He replied that he certainly had no idea there could be any thing wrong; but that as trifles often mar great affairs he thought it best to impart to me his conjecture, that such use might be made of it as should be thought adviseable."

These two accounts of the interview stand in such marked contrast and contradiction to each other that the discrepancy cannot be dismissed as the natural result of misconceptions, misunderstandings, or varying degrees of emphasis on the part of two different reporters, both interested. Clearly, one version or the other is a contrived and deliberate misrepresentation. There can be no doubt that Hamilton's report to Washington is unreliable and calculated to mislead both in its details and in its aim. It falls inexorably into the pattern of his secret relations with Beckwith of the preceding year. In effect what Hamilton did in this letter was exactly what he had done in misrepresenting the interview of the 8th of July: he put words in Beckwith's mouth in order to defend and support his own object. In both instances his aim was to offset the coolness that Washington and Jefferson—as well as Hamilton himself, of course—saw in the posture of the British cabinet. But in this most recent attempt he sought to place the blame for the ministry's aloofness upon Gouverneur Morris' supposed lack of tact and discretion, attributing to Beckwith sole responsibility for a charge that in reality was his own. Again, as in the July episode, he did so by basing this upon a supposed conjecture advanced by the British agent. Further, "the sole object" of the interview, far from being that attributed by Hamilton to Beckwith, was his own and was twofold: (1) to seize the moment of crisis as one in which to take up "seriously and dispassionately, and . . . without loss of time" the matter of a closer connection with England because circumstances favored those who thought the Bourbon compact an example to follow and these circumstances required a counterpoise; and (2) to transfer the negotiations to America where the Secretary of the Treasury himself could keep a close eye on them and have a hand in shaping them. It is scarcely necessary to add that both of these objects were fully disclosed to Beckwith and were withheld from the President, who was led to believe that the agent had sought the interview for the sole purpose of making delicate hints about Gouverneur Morris' conduct. Hamilton's letter can only be regarded as a contrived effort to discredit the agent of the President.

This misrepresentation gave rise to the generally accepted belief that the coolness of the ministry was in fact due in part to Gouverneur Morris' lack of tact and discretion.[133] But this supposition is grounded upon

[133] Bemis, *Jay's Treaty*, p. 68, 80, 84.

the assumption that Beckwith complained of Morris' friendly relations with the French ambassador and with the leader of the opposition, a complaint far less Beckwith's than Hamilton's and one arising from feelings of resentment in New York, not in London. In raising the question in the delicate manner he did, Beckwith was merely responding to Hamilton's observations and his report was not one of a complaint that he had registered but rather one of disappointment that had been expressed to him. There is no evidence that Dorchester or the ministry were affected in their attitudes by anything that Morris did or said, much less that they requested their agent to make observations about his conduct. That Hamilton made so much of so implausible and trivial a factor is an indication of the strength of his desire to counteract the mission to Spain.

Gouverneur Morris, brilliant and self-assured, possessed manners—as Madison had warned the President before the appointment was made —that produced unfavorable opinions of himself both "before . . . known, and where known." Like most foreign envoys, he also rendered accounts in his diplomatic dispatches that did no discredit to his own powers as a negotiator. Leeds and Pitt may well have been offended by some of his blunt rejoinders—if those rejoinders were in fact as blunt as Morris reported them to be. Even so, the general tenor of the negotiation was polite and amicable. The fact is that Morris was not enjoined to secrecy and he was not forbidden to reveal his mission to the French ambassador. It was quite natural that the latter should have made use of the information so as to suggest that France had prompted the move by Washington. This could scarcely have caused surprise either to Morris or to Leeds. Morris himself, indeed, had similar and no higher motives for making the disclosure, though his action has been called honorable but imprudent. Like La Luzerne, he was only engaged in gaining credit on flimsy grounds. He saw the French ambassador before he saw Leeds, though he called on the latter immediately on arrival in London and found him absent. "I communicated to the french Embassador *in Confidence*," Morris reported to Washington, "that you had directed me to call for a performance of the Treaty. He told me at once that they would not give up the Posts. Perhaps he may be right. I thought it best to make such Communication because the Thing itself cannot remain a Secret and by mentioning it to him we are enabled to say with Truth that in every Step relating to the Treaty of Peace we have acted confidentially in Regard to our Ally."[134] Morris at times may have been lacking in tact, but he was too much a man of the world, too experienced in Parisian court and diplomatic circles, to be naive. To reveal in the strictest confidence what he knew could not be kept secret was only an effort to enhance the value of a gesture toward an ally. La Luzerne no doubt penetrated the motive as clearly as he perceived the attitude of the ministry respecting the western posts.

[134] Morris to Washington, 7 Apr. 1790; RC in DLC: Washington Papers. La Luzerne undoubtedly knew this even before Morris told him, for the latter had informed Montmorin of his mission "in the most perfect Confidence" before leaving Paris; Morris, *Diary*, ed. Davenport, I, 374, under 22 Jan. 1790—that is, immediately on receiving Washington's letter of 13 Oct. 1789.

As for Charles James Fox, there seems to be no more substance than this to the report being spread in New York and made pointed in Hamilton's letter to Washington. When Morris later learned of the allegation that the negotiations had been damaged by his indiscretions, he denied this and said that, having deliberately avoided opposition circles, he had dined with Fox only once. There is no reason to doubt this. He reported one of these meetings to Washington in words that could have given Hamilton concern if he had seen them. Morris stated that he dined in company with Fox on the 17th of April and then added:[135]

[135] Morris to Washington, 2 May 1790, "Private"; RC in DLC: Washington Papers. Morris gave substantially the account that appears in his diary, though he omitted the response that he made to Fox about trade with the West Indies: "I tell him that [his] is a solid Principle of Policy, for that our Position renders the Islands so materially dependent on us that they should make it our Interest to keep them in Possession. That further, if we chuse to lay them under Disadvantages in our Ports we can materially injure their Navigation, whereas the Admission of our Vessels into their Islands can do them no Harm in that Respect. All this is true, but I suspect that we shall be obliged in America to give them the Conviction of their Senses"; Morris, *Diary*, ed. Davenport, I, 485-6.

Morris learned of the rumors being spread about his mission from Washington himself in an extremely frank letter written two years later: "That in England you indiscreetly communicated the purport of your Mission in the first instance, to the Minister of France, at that Court, who availing himself in the same moment of the occasion, gave it the appearance of a movement through his Court. This, and other circumstances of a similar nature, added to a close intercourse with the opposition Members, occasioned distrust, and gave displeasure to the Ministry; *which was the cause, it is said, of that reserve which you experienced in negotiating the business which had been intrusted to you*"; Washington to Morris, 28 Jan. 1792, "(Private)," *Writings*, ed. Fitzpatrick, XXXI, 469 (emphasis supplied). These comments Washington presented as "the ideas of [Morris'] political adversaries." Since the letter in which they were couched was drafted by Jefferson himself, it is possible he may have suspected they were the result of rumors spread by Hamilton and perhaps others. Robert Morris was also informed that La Luzerne had rushed to tell Leeds what Gouverneur Morris had told him. The latter indignantly denied the charge, repeating to Robert Morris the substance of what he had said to Fox: "Seriously, my friend, the Obstacle to a Treaty was in the British Cabinet. . . . If you mean to make a good Treaty with Britain, support your pretensions with Spirit *and they will respect you for it*. You must give them *visible Reasons* because they will have *to justify their Conduct*: and it will not do to say to a House of Commons *the American Minister was such a charming Fellow that we could not resist him*. I rather think it would be at least as good Ground to say *The American Legislature would have greatly injured our Navigation and Commerce if we had not by this Treaty have induced them to repeal their Laws, and there was Reason also to apprehend that the United States would connect themselves still more intimately with France, who for the Sake of such Connection would doubtless support them in their Claims as soon as the State of her domestic Affairs would permit her to look abroad*"; undated letter, Gouverneur Morris to Robert Morris, in Morris, *Diary*, ed. Davenport, I, 615-16 (italics in the original). Morris rarely found himself in agreement with Jefferson and Madison, but on this occasion he both negotiated and defended his conduct on precisely the principles that the Secretary of State had advocated.

It is a curious fact that the one time Morris dined with Charles James Fox was at the home of Alexander Hamilton's brother-in-law, John Barker Church. Indeed, as soon as Morris arrived in London, Church went off to seek Fox to have him meet Morris. A few days later he dined at Church's and noted that Fox could not be there that day. A week later he again dined at Church's and *promised* to meet Fox there at dinner the following Saturday. He did so on the 17th—the occasion he reported to Washington; Morris, *Diary*, I, 469, 472, 480, 485. Morris,

The state of french Politics formed of course a large Part of the
Conversation. The situation of other Countries was then passed in
Review, and it became a Question how far Britain might be engaged
in the Affairs of the Continent. At length I took an Opportunity to
ask what System the Administration had adopted respecting America.
He told me that he could not tell but believed they had none, and
would in all Probability be governed by Events. That he did not
believe Mr. Pitt would trouble his Head about the Matter, but would
probably leave it to Lord Hawksbury and Mr. Grenville who are
both of them indisposed to us whereas Pitt himself is he supposes
rather friendly than otherwise. Mr. Fox said farther that he and
Burke are now almost alone in their Opinion that we should be
permitted to trade in our own Bottoms to their Islands, and that this
Opinion loses Ground daily tho for his own Part he persists in it.—
I find that the Ministers apply for Information respecting America,
and particularly American Commerce to a Mr. Irwin who long re-
sided in America and is now here in the Customs. A mighty Sour
Sort of Creature and one who seems to have a mortal Aversion for us.
I met him at Dinner one Day and he took Pains to let me know that he
was doing all he could to prevent any Encouragement from being
given to our Exports by the Corn Bill which is now on the Carpet.
He declared that he would by the force of Starvation oblige the
People of Britain to raise Corn enough for their own Consumption,
and that even the Supply of the West India Islands ought to be provided in this Country.—You will readily perceive Sir from this rude
sketch of influential Characters, that there is but little Disposition for
treating with us at present.

Presumably Washington did not reveal this private letter to Hamilton, but the meeting with Fox was known in New York and given
an interpretation by the Secretary of the Treasury that, so far as the
evidence discloses, was never given it by the ministry. The growing
restrictions of the British customs, the rising influence in the ministry
of Grenville and particularly of Hawkesbury, the apparent justification
of strict mercantilist doctrine by its fruits, the assurances received from
America that a closer connection was desired by the British interest,
that indeed an alliance might be sought to dispossess the Spaniards
from New Orleans—these and other factors were the motivating forces
of British policy, not the trivial one of Gouverneur Morris' diplomatic
manners. In any case, the alleged protest by Beckwith came at the close
of the mission, was made three thousand miles away, and could have
had no effect whatever upon its outcome. Washington was no more
deceived in September than he had been in July, though again he looked
in the wrong direction for hidden motives. His reply of dismissal to the
subject raised by Hamilton was one whose irony even the President

denying the allegations as "totally false," later told Washington that he avoided
going to Church's home solely because he wished to avoid meeting Fox; Morris
to Washington, 10 Apr. 1792, same, I, 614-15. There can be no doubt that the
allegations that Morris disposed of in these two brilliant letters arose from rumors
employed if not originated by the man who had nominated him for the office,
that is, the Secretary of the Treasury.

himself could not have perceived. "The motives . . . by which the Author of the communication to you was actuated," he wrote Hamilton, "although they may have been pure and in that case praiseworthy, do also (but it may be uncharitable to harbour the suspicion) admit of a different interpretation and that by an easy and pretty direct clew."[136] Washington let the matter drop there, leaving Hamilton perhaps to speculate in some anxiety as to the nature of the clue to motives not pure or praiseworthy. The next clue came to the President shortly after this exchange, though the action initiating it took place some weeks earlier. It was indeed an "easy and pretty direct clew" and it should have caused Washington to search for motives in the right and unmistakable direction.

[136] Washington to Hamilton, 10 Oct. 1790, "Private," *Writings*, ed. Fitzpatrick, XXXI, 131-2; Syrett, *Hamilton*, VII, 107-8. Conclusive proof that Hamilton opened the subject of Morris' alleged misconduct lies in the fact that, some months later, Beckwith himself reported this to Grenville as information presumably not known to the minister: "Without wishing to lessen in any shape, the consideration due to a gentleman in Mr. Morris's situation," he wrote, "it becomes my duty to apprize your Lordship, that an intimacy has long subsisted between him and Monsieur de la Luzerne, the French Ambassador, and it has been suggested to me from a respectable quarter here, that Mr. Morris at an early period disclosed to that Minister, the nature of his objects in England; in this undoubtedly I am liable to be misled, but I believe it to be true" (Beckwith to Grenville, 6 Apr. 1791, PRO: FO 4/12, f. 86-7).

VII

Hamilton Hands His Foes
a Weapon

Jefferson's instructions to Gouverneur Morris of 12 Aug. 1790 were explicit. The offer of neutrality in return for pledges was not to be disclosed except in the event of war and after hostilities had begun. The instructions also included expressions approving Morris' conduct of the negotiations. The President had not only sanctioned the instructions thus drafted but, in replying to Morris' dispatches of April and May, he had said: "as far as your intercourse with the british ministry had then gone [permit me] to assure you of my entire approbation of your conduct."[137] An interval of more than three weeks elapsed between the date of these instructions and the time of Humphreys' departure during which Hamilton might have registered his disapproval of Morris' conduct had he chosen to do so. For a part of this time Jefferson and Humphreys were absent with Washington on the tour to Rhode Island, while Hamilton remained in New York. Even so, more than a week remained after their return in which Hamilton might have expressed his disagreement with the administration's position. That he did not do this is clear from his later report of what he supposedly said to Beckwith. For that report is flatly contradicted not only by Beckwith's statements but also by Hamilton's own act at this time. Instead of taking advantage of the interval available to him, Hamilton waited until both the President and the Secretary of State had left New York for Virginia. Both departed on the morning of the 30th of August. The very next day Humphreys was sought out by the Secretary of the Treasury. The envoy to Madrid simultaneously revealed this fact and his own ineptitude as a diplomat in a farewell letter to Washington:[138]

Yesterday, I had two pretty long conversations with the Secretary of the Treasury, in the course of which the general interests of the U.S. were discussed, and the several contingencies that might take place between them and the different European Powers. I was glad to have an opportunity of becoming acquainted with his sentiments, and to have it in my power to compare his reasoning on some important points with that of other political Characters.

137 Washington to Morris, 7 July 1790, *Writings*, ed. Fitzpatrick, XXXI, 68. See Document VIII, below.
138 Humphreys to Washington, 1 Sep. 1790, Humphreys, *Humphreys*, II, 25-7.

If Washington had any doubt about the meaning of the allusion to the discussion about the national interest and the comparison of Hamilton's views with those of other political characters, all ambiguity was removed by the astonishing revelation in Humphreys' next communication, written from London:[139]

> The night after you left New York Col. Hamilton in a very confidential conversation, expressed himself (though still he mentioned his high opinion of the talents and honor of the gentleman in question) not perfectly satisfied with the manner in which Mr. G[ouverneur] M[orris] had conducted the business entrusted to him with the Duke of Leeds, and he desired me, upon investigating the temper of the British administration with regard to the points in agitation between the United States and Great Britain to write you, or him, the result of my Information. This, in the absence of Mr. M[orris] and in the private character it is necesary for me to preserve I have found in a manner impossible, without exposing myself to be considered as a person at least some way or another, employed in political affairs.

What Beckwith quoted Hamilton as saying to him about Morris a few weeks after Humphreys sailed thus stands confirmed and Hamilton's report of that interview discredited by the innocent revelations of an inexperienced envoy. Not the least of the charges to which the Secretary of the Treasury exposed himself in this further act of deception on the President and the Secretary of State is that of misjudging the instrument he had chosen—unless, as is possible, he deliberately made the secret approach to Humphreys because he knew him to be pliable, impressionable, and inept as the envoy of an administration whose policy and instructions to him left no ground whatever for ambiguity. Washington, who had already penetrated the effort to discredit Morris though without guessing its true origin in Hamilton's distortion of Beckwith's words and purpose, took the news of this attempt in characteristic silence.[140]

In urging Humphreys to undertake what Morris was officially authorized to do, Hamilton set in motion an operation that he must have known would result in the disclosure of the public character if not the exact nature of the mission to Spain, as even Humphreys himself be-

[139] Humphreys to Washington, 31 Oct. 1790, same, II, 50-4, "(*Secret*)."
[140] Washington to Humphreys, 16 Mch. 1791, *Writings*, ed. Fitzpatrick, XXXI, 241-2. Humphreys had said that Count Andriani had written things "monstrously absurd and ill founded—that the United States are divided into two factions, Mr. Jefferson and the northern [thus in MS] States in favour of France, the southern [thus in MS] States and New York in favour of Britain . . . that there was no man in Congress but Mr. Madison who argued in a gentlemanlike and solid manner—nor, in short, any man out of it in America, but Col. Hamilton, who possessed abilities." To this Washington replied: "The remarks of a foreign Count are such as do no credit to his judgment and as little to his heart. They are the superficial observations of a few months' residence, and an insult to the inhabitants of a country, where he has received much more attention and civility than he seems to merit." But the idle tales and the insult, so far as these touched upon the relations of the two key figures in the cabinet, were given ample proof in the very communication in which Humphreys reported the differing sentiments of "political Characters."

latedly realized. But there is no evidence that he otherwise violated the secrecy to which he was bound. In the same interview with Beckwith in which Hamilton urged so strongly that arrangements for a commercial treaty be pressed at that moment, the former reported to Dorchester: "It has been asserted here, that Colonel Humphries is gone to Europe to negotiate [the Holland loan]; it is on the other hand supposed that his objects are in England." Sir John Temple learned of the mission by accident or otherwise. "Since I finished my letter," he wrote to Leeds on 2 Sep. 1790, "I have casually learn'd that Colonel Humphreys (a distinguished favorite of General Washington) has taken passage in . . . a Merchant Ship bound for London in two or three days! His going it seems was intended to be a profound secret. This Gentleman was, first, Secretary to the Minister from these States to France . . . it is more than probable that he goes in some Diplomatic Character, if not to our Court, to France, Spain, or some other."[141] The "profound secret" was also known to French as well as British agents, as Humphreys found to his discomfort soon after ariving in London:[142]

I have not even once mentioned the subject to the Marq. de la Luzerne [Humphreys wrote to Washington]. On the contrary, I have judged it expedient to use all the discretion in my power, equally avoiding all appearances of curious enquiry or mysterious reserve, in order to pass for a meer common traveller. Yet somebody has written to Paris, describing a person, once a Colonel, in the American Army, as now employed here in intrigues relative to the Spanish War. This must be absolutely the effect of conjecture, without any ostensible grounds; for I have never opened my lips to any Creature in existence on any matter that led to it since my arrival. I have hitherto escaped all observations in the News Papers here. With this object in sight, I have carefully avoided seeing the Spanish Ambassador, and when I was asked by the Marquis de la Luzerne, if I had come to Europe on public business I answered, as I might with veracity, in the negative.

La Luzerne had reason to believe that the answer was not in fact veracious, but whether the conjectures and reports that arrived simultaneously with Humphreys arose from his own indiscretions before departure, from accident, or from intentional disclosure in New York is not known. Nor could that disclosure have been significant except as it underscored the point made by Hamilton to Beckwith—that he was displeased with Morris' conduct, that the time was ripe for estab-

141 Temple to Leeds, 2 Sep. 1790, PRO: FO 4/8, f. 327.
142 Humphreys to Washington, 31 Oct. 1790, Humphreys, *Humphreys*, II, 50-4, "(*Secret*)." Humphreys, who had known La Luzerne in America, conveyed Washington's letter of 10 Aug. 1790 to the minister. "As you know fully the manner in which that Gentleman has been in my family and connected with me for many years," Washington wrote La Luzerne, "I will say nothing more on his subject, than that he expects to travel in several parts of Europe; and that, if it should be convenient to your excellency to give him letters to any characters of your nation in the Countries or Courts which he may happen to visit, I shall consider the interest you take on his behalf in a very acceptable and obliging point of light"; Washington, *Writings*, ed. Fitzpatrick, XXXI, 85.

lishing a closer connection between England and the United States, that there was no understanding with Spain, that the navigation of the Mississippi was a national interest so vital to the United States as to justify war against Spain as an ally of England to obtain it, and that, most particularly, the negotiations needed to be pressed at that time and to be carried forward in America as a counterpoise to those who leaned toward the house of Bourbon.

The last point Hamilton drove home repeatedly. "I have already mentioned my wish," he told Beckwith, "that when matters shall be brought to a point, and a serious discussion takes place between Great Britain and us, pains may be taken to guard against any jealousies in the manner of it; we are a new people, which may occasion a coyness. Some of us possibly may entertain doubts of your wanting to Mark a Superiority, and such an idea may give a turn to the whole negotiation."[143] Here, at bottom, lies the explanation of the long months of clandestine discussions with a secret agent, the repeated deceptions practised on the administration, the attempt by indirection to thwart the policy agreed upon with respect to Spain. The belief in the possibility of a close and harmonious commercial connection with Great Britain was the paramount object, but the spring of action was an overarching self-confidence, matched by the fear that this great end might be endangered by the imprudent responses of a Gouverneur Morris or by the manners of a new people as embodied in the Secretary of State. The belief at that period was illusory, but the fear was well grounded. Jefferson, however, did not call it coyness: "with those who respect their own dignity so much," he wrote Morris, "ours must not be counted at nought." On this the President agreed. The government of the United States, he instructed Hamilton to remember in his consultation with Beckwith, should be left "entirely free to pursue, unreproached, such a line of conduct in the dispute as her interest (and honor)" should dictate. But neither Washington nor Jefferson ever knew to what extent both the national dignity and the national interest as pursued by the administration had been compromised by Hamilton who had said in the course of the secret discussions: "foreign nations in common are guided solely by their respective interests in whatever concerns their intercourse." In forgetting the national dignity, Hamilton also sacrificed his own honor and official character.

The failure of the house of Bourbon to respect the family compact doomed Jefferson's approach to Spain. But even Hamilton learned in a short time that a proposal to exchange ministers between the United States and Great Britain, whether proceeding from the coyness of a new people or from a sense of national dignity, would have to come first from that power that had ignored the initial advance of the other. Even so, he cannot have realized how greatly he contributed to the decision of the British cabinet to appoint a minister to the United States. For that decision resulted not at all from the proposals and suggestions made so insistently by him through Beckwith and Dorchester for over

[143] Beckwith's report of conversations (ca. 12 Aug. 1790), enclosed in Dorchester to Grenville, 25 Sep. 1790, No. 49, PRO: CO 42/69, f. 28, 30-48.

a year and a half before the appointment was made. It came rather from the fear instilled by the weapon he had unintentionally put in the hands of the member of the cabinet against whom his moves were directed from the beginning. The fear was well justified. When at the opening of the ensuing session of Congress the President asked the Secretary of State to study and report upon the correspondence of Gouverneur Morris, the conclusion arrived at was one that both men had reached months earlier. On the central question Jefferson—revealing that he had taken Hamilton's memorandum of the 8th of July at face value—concluded "That the British court . . . equivocate on every proposal of a treaty of commerce, and authorize in their communications with Mr. Morris the same conclusions which have been drawn from those they had had from time to time with Mr. Adams, and those through Majr. Beckwith: to wit, that they do not mean to submit their present advantages in commerce to the risk which might attend a discussion of them, whereon some reciprocity could not fail to be demanded. Unless indeed we would agree to make it a treaty of *alliance*, as well as of *commerce*, so as to undermine our obligations with France. This method of stripping that rival nation of it's alliances they tried successfully with Holland, endeavored at with Spain, and have plainly and repeatedly suggested to us. For this they would probably relax some of the rigours they exercise against our commerce." Nothing in this analysis appears ill-founded in the light of history save that part based upon the false representations transmitted to the administration by the Secretary of the Treasury as having purportedly come from Major Beckwith.[144]

Jefferson therefore thought it would be dishonorable to the United States, "useless, and even injurious, to renew the propositions for a treaty of commerce, or for the exchange of a minister: and that these subjects should now remain dormant" until brought forward earnestly by Great Britain. On the matter of the posts and indemnification for slaves carried away by the British army, demands for these should not again be made by the United States until the nation was in a position of doing itself the justice that might be refused. He concluded with the recommendation that "Mr. Morris should be informed that he has fulfilled the object of his agency to the satisfaction of the President, inasmuch as he has enabled him to judge of the real views of the British cabinet, and that it is his pleasure that the matters committed to him be left in the situation in which the letter shall find them." Washington acted in complete accord with this advice.[145] The false reports, thanks to

[144] See TJ's report to the President, 15 Dec. 1790.

[145] TJ to Morris, 17 Dec. 1790, in which he terminated the mission and added: "I have it in charge . . . to assure you that your conduct in these communications with the British ministers has met the President's entire approbation, and to convey to you his acknowledgements for your services." Washington wrote to Morris the same date: "An official letter from the Secretary of State . . . acknowledging the receipt of your public dispatches, will discover to you my sentiments on the views and intentions of the british Cabinet. If the exigencies of the national affairs of that kingdom should excite dispositions in it favorable to a commercial treaty with the United States, and to the fulfilment of the treaty of peace, its Ministers will, of themselves, come forward with propositions. Until these are apparent to them, and press, I am satisfied from the communications you have had with them, that it is not only useless, but would be derogatory to push them any farther on

an able envoy and to a perceptive Secretary of State, had misled no one.

But they had furnished those whom Hamilton and his friends in The Senate regarded as being under a French bias with a weapon that could be used. For the moment, writes Setser, "it appeared that Jefferson's star was in the ascendant and that his policy of resistance to Great Britain was to become the avowed policy of the United States Government."[146] The signal for a revival of Madison's "discriminating clauses" was given in the President's address to Congress recommending consideration of the embarrassments lying upon American commerce, suggesting the possibility of "such encouragements to our own Navigation as will render our commerce and agriculture less dependent on foreign bottoms," and directing attention to the Mediterranean trade. Jefferson's hand is evident in the address and Madison's in the House of Representatives framed the response. A committee promptly reported a navigation bill providing that imports into the United States should be permitted only in American bottoms and in those of the country of production for articles imported. In addition, a special duty was proposed of one cent per gallon on rum and twelve and a half cents per gallon on other distilled spirits coming from ports from which American vessels were not allowed to export them.

The signal came as an alarm to Beckwith. On the 19th of January he called on Hamilton, who again described the cleavage of parties on this issue, but gave the agent little comfort. "I think in the course of the present Sessions," the Secretary said, "we shall adopt in a degree the idea furnished by your Navigation Act, the effect of which will be to restrain your Shipping from being the carriers to our markets of other produce or manufacture than that of your own dominions (in all parts of the world) or of carrying from hence, excepting to your possessions, either at home or abroad." Hamilton sought to brighten the gloomy news by saying that there would be no prohibited articles and that, judging from returns in his office, such regulations would not be of any consequence to the shipping of Great Britain. That very day the December packet arrived bringing private rumors that the British ministry had decided to send a minister to the United States. On the following day when Beckwith called again, Hamilton spoke with confidence. "Upon the subject of commerce and navigation, which I mentioned to you yesterday," he said, "I think I can assure you that nothing will take place during the present session, to the injury of your trade."[147] But the elation that this brought was short-lived. During the next few weeks as the scene unfolded Beckwith was kept fully informed by his friends in the Senate, even to the extent of being told about debates there from which the American press and public were excluded.

Early in February a Senator disclosed to him that William Short,

the first point or to say anything more on the latter, *until we are in a situation to speak with more decision*" (Washington to Morris, 17 Dec. 1790, *Writings*, ed. Fitzpatrick, XXXI, 172-3; emphasis supplied).

146 Vernon G. Setser, *The Commercial Reciprocity Policy of the United States 1774-1829* (Philadelphia, 1937), p. 110.

147 Beckwith to Grenville, 23 Jan. 1791, covering enclosure concerning the conversations with Hamilton, PRO: FO 4/12, f. 23-30, endorsed as received 17 Mch. 1791.

chargé d'affaires in Paris, had informed the Secretary of State of the complaint of the National Assembly to the effect that the whole of the American trade was being given to England and that France would "alter their present system, which favors the admission of salted provisions into their West india islands, and the advantages which arise from the Ordinances now in force, relative to oil, spermaceti, and other indulgencies in the article of shipping &c. &c., unless the States . . . come forward with certain specific advantages in favor of the commercial interest of France." The Senator informed Beckwith that the papers on this subject had been laid before the Senate the preceding day. In the ensuing debate, he said, "It was observed that the application was absurd and impracticable; if the French merchants would trade to this country as those of England did, if they would send their property here and trust us as long with it, and if their goods would sell, we were equally disposed to be connected with them, as with England; if they would not, or could not do this, and if it was notorious that they had not shipping sufficient for their own commerce, was it to be expected that the States could grant exclusive privileges to them, privileges for which their nature, must produce one of two things, either an extension of similar advantages to other countries, with whom we trade largely, or a war of commerce with those countries, which would prove extremely injurious to the interests of the States."

Beckwith declared that this argument was offered in the Senate "to oppose an attempt of Mr. Jefferson . . . and of the French party connected with him to favor France, and to try to bring forward the discriminating system of duties in a different mode."[148] Such was the interpretation placed upon a move that had originated when the French chargé d'affaires presented to Jefferson a protest against the American tonnage laws of 1789 and 1790 and claimed exemption for France under the treaty of amity and commerce of 1778. What Beckwith presumably did not know was that Jefferson in his report to the President had declared the claim unwarranted, and—in order to retain special favors granted by France in the admission of whale and fish oils, as well no doubt as to achieve the admission of salt provisions for which he had so long labored—had submitted alternative proposals that clearly required action by the body that had passed the tonnage laws, all of which he laid before the Secretary of the Treasury prior to handing the report in to Washington. Nor could he have known that Hamilton, agreeing that the claim was unwarranted, had rejected Jefferson's alternatives and suggested instead of remedy by law the negotiation of a new treaty with France—a course clearly impossible of realization.[149]

It was in these circumstances that Beckwith learned in mid-February that the President had laid Gouverneur Morris' reports before the

---

148 Beckwith to Grenville, 3 Mch. 1791, covering enclosures concerning conversations with members of Congress and with Hamilton from 3 Feb. to 26 Feb. 1791, together with texts of the President's message to Congress of 14 Feb. 1791, of Beckwith's letter to Hamilton of 17 Feb. 1791, and of Madison's bill on commerce; PRO: FO 4/12, f. 36-50; endorsed as received 1 May 1791.
149 TJ's report to Washington, 18 Jan. 1791; Hamilton to TJ, 11 Jan. 1791; TJ to Madison, [1 Jan. 1791]; TJ to Hamilton, 13 Jan. 1791. See Malone, *Jefferson*, II, 328-30.

Senate. These papers, his informant declared, "were submitted to us yesterday, at the instigation I believe of Mr. Jefferson, and in order to induce us to favor a French interest, from a certain coldness which runs through Mr. Morris's communications, as they regard the disposition of your Ministry towards us." The Senator made himself very explicit: "I wish to impress you with its being my conviction that there is an absolute necessity of following up this business during the summer; a delay I do assure you will at least be dangerous and may throw us into a French interest."

Beckwith, alarmed at this turn of events, immediately requested an interview with the Secretary of the Treasury. The two men had a lengthy conversation on the morning of the 16th. Beckwith said nothing of his information from the Senator, but based his remarks on brief newspaper statements about the President's communications to the two houses on the subject of a commercial treaty with Great Britain. "Although no particulars are stated," he said, "yet enough is expressed to convey an impression to the public mind, that we are not disposed to form any such treaty." He recalled the opinion of Gouverneur Morris' he had expressed in a former conversation—an opinion almost identical with what he had reported the preceding autumn as being that of Hamilton. "I assume it as a fact," he said, "that the information laid before your Legislature, is founded on Mr. Morris's communications, and as there have been no late arrivals from England, I am further led to conceive, that this information is not recent, and that it refers to accounts from thence, pending our negotiations with Spain." He then felt obliged to probe the motives that had led the President to make such communications to Congress. His conclusion was phrased in polite diplomatic terms but its meaning was unmistakable: "It is my duty and my wish to speak in terms of the highest respect of the Chief Magistrate of this Country, as well as of the government itself. But I should be guilty of insincerity, if I did not declare, I cannot avoid suspecting, that this communication (tending as it does to convey an impression of there being a coldness in our Administration towards The States) has been made in order to influence gentlemen in a popular Assembly with ideas which may operate on other questions; whether this may have been the effect of accident or of design, I do not presume to determine."[150]

Hamilton recalled to the agent their conversations in which he had frequently mentioned the differences of opinion existing in the government "respecting our having a strict national or commercial friendship with Great Britain." He could not bring himself to believe that the President's mind was in the least influenced by any set of prejudices. "He indeed is of opinion," Hamilton stated, "from Mr. Morris's letters, *that no Commercial treaty is attainable with England*, but I am sure he is not led to make these communications to the Legislature at this time, from any idea of assimilating this with other questions."[151] Yet he did not "pretend to say that such views may not have struck the minds of certain persons, who have recommended this measure." He did not anticipate hostile legislation. "In the Senate," he added confi-

---

[150] See note 148.
[151] Emphasis in MS; see note 148.

dently, "I am sure, none will be effected." In the present state of affairs nothing had happened to give a colorable pretext for breaking off the treaty of alliance with France and immediately forming another with Great Britain. "A regard for National decorum," he said, "puts such a decisive step as this, out of our Reach, but I tell you candidly as an individual, that I think the formation of a treaty of commerce, would by degrees have led to this measure, which undoubtedly that Party with us, whose remaining Animosities and French partialities influence their whole political conduct, regard with dissatisfaction."

Beckwith reminded him that Morris' communications reflected his opinion formed during the threat of war. He then asked a question and answered it with a reference to his instructions from Dorchester phrased in direct contradiction to what Hamilton had said of those instructions to the President: "Is it quite clear that this gentleman is really thoroughly acquainted with the intentions of our Government? For my own part my instructions from Lord Dorchester authorise me to think and to say, that we have the most friendly dispositions towards the States, of which our liberality in Commercial matters is a decisive proof, notwithstanding the existing difficulties, relative to the treaty of peace; I know that Gentlemen in a French interest, are not disposed to admit the force of this, as they do not view our commercial conduct in this light, but I am instructed to hold a different language on this subject." The remarks were almost a paraphrase of Dorchester's instructions. There can be no doubt that on all occasions when it was necessary to cite them the able officer did so accurately and with exactitude.

Beckwith now for the first time took it upon himself to speak as if he were in fact clothed with some public authority. He made it plain that he did so because he looked upon the President's communication to the two houses as an attempt to check the growing friendship between his country and the United States, as a threat to their exchange of ministers, and as a strengthening of the French interest in America. Hitherto, he said, "I have thought it my duty to be silent on all political matters, and have shunned explanations even to gentlemen in your Legislature, but in the present moment, I should think it wrong to adhere to this. I feel myself compelled to speak out, and I wish to have my sentiments on this subject known, where they ought to be." To accomplish this he proposed to write Hamilton on this important question, authorizing him to make what use of it he pleased. "I shall state my sentiments candidly," he concluded, "and I trust in a way not to give any offense to your Government."

Beckwith's letter to Hamilton, like his remarks in the interview, was ostensibly based on newspaper reports rather than on what he had heard from friends in the Senate. On the 17th of February Washington's message to the two houses had appeared in the press: "Soon after I was called to the administration of the government, I found it important to come to an understanding with the Court of London, on several points interesting to the United States, and particularly to know, whether they were disposed to enter into arrangements by mutual consent, which might fix the commerce between the two nations on principles of reciprocal advantage. For this purpose I authorised informal conferences with their ministers; and from these, I do not infer any disposition on their part, to enter into any arrangements merely commercial. I have thought it proper to give you this information as it might at some time have influence on matters under your consideration."[152] Beckwith did not know, but he and his advisors strongly suspected, that Jefferson's hand was in this move. The Secretary of State had, in fact, drafted the message.

Beckwith's alarm is understandable. But in his letter to the Secretary of the Treasury his concern was hidden in diplomatic language:[153]

> It is with the most perfect deference for the general government of this country [he wrote], and with the highest respect for the Office and Character of the Chief Magistrate who presides at the head of it, that I take the liberty of submitting any ideas of mine, on so important a question; but from the nature of my Lord Dorchester's instructions to me, I am free to own, I have always been led to believe, that a most sincere and favorable disposition did and does exist on the part of Great Britain towards the United States, of which her liberality in commercial matters, affords the most convincing proofs, notwithstanding the still existing difficulties relative to the treaty of peace; the improvement of this disposition to its utmost extent, and the giving it a permanent effect, is a work, to which our mutual wants, as well as ancient friendships strongly stimulate; it involves the interests of two countries, where natural habits of commerce, cannot escape the observation of the most limited comprehension, where even distance is advantage, and where the immense commercial capital of the one Country, feeds the enterprize of the other.
>
> But I have done—flattering myself that neither the manner nor the substance of this letter may give offence, where my duty and my wishes unite in a desire to pay every possible mark of attention and respect.

Again the paraphrase of the instructions from Dorchester was exact, though Beckwith's innate tact led him to screen out the harsher expressions of the Governor General. The agent delivered the letter to Hamilton on the morning of the 18th of February. In drafting it, Beckwith told Grenville, he had carefully avoided "any expressions which might furnish the smallest pretext for complaint on the part of those who were pushing a French interest." He was told—presumably by Hamilton—that the letter was immediately laid before the President. Possibly it was, but no copy survives in the papers of Washington and his diary for this period is missing, so that verification is not possible. The general terms of the letter could not have caused any embarrassment to Hamilton even if it had been shown.

Beckwith was far from content with making this delicate protest. It

152 The text is that transcribed by Beckwith (note 148); see Washington, *Writings*, ed. Fitzpatrick, XXXI, 214.
153 See note 148.

was prudent to write in such guarded terms in a letter obviously intended for the Chief Executive, but, as he informed Grenville, he "conceived it equally proper and necessary to hold a different language in conversation." He said in private that if those who seemed to be pressing violent measures thought the trade of the United States indispensable to Great Britain, it was necessary for him to "say plainly that the fact was not so"; that its importance was merely relative and on certain conditions; and that "such a fallacious principle acted upon at this juncture, could never advance, but must retard, and might finally prevent an amicable arrangement of the differences" between the two countries. Moreover, he reminded his friends in office, "when [in 1789] the system for the discrimination of duties with different nations had been in agitation in the States soon after the formation of the present government," Great Britain had been prepared to meet it.[154]

The violence of the reaction by Beckwith to the use made by Madison and Jefferson of the failure of the Morris mission was itself a testimony to the confidence of the Secretary of State that means were available and infallible for protecting the national interests. By the end of February a Senator told Beckwith gloomily: "I do not think a treaty of Alliance practicable at this moment; I am really of opinion that a Majority of the sensible, cool headed Men in this Country would prefer it, but Mr. Jefferson's influence and his exertions would defeat it. . . . Mr. Jefferson is making every possible exertion to turn the commerce of this Country into the scale of France."[155] Others in Congress pressed Beckwith "to return home immediately, from an idea which these gentlemen entertain of the importance of an attention to the affairs of this Country, as well as from their Anxiety on the subject."[156] Beckwith's instructions from Dorchester permitted such a move, but he decided against it, feeling that he could serve a more useful purpose by remaining in Philadelphia. The picture that he drew for Grenville of the divisive tendencies in the administration reflected his anxiety:[157]

The talents of General Washington are greatly overrated in the world. His public reputation has hitherto been supported by reserve, caution, temper, firmness, and a plain understanding, with a good choice of men around him; his present high station has lately become extremely embarrassing from a difference in the political opinion of the officers at the head of the executive departments, which affects more or less every measure of this government. If the concerns of the States, were transacted in a cabinet, the chief magistrate would be compelled to a choice, the one influence or the other would obtain a complete ascendancy; but as the President by the Constitution, can do wrong, may be impeached, and (although he practices it) is not under the necessity of demanding the opinions of the heads of departments . . . the condition of things . . . does not press to such an extremity, and he balances amidst discordant advice, sometimes lean-

154 See note 148.
155 See note 148.
156 Beckwith to Grenville, 11 Mch. 1791, PRO: FO 4/12, f. 76-81; endorsed as received 1 May 1791.
157 Same.

ing to one party, and occasionally to the other. The great point of difference is on an English and a French connexion; the gentleman at the head of the former, conceives the best interests of this country will be greatly promoted by a solid and permanent friendship with Great Britain, and in this opinion he is supported by the most enlightened men in the legislature; this party think that the condition of the two Countries is such as render the formation of a commercial treaty very practicable and to the benefit of both nations and they are extremely desirous to promote it: Mr. Jefferson . . . is at the head of the latter, he is blindly devoted to a French influence, which he does not take common pains to conceal and there are no lengths in his power to which he will not go to favor the interests of that kingdom.

Thus, perfectly reflecting the views and prejudices of William Samuel Johnson and others in the Senate with whom he had been in intimate contact since 1789, Beckwith succeeded in persuading himself, and endeavored to persuade the British Secretary for Foreign Affairs, that the Secretary of State was a narrow partisan under the influence of France, bitterly hostile to England.

It is a mistake, however, to conclude that at this point the forces in the House of Representatives led by Madison stayed their hand because of the rumors that Britain was about to send a minister to the United States.[158] The virulence of the debate over the bill for a national bank, the narrow division in the house, the disinclination to press matters to an extremity when plans for the permanent seat of government were being projected—these and a number of other factors, tangible and intangible, must have caused the weapon to be sheathed. Deeply as they believed the national interest and dignity to be involved, however, Madison and Jefferson at no time in the long battle for commercial reciprocity dared employ the threats that had been sounded so ominously in the preceding session when Hamilton's assumption bill hung in the balance—the warnings of disunion. Their nationalism was of a tougher fibre. The issue was not forced. Had a vote been compelled in the evenly-divided House of Representatives, Beckwith reported, the opposition were determined "not only to debate the validity and propriety of Mr. Morris's proceedings, arising from his conversations with Mr. Pitt, but to investigate at large, in how far his opinions supported the inference drawn from them by the Executive in this Country, and whether all circumstances considered, they ought to have been made the basis of a legislative procedure." This, Beckwith declared, "would have produced a very delicate discussion indeed, as it respected the President personally, rather than have suffered any strong measure to have taken place at this time."[159]

Yet the President's message to Congress and the response had sounded warning signals that were heard across the Atlantic. Beckwith's full reports of the proceedings in Congress and of his delicate

[158] See for example, Vernon G. Setser, *The Commercial Reciprocity Policy of the United States 1774-1829* (Philadelphia, 1937), p. 110.
[159] Beckwith to Grenville, 14 Mch. 1791, PRO: FO 4/12, f. 82-3.

letter of protest to Hamilton arrived in London on the first of May. Within a month Lord Grenville had directed George Hammond to return as speedily as possible from his post in Madrid. His next mission would be that of minister to the United States.

Thus, ironically, by a course of deception begun when he recommended Gouverneur Morris for appointment in 1789, Hamilton had succeeded only in furnishing the Secretary of State with a powerful instrument that came very close to bringing success to his and Madison's commercial policy. No advance toward a *rapprochement* had been made but the ministry had been filled with apprehension. Back of their fear lay the possibility that the Secretary of State, preferring amicable to adversary relations in commerce, might be able to employ the means that he considered both available and infallible. The West India planters doubtless would have agreed, and the swiftness with which the ministry responded to the mere threat indicates how clearly they grasped the reality of the danger. Hamilton's duplicity had in fact come very near wrecking his own policy. But when the exchange of ministers ultimately came about, he moved on undaunted along the same course, saying one thing to the administration and another to the envoy of Great Britain. The manoeuver that had begun immediately on the signing of Jefferson's commission as Secretary of State was repeated in one form or another in almost every aspect of foreign affairs for the next four years, foredooming the major objectives of Jefferson's policy to failure and making his continuance in office intolerable once the President shifted the immense weight of his influence to the other side of the scales. The calculated and continuing use of deception by the Secretary of the Treasury is thus a major factor that must be reckoned with in the assessment of foreign policy in the first administration and beyond.

Documents on the War Crisis

I. Secretary of State to the President, enclosing Opinion

July 12. 1790.

Th: Jefferson had a conference yesterday with Mr. Madison on the subject recommended by the President. He has the honor of inclosing him some considerations thereon, in all of which he believes Mr. Madison concurred. He has sketched the heads only, as the President's mind will readily furnish the developement of each. He will wait on the president at one aclock on some other business, and then and at all other times be ready to enter more into the details of any part of the subject the president may chuse.

RC (DNA: RG 59, MLR); addressed: "The President of the United States"; endorsed by Washington: "From Thoms. Jefferson Esqr. 12th July 1790 on the Subject of the War between Great Britain and Spain. Opinion." Entry in SJPL reads: "Opn. Th: J. on conduct of U.S. in War between Spain & Gr. Br."

ENCLOSURE

Jefferson's Outline of Policy Contingent on War between England and Spain

Heads of consideration on the conduct we are to observe in the war between Spain and Gr. Britain and particularly should the latter attempt the conquest of Louisiana and the Floridas.

The dangers to us should Great Britain possess herself of those countries.

She will[1] possess a territory equal to half ours, beyond the Missisipi[2]

She will seduce that half of ours which is on this side the Missisipi[3]

    by her language, laws, religion, manners, government, commerce, capital.

    by the possession of N. Orleans, which draws to it the dependance of all the waters of Misspi

    by the markets she can offer them in the gulph of Mexico and elsewhere.

She will take from the remaining part of our States the markets they now have for their produce by furnishing those markets cheaper with the same articles. Tobacco, rice, indigo, bread, lumber, naval stores, furs.

She will have then possessions double the size of ours, as good in soil and climate.

She will encircle us compleatly, by these possessions on our landboard, and her fleets on our sea-board.

Instead of two neighbors balancing each other, we shall have one, with more than the strength of both.

Would the prevention of this be worth a war?

Consider our abilities to take part in a war.

[89]

Our operations would be by land only.

How many men should we need to employ?—Their cost?

Our resources of taxation and credit equal to this.

Weigh the evil of this new accumulation of debt

Against the loss of markets, and eternal expence and danger from so overgrown a neighbor.

But this is on supposition that France as well as Spain shall be engaged in the war. For with Spain alone, the war would be unsuccessful, and our situation rendered worse.[4]

No need to take a part in the war as yet. We may chuse our own time.

Delay gives us many chances to avoid it altogether.

In such a choice of objects, Gr. Britain may not single out Louisiana and the Floridas.

She may fail in her attempt on them.

France and Spain may recover them.

If all these chances fail, we should have to re-take them.[4]

The difference between retaking, and preventing, overbalanced by the benefits of delay.

Delay enables us to be better prepared:

To obtain from the allies a price for our assistance.[5]

Suppose these our ultimate views. What is to be done at this time?

1. As to Spain?

If she be as sensible as we are that she cannot save Louisiana and the Floridas,

Might she not prefer their Independance to their Subjection to Grt. Britain?

Does not the proposition of the Ct. d'Estaing furnish us an opening to communicate our ideas on this subject to the court of France, and thro them to that of Madrid? And our readiness to join them in guaranteeing the independance of those countries?

This might save us from a war, if Gr. Britain respects our weight in a war.

And if she does not, the object would place the war on popular ground with us.[6]

2. As to England? Say to Beckwith

'that as to a Treaty of commerce, we would prefer amicable, to adversary arrangements, tho the latter would be infallible, and in our own power:[7]

That our ideas are that such a treaty should be founded in perfect reciprocity; and would therefore be it's own price:

That as to an Alliance, we can say nothing till it's object be shewn, and that it is not to be inconsistent with existing engagements:[8]

That in the event of war between Gr. Brit. and Spain we are disposed to be strictly neutral:[9]

That however, we should view with extreme uneasiness any attempts of either power to seize the possessions of the other on our frontier, as we consider our own safety interested in a due balance between our neighbors.' [It might be advantageous to express this latter sentiment, because if there be any difference of opinion in their councils, whether to bend their force against North or South America, or the islands, (and certainly there is room for difference) and if these opinions be nearly balanced, that balance might be determined by the prospect of having an enemy the more or less, according to the object they should select.]

TH: JEFFERSON
July. 12. 1790.

MS (DNA: RG 59, MLR); in TJ's hand; endorsed by Washington: "The Secretary of State 12th July 1790"; brackets in MS. Dft (DLC); in TJ's hand; text varies from that above, principally in phraseology, but some of more important differences are noted below (full text printed, though not with complete accuracy, in Ford, v, 199-203; e.g. "reduce" instead of "seduce"). FC (DNA: RG 59, SDC).

¹ In this and the succeeding four heads, Dft reads: "She would."
² This head in Dft reads: "Beyond the Missi. a territory equal to half ours."
³ This head in Dft reads: "She would seduce ⟨draw to it⟩ our Cis-Missi. possessions."
⁴ This head not in Dft.
⁵ This head in Dft reads: "To stipulate with Spain and France advantages

for our assistance."
⁶ Preceding two words not in Dft.
⁷ This head takes on a more expanded form in Dft: "That as to a treaty of commerce, we had never desired it but on terms of perfect reciprocity.—That therefore we never thought to give any price for it but itself.—That we had wished for it to avoid giving mutual wounds to the commerce of both nations.—But that we have the measures in our own power which may save us from loss."
⁸ In Dft this head reads: "⟨That no considerations⟩ ⟨France as well as Spain will be involved⟩ That as to the Alliance they propose, it would involve us against France and Spain and considered even in a moral view, no price could repay such an abandonment of character."
⁹ In Dft this head reads: "That we are truly disposed to remain neutral."

II. Secretary of State to William Carmichael, enclosing Outline of Policy

DEAR SIR   New York August 2d. 1790.

This letter will be delivered you by Colo. Humphreys, whose character is so well known to you as to need no recommendations from me. [The present appearances of war between our two neighbours, Spain and England, cannot but excite all our attention. The part we are to act is uncertain, and will be difficult. The unsettled state of our dispute with Spain may give a turn to it very different from what we would wish. As it is important that you should be fully apprised of our way of thinking on this subject, I have sketched, in the enclosed paper, general heads of consideration arising from present circumstances; these will be readily developed by your own reflections]¹ and in conversations with Col. Humphreys, who possessing the sentiments of the Executive on this subject, being well acquainted with the circumstances of the Western Country in particular, and of the State of our affairs in general, comes to Madrid expressly for the purpose of giving you a thorough communication of them: he will therefore remain there as many days, or weeks, as may be necessary for this purpose. [With this information,][1] written and oral, [you will be enabled to meet the minister in conversations on the subject of the navigation of the Missisippi to which we wish you to lead his attention immediately. Impress him thoroughly with the necessity of an early and even an immediate settlement of this matter, and of a return to the field of negociation for this purpose: and though it must be done delicately, yet he must be made to understand unequivocally that a resumption of the negociation is not desired on our part, unless he can determine, in the first opening of it, to yield the immediate and full enjoyment of that navigation. (I say nothing of the claims of Spain to our Territory north of the 31st. degree, and east of the Missisippi: they never merited the respect of an answer; and you know it has been admitted at Madrid that they were not to be maintained.) It may be asked what need of negociation, if the navigation is to be ceded at all events? You know that the navigation cannot be practised without a port where the sea and river vessels may meet and exchange loads, and where those employed about them may be safe and unmolested. The right to use a thing comprehends a right to the means necessary to it's use, and without which it would be useless: the fixing on a proper port, and the degree of freedom it is to enjoy in it's operations, will require negociation, and be governed by events. There is danger indeed that even the unavoidable delay of sending a negociator here, may render the mission too late for the preservation of peace: it is impossible to answer for the forbearance of our western citizens. We endeavor to quiet them with the expectation of an attainment of their rights by peaceable means, but should they, in a moment of impatience, hazard others, there is no saying how far we may be led: for neither themselves nor their rights will ever be abandoned by us.

You will be pleased to observe that we press these matters warmly and firmly under this idea, that the war between Spain and Great Britain will be begun before you receive this; and such a moment must not be lost. But should an accommodation take place, we retain indeed the same object, and the same resolutions unalterably; but your discretion will suggest that, in that event, they must be pressed more softly; and that patience and persuasion must temper your conferences, till either these may prevail, or some other circumstance turn up which may enable us to use other means for the attainment of an object, which we are determined in the end to obtain at every risk.]¹ I have the honor to be with great esteem Dear Sir &c.

FC (DNA: RG 59, PCC No. 121); at foot of text: "(signed) Thomas Jefferson." Entry in SJL designates this letter as "(secret)." Tr of Extract (CLU); in TJ's hand, with the following caption: "Extracts from a letter to Mr. Carmichael dated Aug. 2. 1790" (see note 1 below).

¹ This and other passages enclosed in brackets (supplied) comprise the

text of the continuous document described above as Tr of Extract. It is to be noted that, aside from the complimentary close, the only passages not included in the text of the extract are those alluding to David Humphreys' mission. This extract was sent by TJ to Short, 10 Aug. 1790, after Washington had given his approval. See TJ to Washington, 8 Aug. 1790 (Document V).

ENCLOSURE

Jefferson's Outline of Policy on the Mississippi Question

Heads of consideration on the Navigation of the
Missisipi for Mr. Carmichael.

We have a *right* to the navigation of the Missisipi   1. by Nature:
                                                        2. by Treaty.

It is *necessary* to us.

More than half the territory of the U.S. is on the waters of that river. 200,000 of our citizens are settled on them, of whom 40,000 bear arms.¹

These have no other Out-let for their tobacco, rice, corn, hemp, lumber, house timber, ship timber.

We have hitherto respected² the indecision of Spain, because we wish peace: because our Western citizens have had vent at home for their productions.

A surplus of production begins now to demand foreign markets.

Whenever they shall say 'We cannot, we will not, be longer shut up'

The U.S. will be reduced to the following dilemma:

1. To force them to acquiescence:
2. To separate from them, rather than take part in a war against Spain:
3. Or to preserve them in our union, by joining them in the war.

The 1st. is neither in our principles, nor in our power:

2. A multitude of reasons decide against the 2ᵈ.

It may suffice to speak out one: were we to give up half our territory rather than engage in a just war to preserve it, we should not keep the other half long.³

3. The 3ᵈ. is the⁴ alternative we must necessarily adopt.

How are we to obtain that navigation?[5]

(A) By *Force*

1. Acting *separately.*

That we can effect this with certainty and promptitude, circumstances decide.

Objection. We cannot retain New Orleans, for instance, were we to take it.

Answer. A moderate force may be so secured, as to hold out till succoured.

Our succours can be prompt and effectual

Suppose, after taking it, we withdraw our force.

If Spain retakes it by an expedition, we can recover it by a counter-expedition and so as often as the case shall happen. Their expeditions will be slow, expensive, and lead to catastrophes: Ours sudden, economical, and a check have no consequences.[6]

We should associate the country to our union.

The inhabitants wish this.

They are not disposed to be of the Spanish government.

It is idle in Spain to suppose our Western inhabitants will unite with them.[7]

They could be quiet but a short time under a government so repugnant to their feelings.

Were they to come under it for present purposes, it would be with a view to throw it off soon.[8]

Should they remain, they would communicate a spirit of Independence to those with whom they should be mixed.

II. Acting in *conjunction* with Great Britain, and with a view to partition.

The Floridas and island of New Orleans[9] would be assigned to us.

Louisiana (or all the Western waters of the Missisipi) to them.

We confess that such an Alliance is not what we would wish.

Because it may eventually lead us into embarrassing situations with our best friend.

And put the power of two neighbors into the hands of one.

Ld. Lansdowne has declared he gave the Floridas to Spain rather than the U. S. as a bone of discord with the House of Bourbon, and of reunion[10] with Gr. Britain.

Connolly's attempt (as well as other facts) proves they keep it in view.

(B.) By *Negociation.*

1. What must Spain do[15] of *Necessity*?[11]

The conduct of Spain has proved that the occlusion of the Missisipi is system with her.

If she opens it now, it will be because forced by imperious circumstances.

She will consequently shut it again when these circumstances cease.

Treaty will be no obstacle.

Irregularities, real or pretended, in our navigators, will furnish colour enough.

Perpetual broils, and finally war will ensue.

Prudence, and even necessity, imposes on us the law of settling the matter now *finally*, and not by *halves*.

With experience of the past, and prospect of the future, it would be imbecility in us to accept the naked navigation.

With that, we must have what is necessary 1. to it's use, and without which it would be useless: 2. to secure it's continuance.[12]

That is, a port near the mouth to recieve our vessels, and protect the navigation. So well separated in jurisdiction and fact as to avoid the danger of broils.[13]

But even this will not secure the Floridas, and Louisiana against Great Britain.

If we are neutral, she will wrest those possessions from Spain.

The inhabitants (French, English, Scotch, American)[14] would prefer England to Spain.

II. What then had Spain better do[15] of *choice?*

Cede to us all territory on our side of the Missisipi:[16]

On condition that we guarantee all her possessions on the Western waters of that river:

She agreeing further, to subsidize us, if the guarantee brings us into the war.

Should Gr. Britain possess herself of the Floridas and Louisiana,

Her governing principles are Conquest, Colonization, Commerce, Monopoly.

She will establish powerful colonies in them.

These can be poured into the gulph of Mexico, for any sudden enterprize there.

Or invade Mexico, their next neighbor, by land.

Whilst a fleet co-operates along shore, and cuts off relief.

And proceed successively from colony to colony.

With respect to us, if Gr. Britain establishes herself on our whole land-board

Our lot will be bloody and eternal war; or indissoluble confederacy.

Which ought we to chuse?

what will be the lot of the Spanish colonies, in the jaws of such a confederacy?

What will secure the Ocean against Monopoly?

Safer for Spain that we should be her neighbor, than England.

Conquest not in our principles: inconsistent with our government.

Not our interest to cross the Missisipi for ages.

And will never be our interest to remain united with those who do.

Intermediate chances save the trouble of calculating so far forward.

Consequences of this Cession, and Guarantee.[17]

1. Every subject of difference will be removed from between Spain and the U. S.
2. Our interest will be strongly engaged in her retaining her American possessions.
3. Spain will be quieted as to Louisiana, and her territories West of that.
4. She may employ her whole force in defence of her islands and Southern possessions.
5. If we preserve our neutrality, it will be a very partial one to her.
6. If we are forced into the war, it will be, as we wish, on the side of the H. of Bourbon.
7. Our privateers will commit formidable depredations on the Brit. trade, and occupy much of their force.
8. By withholding supplies of provision, as well as by concurring in expeditions, the British islands will be in imminent danger.
9. Their expences of precaution, both for their continental and insular possessions will be so augmented as to give a hope of running their credit down.

In fine, for a narrow slip of barren, detached, and expensive country, Spain secures the rest of her territory, and makes an Ally, where she might have a dangerous enemy.

Th: Jefferson
Aug. 2. 1790

PrC (CLU); in TJ's hand, being a fair copy of texts indicated below as Dft and MS, but having important variations which are indicated in the textual notes. Tr (DNA: RG 59, DD); filed with Humphreys' letter to TJ, 17 Aug. 1791; in clerk's hand. Dft (DLC); with numerous alterations, some of which are indicated in notes below; at head of text: "Aug. 2. 1790." MS (MHi); in TJ's hand. FC (DNA: RG 59, SDC). Internal evidence in Dft shows that TJ copied it from some previous text, but with alterations being made in the course of transcription, and it is plain that he utilized the draft of the statement of policy transmitted to Washington on 12 July 1790 in preparing this outline for Carmichael. In his letter to Washington of 8 Aug. 1790 TJ stated that the text drawn up earlier that had been left with the president contained "two or three small differences" from that then enclosed. A collation of the various texts shows clearly that Dft, MS, and FC represent the earlier state and that PrC and Tr represent the state enclosed in the letter to Washington on 8 Aug. 1790. The missing RC from which PrC was executed was evidently the text sent to Carmichael.

1 The words ". . . of whom 40,000 bear arms" are not in Dft, MS, or FC.

2 Instead of "respected," Dft, MS, and FC read "borne."

3 Dft reads: "One only shall be spoken out. The Nation that gives up half it's territory, rather than engage in a just war to preserve it, will not keep the other half long." All other texts read as above.

4 In Dft TJ first wrote, and then deleted, "only."

5 In Dft TJ first wrote ". . . obtain the enjoyment of our right of navigation," and then altered the passage to read as above.

6 Dft and MS both read originally: ". . . a check of little consequences," and in the course of transcribing the latter from the former TJ altered the text in both to read as above.

7 This passage in Dft reads: "⟨unite with them⟩ submit to their government." TJ thus restored the earlier reading in PrC.

8 Dft originally read: ". . . with a view soon to set up for themse[lves]," and TJ altered the text to read as above.

9 All texts save PrC read: "The Floridas (including N. Orleans)," &c.

10 This word interlined in Dft in substitution for "coalition," deleted.

11 Dft originally read: "What are the lowest terms we could admit?" TJ then altered the query to read as above.

12 Dft, MS, and FC read: "We must have what will secure it's continuance: That is a port near the mouth, to recieve our vessels, and protect the navigation."

13 This sentence not in Dft, MS, or FC.

14 Tr alone of all texts reads "German" for "American," clearly a clerk's error.

15 This word interlined in Dft in substitution for "yield," deleted.

16 Dft originally read: "cede to us the Floridas, i.e. all her possessions East of the Missisipi," and then TJ altered the passage to read as above.

17 Dft originally read: "Consequences of this cession of the Floridas to us, and guarantee of Louisiana to Spain," and then TJ altered the passage to read as above.

III. Thomas Jefferson to Luis Pinto de Souza

SIR   New York August 7th. 1790.

Under cover of the acquaintance I had the honor of contracting with you, during the negociations we transacted together in London, I take the liberty of addressing you the present letter. The friendly dispositions you were then pleased to express towards this Country, which were sincerely and reciprocally felt on my part towards yours, flatter me with the hope you will assist in maturing a subject for their common good. As yet we have not the information necessary to present it to you formally, as the Minister of her most faithful Majesty; I beg therefore that this letter may be considered as between two individual friends of their respective Countries, preliminary to a formal proposition, and meant to give an acceptable shape to that.

It is unnecessary, with your Excellency, to go through the history of our first experiment in Government, the result of which was a want of such tone in the governing powers, as might effect the good of those committed to their care: the nation became sensible of this, have changed it's organization, made a better distribution of it's powers, and given to them more energy and independence. The new Government has now for some time been under way, and so far gives a confidence that it will answer it's purposes: abuses under the old forms have led us to lay the basis of the new in a rigorous economy of the public contributions. This principle will shew itself in our diplomatic establishments, and the rather as, at such a distance from Europe, and with such an ocean between us, we hope to meddle little in it's quarrels or combinations: it's peace and it's commerce are what we shall court; and to cultivate these, we propose to place at the Courts of Europe most interesting to us, diplomatic characters of economical grade, and shall be glad to receive like ones in exchange. The important commerce carried on between your Country and ours, and the proofs of friendly disposition towards us which her Majesty has manifested, induce us to wish for such an exchange with her, to express our sensibility at the intimations heretofore received of her readiness to meet our wish in this point, and our regret at the delay which has proceeded from the circumstances before touched on. The grade to be exchanged is the present question, and that on which I ask a friendly and informal consultation with you: that of Chargé des affaires is the one we would prefer; it is that we employ at the Court of Madrid. But it has been said that, by the etiquette of your Court, that grade cannot be received there under a favorable countenance. Something like this existed at the Court of Madrid but his most Catholic Majesty, in consideration of our peculiar circumstances, dispensed with a general rule, in our favor, and in our particular case; and our Chargé des affaires there enjoys at Court the privileges, the respect and favor due to a friendly nation, to a nation whom distance and difference of circumstances liberate in some degree from an etiquette to which it is a stranger at home as well as abroad. The representative of her Majesty here, under whatever name mutual convenience may designate him, shall be received in the plenitude of friendship and favor. May we not ask a reciprocal treatment of ours with you? The nations of Europe have already seen the necessity of distinguishing America from Europe, even in their Treaties: and a difference of commerce, of government, of condition and character must every day evince, more and more, the impracticability of involving them under common regulations. Nor ought a difference of arrangement with respect to us to excite claims for others whose circumstances bear no similitude to ours.

I beg leave to submit these considerations to your Excellency's wisdom and goodness. You will see them to be such as could not be offered formally. They must shield themselves under the protection of those sentiments of veneration and esteem with which your character heretofore inspired me, and which I flattered myself were not merely indifferent to you. Be so good as to honor, with a conference hereon, the bearer Col. Humphreys (who was known to you in London) a gentleman who has long been of the President's family, and whose worth has acquired so much of our confidence that whatever shall be arranged with him, on this subject, may be considered as settled. Presuming on a continuance of her Majesty's dispositions, accept this private assurance that a proper person shall be appointed in due form to reside with you, as soon as we shall know the result of your deliberations with Colonel Humphreys, who I beg leave to present to your notice; adding the homage of those sentiments of respect and attachment, with which I have the honor to be your Excellency's most obedient and most humble servant,

THOMAS JEFFERSON

FC (DNA: RG 59, PCC No. 121). On its face this was a private letter. But the text is recorded in the files of the Department of State; it was sent to the President for his approval; and it had the same secret status as other dispatches carried by Humphreys on his urgent mission—facts which give it an official character while stamping it as a typical example of TJ's flexible and indirect diplomacy. While negotiating with De Pinto for a treaty of commerce in 1786, TJ had formed the opinion that the minister from Portugal was "sensible, candid," and favorably disposed toward America. He had also supposed that De Pinto might be promoted to the post of foreign minister at Lisbon and that this would be favorable for the adoption of the treaty and for the admission of American flour into Portugal (Vol. 9: 410-33; 10: 242). The sanguine attitude was characteristic, but the hopes were disappointed.

IV. Secretary of State to Joshua Johnson

SIR   New York Aug. 7. 1790.

The President of the United States, desirous of availing his country of the talents of it's best citizens in their respective lines, has thought proper to nominate you Consul for the U.S. at the port of London. The extent of our commercial and political connections with that country marks the importance of the trust he confides to you, and the more as we have no diplomatic character at that court. I shall say more to you in a future letter on the extent of the Consular functions, which are in general to be confined to the superintendance and patronage of commerce, and navigation; but in your position we must desire somewhat more. Political intelligence from that country is interesting to us in a high degree. We must therefore ask you to furnish us with this as far as you shall be able; to send us moreover the gazette of the court, Woodfall's parliamentary paper, Debrett's parliamentary register: to serve sometimes as a center for our correspondencies [with] other parts of Europe, by receiving and forwarding letters sent to your care. It is desireable that we be annually informed of the extent to which the British fisheries are carried on within each year, stating the number and tonnage of the vessels and the number of men employed in the respective fisheries: to-wit the Northern, and Southern whale fisheries, and the Cod-fishery. I have as yet no statement of them for the year 1789. with which therefore I will thank you to begin.— While the press of seamen continues, our seamen in ports nearer to you than to Liverpool (where Mr. Maury is Consul) will need your protection. The liberation of those impressed should be desired of the proper authority, with due firmness, yet always in temperate and respectful terms, in which way indeed all applications to government should be made.

The public papers herein desired may come regularly once a month by the British packet, and intermediately by any vessels bound directly either to Philadelphia or New York. All expences incurred for papers, and postages shall be paid at such intervals as you chuse either here on your order, or by bill on London whenever you transmit to me an account.

There was a bill brought into the legislature for the establishment of some regulations in the Consular offices: but it is postponed to the next session. That bill proposed some particular fees for particular services. They were however so small as to be no object. As there will be little or no legal emolument annexed to the office of Consul, it is of course not expected that it shall render any expence incumbent on him. I have the honor to be with great esteem, Sir Your most obedient & most humble servant,

Th: Jefferson

RC (DNA: RG 59, CD); slightly mutilated, with loss of one or two words being supplied from FC; addressed: "Mr. Joshua Johnson Merchant London"; endorsed as "Received 14 October Answerd 2 November. [1790] ℗ the Two Brothers Capt. Sely." FC and Tr (DNA: RG 59, PCC No. 121).

V. Secretary of State to the President

Aug. 8. 1790.

Th: Jefferson has the honor to inclose to the President the following papers.

1. The secret letter and paper of Aug. 2. for Mr. Carmichael.
2. The secret letter for the Chevalr. de Pinto.
3. A letter for Mr. Joshua Johnson.

On supposition that, delivering them himself to Colo. Humphreys, he might wish to comment to him on their contents, and particularly as to the 1st. to qualify such of the considerations as he may think need qualification, and to enlarge such as are too restrained. He will observe two or three small differences between the considerations of Aug. 2. now inclosed, and the first copy left with the President which are submitted to him.

The letter of Aug. 7.[1] to Mr. Carmichael and the cyphers, are all that will remain of the dispatches necessary for Colo. Humphreys for London, Lisbon, and Madrid, as Th: J. supposes.

Will the President be pleased to consider, at his leisure, how far it might be safe and useful to communicate the letter and considerations of Aug. 2. to Mr. Short, or the M. de la Fayette?

RC (NjP); endorsed. PrC (DLC). Enclosures: (1) TJ to Carmichael, 2 Aug. 1790 and its enclosure. (2) TJ to De Pinto, 7 Aug. 1790. (3) TJ to Johnson, 7 Aug. 1790.
On the TWO OR THREE SMALL DIF-
FERENCES, see notes to TJ's outline of policy on the Mississippi Question, enclosed in TJ to Carmichael, 2 Aug. 1790 (Document II, enclosure).

[1] I.e., 6 Aug.

VI. Secretary of State to William Short

DEAR SIR   New York Aug. 10. 1790.

This letter, with the very confidential papers it incloses, will be delivered you by Mr. Barrett with his own hands. If there be no war between Spain and England, they need be known to yourself alone. But if that war be begun, or whenever it shall begin, we wish you to communicate them to the Marquis de la Fayette, on whose assistance we know we can count in matters which interest both our countries. He and you will consider how far the contents of these papers may be communicated to the Count de Montmorin, and his influence be asked with the court of Madrid. France will be called into the war, as an ally, and not on any pretence of the quarrel being in any degree her own. She may reasonably require then that Spain should do every thing which depends on her to lessen the number of her enemies. She cannot doubt that we shall be of that number, if she does not yield our right to the common use of the Missisipi, and the means of using and securing it. You will observe we state in general the necessity, not only of our having a port near the mouth of the river (without which we could make no use of the navigation at all) but of it's being so well separated from the territories of Spain and her jurisdiction, as not to engender daily disputes and broils between us. It is certain that if Spain were to retain any jurisdiction over our entrepot her officers would abuse that jurisdiction, and our people would abuse their privileges in it. Both parties must foresee this, and that it will end in war. Hence the necessity of a well defined separation. Nature has decided what shall be the geography of that in the end, whatever it might be in the beginning, by cutting off from the adjacent countries of Florida and Louisiana, and inclosing between two of it's channels, a long and narrow slip of land, called the island of New Orleans. The idea of ceding this could not be hazarded to Spain, in the first step; it would be too disagreeable at first view: because this island, with it's town, constitutes at present their principal settlement in that part of their dominions, containing about 10,000 white inhabitants of every age and sex. Reason and events however, may, by little and little, familiarize them to it. That we have a right to some spot as an entrepot for our commerce, may be at once affirmed. The expediency too may be expressed of so locating it as to cut off the source of future quarrels and wars. A disinterested eye, looking on a map, will remark how conveniently this tongue of land is formed for the purpose; the Ibberville and Amit channel offering a good boundary and convenient outlet on the one side for Florida, and the main channel an equally good boundary and outlet on the other side for Louisiana; while the slip of land between is almost entirely morass or sand-bank; the whole of it lower than the water of the river, in it's highest floods, and only it's Western margin (which is the highest ground) secured by banks and inhabited. I suppose this idea too much even for the Count de Montmorin at first, and that therefore you will find it prudent to urge, and get him to recommend to the Spanish court only in general terms 'a port near the mouth of the river, with a circumjacent territory sufficient for it's support, well defined, and extraterritorial to Spain,' leaving the idea to future growth.

I inclose you the copy of a paper distributed by the Spanish commandant on the West side of the Missisipi, which may justify us to M. de Montmorin for pushing this matter to an immediate conclusion. It cannot be expected we shall give Spain time, to be used by her for dismembering us.

It is proper to apprise you of a circumstance which may shew the expediency of being in some degree on your guard even in your communications to the court of France. It is believed here that the Count de Moustier, during his residence with us, concieved a project of again engaging France in a colony upon our continent, and that he directed his views to some of the country on the Missisipi, and obtained and communicated a good deal of matter on the subject to his court. He saw the immediate advantage of selling some yards of French cloths and silks to the inhabitants of N. Orleans. But he did not take into account what it would cost France to nurse and protect a colony there till it should be able to join it's neighbors, or to stand by itself; and then what it would cost her to get rid of it. I hardly suspect that the court of France could be seduced by so partial a view of the subject as was presented to them; and I suspect it the less since the National assembly has constitutionally excluded conquest from the objects of their government. It may be added too that, the place being ours, their yards of cloth and silk would be as freely sold as if it were theirs.

You will perceive by this letter, and the papers it incloses, what part of the ideas of the Count d'Estain coincide with our views. The answer to him must be a compound of civility and reserve, expressing our thankfulness for his attentions; that we consider them as proofs of the continuance of his friendly dispositions, and that tho' it might be out of our system to implicate ourselves in trans-Atlantic guarantees, yet other parts of his plans are capable of being improved to the common benefit of the parties. Be so good as to say to him something of this kind, verbally, and so as that the matter may be ended as between him and us.

On the whole, in the event of war, it is left to the judgment of the Marquis de la Fayette and yourself how far you will develope the ideas now communicated to the Count de Montmorin, and how far you will suffer them to be developed to the Spanish court.

I inclose you a pamphlet by Hutchins for your further information on the subject of the Missisipi, and am with sentiments of perfect esteem & attachment Dr. Sir Your most obedient & most humble servt.,   TH: JEFFERSON

RC (CLU). FC (DNA: RG 59, PCC No. 121). Enclosures: (1) TJ to Carmichael, 2 Aug. 1790 (the text enclosed is the item there described as Tr of Extract, which omitted the references to Humphreys' mission). (2) TJ's outline of policy on the Mississippi Question, enclosed in the foregoing (the text sent Short is presumably that approved by Washington: for its identity, see notes to enclosure, TJ to Carmichael, 2 Aug. 1790). (3) Thomas Hutchins, *An historical and topographical description of Louisiana, and West Florida* (Philadelphia, 1784).

VII. Secretary of State to David Humphreys

The President having thought proper to confide several special matters in Europe to your care, it will be expedient that you take your passage in the first convenient vessel bound to the port of London.

When there you will be pleased to deliver to Mr. G. Morris and to Mr. Johnson the letters and papers you will have in charge for them, to communicate to us from thence any interesting public intelligence you may be able to obtain, and then take as early a passage as possible to Lisbon.

At Lisbon you will deliver the letter with which you are charged for the Chevalier Pinto, putting on it the address proper to his present situation. You know the contents of this letter, and will make it the subject of such conferences with him as may be necessary to obtain our point of establishing there the diplomatic grade which alone coincides with our system, and of ensuring it's reception and treatment with the requisite respect. Communicate to us the result of your conferences, and then proceed to Madrid.

There you will deliver the letters and papers which you have in charge for Mr. Carmichael, the contents of all which are known to you. Be so good as to multiply as much as possible your conferences with him in order to possess him fully of the special matters sketched out in those papers, and of the state of our affairs in general.

Your stay there will be as long as it's objects may require, only taking care to be returned to Lisbon by the time you may reasonably expect that our answers to your letters to be written from Lisbon may reach that place. This cannot be earlier than the first or second week of January. These answers will convey to you the President's further pleasure.

Thro' the whole of this business it will be best that you avoid all suspicion of being on any public business. This need be known only to the Chevalier Pinto and Mr. Carmichael. The former need not know of your journey to Madrid, or if it be necessary, he may be made to understand that it is a journey of curiosity to fill up the interval between writing your letters and recieving the answers. To every other person it will be best that you appear as a private traveller.

The President of the United States allows you from this date at the rate of two thousand two hundred and fifty dollars a year for your services and expences, and moreover what you may incur for the postage of letters; until he shall otherwise order.

TH: JEFFERSON

RC (NjP); at head of text: "To Colonel David Humphreys"; endorsed. FC (DNA: RG 59, PCC No. 121). It is possible that some or all of the letters and papers carried by Humphreys were enclosed with the above, but it is also possible that Washington himself handed the more important ones to the envoy (see TJ to Washington, 8 Aug. 1790). In addition to ciphers, newspapers, &c. these included: (1) TJ to Carmichael, 2 and 6 Aug. 1790 and their enclosures. (2) TJ to De Pinto, 7 Aug. 1790. (3) TJ to Johnson, 7 Aug. 1790. (4) TJ to Morris, 12 Aug. 1790. (All of the foregoing are printed in the present series.) (5) Circular of Secretary of State to American Consuls in Europe, 25 Aug. 1790. (6) Secretary of the Treasury to Wilhem & Jan Willink, N. & J. Van Staphorst & Hubbard, 28 Aug. 1790, enclosing a commission of the same date ratifying and confirming the provisional loan of 3,000,000 florins notified in their letter of 25 Jan. 1790 and informing them that half of this sum was destined as a payment on the American Debt to France and to be applied by direction of William Short as chargé d'affaires (text of letter and enclosure in Syrett, *Hamilton*, VI, 580-5). (7) Secretary of the Treasury to William Short, 29 Aug. 1790 (printed in same, VI, 585-6; Short was by this letter referred to the Secretary of State "for instructions with regard to the timing of the intended payment" to France). Humphreys also carried various letters written by Washington (see below).

TJ took pains to see that his own secret dispatches to Short did not go by way of London with Humphreys. His public and private letters to Short of 9, 10, 12, 25, 26, and 31 Aug. 1790 were carried by a trusted individual, Nathaniel Barrett, with instructions that they were to be "delivered . . . with his own hands" to Short in Paris (TJ to Short, 10 Aug. 1790, Document VI in present series). Hamilton, on the other hand, instructed Humphreys to place his dispatches for Short in the custody of his brother-in-law, John Barker Church, a member of Parliament. Shortly after arriving in London, Humphreys wrote Short a letter revealing this fact and giving a hint of the effect Hamilton's confidential conversations had had upon him: "To get the public debt into manageable way, if I may so express myself, seems now to be the great desideratum with our wisest and best political characters. On this subject you will be more particularly informed from some dispatches addressed to you by the Secretary of the Treasury, and which by his direction I am going to put into the hands of Mr. Church in order to be forwarded by a safe conveyance" (Humphreys to Short, 14 Oct. 1790, Humphreys, *Humphreys*, II, 31-2). It was rumored in New York before Humphreys departed that he had gone to Europe to "negotiate [the Holland loan]" (see above, p. 75).

In his capacity as a private traveler, which the administration took exceptional precautions to establish in order to conceal the public nature of his mission, Humphreys carried letters written by Washington on 10 and 11 Aug. 1790 to Paine, D'Estaing, Gardoqui, Rochambeau, La Luzerne, Lafayette, and (on personal matters) Gouverneur Morris (texts in Washington, *Writings*, ed. Fitzpatrick, XXXI, 80-8, 92-3). The longest and most carefully composed of these letters—that to Lafayette—bears almost unmistakable evidence of TJ's influence if not indeed of his hand. Washington touched first on affairs in France and the leadership manifested by Lafayette, revealing both in this letter and in that to Rochambeau that TJ had given a corrective to accounts of the progress of the Revolution in English newspapers both by his own testimony and by calling attention to the accounts in the *Gazette de Leide*. He then adverted to American affairs, reported them on the whole to be satisfactory, and asserted that the treaty with the Creeks would "leave us in peace from one end of our borders to the other," except for a small "banditti" of Shawnee and Cherokee that could easily be punished or destroyed. He then came to the main point—the threat of war, the policy of neutrality, the relations with Spain, and the mission of

Humphreys. In France TJ had unquestionably influenced Lafayette's letters to Washington and there can be little doubt that he exercised a similar influence in the reverse direction as Secretary of State.

VIII. Secretary of State to Gouverneur Morris

DEAR SIR   New York August 12th. 1790.

Your letter of May 29th. to the President of the United States has been duly received. You have placed their proposition of exchanging a Minister on proper ground. It must certainly come from them, and come in unequivocal form; with those who respect their own dignity so much, ours must not be counted at nought. On their own proposal formerly to exchange a Minister, we sent them one; they have taken no notice of that, and talk of agreeing to exchange one now, as if the idea were new. Besides what they are saying to you, they are talking to us through Quebec; but so informally that they may disavow it when they please; it would only oblige them to make the fortune of the poor Major whom they would pretend to sacrifice; through him they talk of a Minister, a treaty of commerce *and alliance*. If the object of the latter be honorable, it is useless; if dishonorable, inadmissible. These tamperings prove they view a war as very possible; and some symptoms indicate designs against the Spanish possessions adjoining us. The consequences of their acquiring all the country on our frontier from the St. Croix to the St. Mary's are too obvious to you to need developement. You will readily see the dangers which would then environ us. We wish you therefore to intimate to them that we cannot be indifferent to enterprizes of this kind, that we should contemplate a change of neighbours with extreme uneasiness; and that a due balance on our borders is not less desireable to us, than a balance of power in Europe has always appeared to them. We wish to be neutral, and we will be so, *if they will execute the treaty fairly*, and *attempt no conquests adjoining us*. The first condition is just; the second imposes no hardship on them; they cannot complain that the other dominions of Spain would be so narrow as not to leave them room enough for conquest. If the war takes place, we would really wish to be quieted on these two points, offering in return an honorable neutrality; more than this they are not to expect. It will be proper that these ideas be conveyed in delicate and friendly terms; but that they be conveyed, if the war takes place; for it is in that case alone, and not till it be begun, that we would wish our dispositions to be known; but in no case need they think of our accepting any equivalent for the posts. I have the honor to be with great respect and esteem Dear Sir &c.

Th: Jefferson

FC (DNA: RG 59, PCC No. 121). For note on Morris' LETTER OF MAY 29TH and other reports by him, see TJ's memorandum to Washington, 15 Dec. 1790. The dispatch of 29 May 1790 came by the June packet which arrived late in July—that is, after Hamilton's interview with Beckwith on the 8th. The above dispatch, it is to be noted, does not refer to the mission of David Humphreys, by whom it was conveyed. This was an intended omission, for Humphreys' instructions permitted him to reveal his object only to "the Chevalier Pinto and Mr. Carmichael" (TJ to Humphreys, 11 Aug. 1790). Morris had left for the continent before Humphreys arrived and so did not receive the dispatch until 23 Dec. 1790 on his return (Morris to TJ, 24 Dec. 1790).

IX. Queries from the President to Members of the Cabinet

(*Secret*)

United States August 27th. 1790

Provided the dispute between Great Britain and Spain should come to the decision of Arms, from a variety of circumstances (individually unimportant and inconclusive, but very much the reverse when compared and combined) there is no doubt in my mind, that New Orleans and the Spanish Posts above it on the Mississippi will be among the first attempts of the former, and that the reduction of them will be undertaken by a combined operation from Detroit.

The *Consequences* of having so formidable and enterprizing a people as the British on both our flanks and rear, with their navy in front, as they respect our Western Settlements which may be seduced thereby, as they regard the Security of the Union and its commerce with the West Indies, are too obvious to need enumeration.

What then should be the Answer of the Executive of the United States to Lord Dorchester, in case he should apply for permission to march Troops through the Territory of the said States from Detroit to the Mississippi?

What notice ought to be taken of the measure, if it should be undertaken without leave, which is the most probable proceeding of the two?

The Opinion of the Secretary of State is requested in writing upon the above statement.

Go: Washington

RC (DLC); in Lear's hand, signed by Washington. Recorded in SJPL but not in SJL. Another RC (DLC: Hamilton Papers). Dft (DLC: Washington Papers); in Humphreys' hand, with space left blank for designation of officer addressed and with following note at foot of text: "(Addressed thus separately to the Secretary of State, the Secy. of the Treasury, and the Secretary of War. Addressed to Mr. Jay thus: 'Mr. Jay will oblige the Presidt. of the United States by giving his opinion in writing on the above Statement' "; accompanied by wrapper docketed by Lear: "Quaeries to and Opinions of the Vice-President, the heads of the Departments and Chief Justice of the U.S. of what Answer should be given if a Request should be made to March troops from the British territory to the Mississippi. 27th Augt. 1790."

X. First Opinion of the Secretary of State

Opinion on the Questions stated in the President's note of August 27. 1790.

I am so deeply impressed with the magnitude of the dangers which will attend our government if Louisiana and the Floridas be added to the British empire, that in my opinion we ought to make ourselves parties in the *general war* expected to take place, should this be the only means of preventing the calamity.

But I think we should defer this step as long as possible; because war is full of chances which may relieve us from the necessity of interfering; and if necessary, still the later we interfere the better we shall be prepared.

It is often indeed more easy to prevent the capture of a place, than to retake it. Should it be so, in the case in question, the difference between the two operations of preventing, and retaking, will not be so costly, as two, three or four years more of war.

So that I am for preserving neutrality as long, and entering into the war as late, as possible.

If this be the best course, it decides, in a good degree, which should be our conduct, if the British ask leave to march troops thro' our territory, or march them without leave.

It is well enough agreed, in the Law of Nations, that for a Neutral power to give or refuse permission to the troops of either belligerent party to pass through their territory, is no breach of neutrality, provided the same refusal or permission be extended to the other party.

If we give leave of passage then to the British troops, Spain will have no just cause of complaint against us, provided we extend the same leave to her when demanded.

If we refuse (as indeed we have a right to do) and the troops should pass notwithstanding, of which there can be little doubt, we shall stand committed. For either we must enter immediately into the war, or pocket an acknowledged insult in the face of the world: and one insult pocketed soon produces another.

There is indeed a middle course, which I should be inclined to prefer. That is, to avoid giving any answer. They will proceed notwithstanding. But to do this under our silence, will admit of palliation, and produce apologies, from military necessity; and will leave us free to pass it over without dishonor, or to make it a handle of quarrel hereafter, if we should have use for it as such.—But if we are obliged to give an answer, I think the occasion not such as should induce us to hazard that answer which might commit us to the war at so early a stage of it; and therefore that the passage should be permitted.

If they should pass without having asked leave, I should be for expressing our dissatisfaction to the British court, and keeping alive an altercation on the subject, till events should decide whether it is most expedient to accept their apologies, or profit of the aggression as a cause of war.

TH: JEFFERSON
Aug. 28. 1790.

RC (DLC: Washington Papers); endorsed by Washington: "The Secretary of State 27th. Augt. 1790." Recorded in SJPL but not in SJL. PrC (DLC).

At the time he wrote this opinion TJ's expectation of a general war was stronger than here indicated—he thought that war was "almost a certain event" and viewed it as tolerably certain that France would join in as an ally of Spain (TJ to Randolph, 29 Aug. 1790). In view of this and of Hamilton's extended argument against allowing such sentiments as gratitude to influence decisions in foreign affairs—an argument that could only have been aimed at the

position he assumed TJ would adopt—the strength of his attachment to the policy of neutrality and of his counsel to avoid involvement except as a last recourse against a calamitous encirclement becomes all the clearer. The essential difference between the two men on this and other issues in foreign affairs is that the Secretary of State followed the policy of neutrality consistently and out of profound conviction, whereas the Secretary of the Treasury supported the doctrine outwardly but endeavored steadily and unceasingly to insinuate a pro-British policy into almost all measures of the government.

XI. Second Opinion of the Secretary of State

On considering more fully the question Whether it will be expedien[t] to Notify to Ld. Dorchester the real object of the expedition preparing by Governor St. Clair, I still think it will not be expedient. For

If the Notification be early, he will get the Indians out of the way, and defeat our object.

If it be so late, as not to leave him time to withdraw them before our stroke be struck, it will then be so late also, as not to leave him time to withdraw any secret aids he may have sent them. And the Notification will betray to him that he may go on without fear in his expedition against the Spaniard[s] and for which he may yet have sufficient time after our expedition is over.

On the other hand, if he should suspect our preparations are to prevent his passing our territory, these suspicions may induce him to decline his expedition; as, even should he think he could either force or steal a passage, he would not divide his troops, leaving (as he would suppose) an enemy between them able to take those he should leave, and cut off the return of those he should carry.

These suspicions too would mislead both him and the Indians; and so enable us to take the latter more completely by surprise; and prevent him from sending secret aid to those whom he would not suppose the objects of the enterprise, thus effecting a double purpose of preventing his enterprize, and securing our own.

Might it not even be expedient, with a view to deter his enterprize, to instruct Gov. St. Clair either to continue his pursuit of the Indians till the season be too far advanced for Ld. Dorchester to move, or, on disbanding his militia, to give them general orders (which might reach the ears of Ld. Dorchester) to be ready to assemble at a moment's warning, tho' no such assembly be really intended? Always taking care neither to say nor do, against their passage, what might directly commit either our Peace, or Honour.

TH: JEFFERSON
Aug. 29. 1790.

FC (DNA: RG 59, SDC). PrC (DLC); in TJ's hand, and arranged in heads as in the case of the original opinion. Not recorded in SJL but entry in SJPL for this and preceding two documents reads: "[1790. Aug.] 27. GW. his Qu? if British wish to march thro' our territory to attack Spain. 28. Th:J.'s answer to that Question. 29. P.S. to do."

Although Washington had sought the opinions of Adams, Jay, and members of the administration on the stand to be taken if British troops moved across American territory against Spanish possessions, there is no evidence that he asked anyone except TJ whether the object of the expedition against the Shawnee and Miami Indians should be disclosed to Lord Dorchester. This may be significant, and the fact that Harmar's stroke at harvest time was in-

tended to be both punitive and a calculated surprise is certainly so. "While, on the one hand, your movements and execution should be so rapid and decisive as to astonish your enemy," Secretary of War Knox wrote General Harmar, "so, on the other, every possible precaution in the power of human foresight should be used to prevent surprise" (Henry Knox to Josiah Harmar, 24 Aug. 1790, *ASP, Indian Affairs*, I, 99). TJ's emphasis on this point in the above opinion obviously coincided with Washington's desire for an expeditious and hidden move. Yet, as historians have long known, the request for the opinion and TJ's response had already been rendered needless by the fact that, in a secret interview with Beckwith, the Secretary of the Treasury gave the agent in confidence what TJ here strongly urged the President to withhold. Naturally neither Washington nor TJ knew that Hamilton had done this or that Dorchester would be in possession of the information less than a fortnight after the Secretary of State urged that he be kept in the dark. While the fact of Hamilton's disclosure has been known, some of its most serious implications have been obscured because the date of the secret interview has not been established with precision. The chronology of the episode sheds some light on this but also raises disturbing questions. At Pittsburgh on 16 Aug. 1790, Governor Arthur St. Clair, on his way to New York for consultation and approval of his plans, urged the militia of Virginia and Pennsylvania to rendezvous early in September for a sixty-day tour of duty. The governor travelled in such urgency both going and returning that he was back in Marietta just thirty days from the date of these instructions. He must, in fact, have left Pittsburgh that day, for he arrived in New York on Friday, 20 Aug. 1790—an astonishing feat for a man of fifty-four, surpassing that of the much younger Beckwith on his journey from Quebec in July (*New-York Journal*, 24 Aug. 1790). When he arrived, both the President and the Secretary of State were in Rhode Island, the Secretary of War and the Secretary of the Treasury in New York. There can be no doubt that St. Clair saw both Knox and Hamilton immediately.

On Saturday the 21st, about sundown, the President and his party returned to the city. On the 23d St. Clair wrote the Secretary of War outlining his plans for the expedition, enclosing the journal of Antoine Gamelin who had carried his fruitless messages of peace to the Indians the preceding April. Two facts in Gamelin's journal are significant. At the Miami village he saw five Potawatomi bring in two Negro prisoners whom they sold as indentured servants to Indian traders. On the 25th of April Blue Jacket of the Shawnee returned the two proffered pieces of wampum and said to him: "we can not give an answer without hearing from our father, at Detroit"; three days later Le Gris, chief of the Miami, told him: "we can not give a definitive answer without consulting the commandant of Detroit" (Arthur St. Clair to Henry Knox, 23 Aug. 1790, with Gamelin's journal, *ASP, Indian Affairs*, I, 92-4). Knox transmitted these documents to the President, Washington immediately gave his approval and his views concerning the expedition, and

Knox furnished St. Clair with his instructions. All of this took place on Monday, the 23rd. Further, on that same day Knox gave Hamilton an estimate of the cost of maintaining 1700 militia and 400 troops in the field for three months ($100,000); procured an advance from the Treasury for the contractors in order to enable them to obtain provisions and quartermaster's supplies; wrote to Samuel Hodgdon, commissary of military stores at Philadelphia, instructing him to send forward to the Northwest Territory, immediately, two tons of rifle and musket powder, four tons of lead bullets, and artillery shot; and gave orders for the transportation of these articles from Pittsburgh (Knox to St. Clair, 23 Aug. 1790, *ASP, Indian Affairs*, I, 98-9). Thus two days after the President's return the whole object of St. Clair's urgent journey had been accomplished. There was no need for him to remain longer in the city save perhaps to receive for Harmar the instructions that Knox wrote on the 24th. Beckwith later reported that the governor's stay in the city was "very short" (Dorchester to Grenville, 10 Nov. 1790, enclosing Beckwith's undated report, received at Quebec 27 Oct. 1790, PRO: CO 42/72, f.59, 61). There can be little doubt that St. Clair left New York on the 24th.

It is this brief chronology between the 20th and the 24th that fixes the time of Hamilton's interview with Beckwith, for it is clear that this took place while St. Clair was still in the city and before the expedition had been approved. Obviously, therefore, Beckwith sought out Hamilton on Saturday the 21st or on Sunday the 22d. The former seems more plausible. For Beckwith told Hamilton that he had heard "that very morning" an "officer attached to the person of the President" quote St. Clair in the presence of witnesses to the effect that traders under British protection at Detroit were encouraging Indian hostilities by purchasing prisoners as indentured servants. Beckwith admitted that he had heard instances of this, but stated that he had sought out Hamilton to give an explanation. Such transactions, he declared, were not only "done upon principles honourable to the parties, and to the general feeling of humanity," but "a procedure of the nature suggested" by St. Clair's information was contrary both to Dorchester's dispositions and to the spirit of his instructions to officers at the upper posts. To this Hamilton replied that St. Clair had brought information of many "excesses committed by the Savages, to which the Government had previously been strangers" and that, while nothing hostile to the United States had been expressed in the talks with the Indians "they indeed had said when proposals were made to them, that they must consult their father at Detroit, but nothing further." Then Hamilton added "that circumstances rendered it probable, measures would shortly be taken for an Expedition into the Indian Country in that quarter." Beckwith concluded with this information to Dorchester: "he mentioned it to prevent any alarm at our posts, *although he relied on my not speaking of it here*; but he did not say against which of the nations beyond the Ohio this expedition was intended to be directed." The dispatch was received in Quebec on 11 Sep. 1790 (Dorchester to Grenville, 25 Sep. 1790, PRO: CO 42/69, f. 28, 30-48; italics supplied; this conversation is the last recorded in a lengthy report covering interviews with various persons, beginning about 8 Aug. 1790; endorsed as received 4 Nov. 1790).

From this it is to be noted first of all that Hamilton anticipated action by the government just as he may have done when he discussed the appointment of an agent to London in the fall of 1789. Second, it is clear that he was privy to the information St. Clair brought in Gamelin's journal. This was natural, for Hamilton, Knox, and St. Clair all had official responsibilities connected with the proposed expedition. Consultation among them in the President's absence was essential. Third, it seems equally certain that from the moment Hamilton gave his voluntary assurance to Beckwith about the limited object of the campaign, he endeavored to have this assurance made official by the government. In this he succeeded with the Secretary of War but not, as the above opinion indicates, with the Secretary of State.

It is sometimes assumed that Washington learned of St. Clair's letter to the commandant at Detroit notifying him of the object of the expedition only after it was written (Freeman, *Washington*, VI, 284). This is in error. The fact is that Knox gave authority for this notification in his instructions to St. Clair: "There are existing jealousies in the minds of the British officers in Canada," he wrote, "of the designs of the United States respecting the posts

to have been relinquished by the last peace. It will be a point, therefore, of delicacy, that you should take measures, by sending some officer or messenger, at a proper time, to assure the commanding officer of the real object of the expedition. That the Shawanese, and some others joined with them, have committed such enormous offences against the citizens of the United States, as are any longer insupportable; but, to assure him of the entire pacific disposition of the United States towards Great Britain and its possessions" (Knox to St. Clair, 23 Aug. 1790, *ASP, Indian Affairs*, I, 98). St. Clair wrote to the commandant on 19 Sep. 1790, stating that he was commanded to do so by the President. He sent a copy of this letter to Knox and Knox in turn forwarded the covering letter and presumably its enclosure to Washington (St. Clair to Knox, 19 Sep. 1790, enclosing his of the same date to the commandant at Detroit, same, I, 95-6). It is certain, therefore, that Washington gave the authorization to St. Clair to say to the commandant what Hamilton had already said to Beckwith. When he learned that the governor had done this with so little regard for the central element in the instructions, he was filled with apprehension. The instructions had stipulated that the notification be made "at a proper time," and Washington thought that St. Clair's revelation had been "unseasonable"—that it "was certainly premature to announce the operation intended until the troops were ready to move; since the Indians, through that channel, might receive such information as would frustrate the expedition" (Washington to Knox, 4 Nov. 1790, *Writings*, ed. Fitzpatrick, XXXI, 144). What Washington was concerned about was the timing of the notification to Major Murray at Detroit. This also was the basic reason for the above opinion by TJ. And it was this fundamental requirement of successful strategy that Hamilton blandly disregarded in his clandestine conference with Dorchester's agent.

The news of the expedition, of course, was spread throughout the Northwest Territory. Major Murray replied to St. Clair's letter on 14 Oct. 1790. Three days later a private letter from Detroit described the effects of the projected expedition on British merchants engaged in the Indian trade. And soon St. Clair's letter of 8 Sep. to the Seneca and that of 19 Sep. 1790 to the Wyandots were in Dorchester's hands along with other reports from the upper posts (Dorchester to Grenville, 10 Nov. 1790, PRO: CO 42/72, f. 73, 75-88, with seven enclosures; endorsed as received 18 Dec. 1790). The military preparations on such a scale could not have been concealed in any event, but what British officers in the upper posts now knew with certainty because of St. Clair's premature disclosure and because of Hamilton's voluntary assurance to Beckwith was precise. An expedition of considerable force was imminent and its objective was the group of Indians who had been troublesome, who had struck no major blow against the Americans, but who looked to Detroit for protection.

The ill-fated force under General Harmar produced a noteworthy series of coincidences on the 4th of November 1790. On that day Washington at Mount Vernon learned with apprehension of St. Clair's premature disclosure, fearing the surprise which Harmar had been so solemnly warned to avoid. On that day at Whitehall the Secretary for Home Affairs learned that the Secretary of the Treasury had told a British agent in confidence that the expedition was about to be undertaken and that its object was only the Indian nations. And on that day at Fort Washington General Harmar tabulated the list of officers and men killed in the engagements against the Miami towns. The total was 183, far more than anyone expected and approximately twice what he had calculated on 22 Oct. 1790 at the camp on the night after the destruction of the Indian harvests and towns. This he lamented but added on that day of battle: "it is the fortune of war" (*ASP, Indian Affairs*, I, 106; Washington to Knox, 4 Nov. 1790, *Writings*, ed. Fitzpatrick, XXXI, 144; Dorchester to Grenville, 25 Sep. 1790, enclosing Beckwith's dispatch containing the conversation with Hamilton of 21 or 22 Aug. 1790, endorsed as received 4 Nov. 1790; PRO: CO 42/69, f. 28, 30-48). There had been three ambushes. The chain of coincidence closed exactly a year later, 4 Nov. 1791, when St. Clair suffered his crushing defeat—caused by surprise.

XII. Opinion of the Chief Justice

SIR   New York 28 Augt. 1790

The Case which I had Yesterday the Honor of recieving from you gave occasion to the following Remarks and Reflections.

Whether the Issue of the Negociations depending between the british and spanish Courts be Peace or War, it certainly is prudent to anticipate and be prepared for the consequences of either Event. In the present State of Things it would doubtless militate against the Interests of the U.S. that the spanish Territories in question should be reduced, and remain under the Government of his B. Majesty; and probably that circumstances would strongly unite with those others which must naturally lead him to regard the Possession of those countries as a desireable object.

If permission to march Troops for that Purpose, thro' the Territories of the U.S. should be requested, it will be necessary to consider

1. Whether the Laws of Nations entitle a *belligerent* Power to a free Passage for Troops thro' the Territories of a *Neutral* Nation? and

2. In Case the Right to such Passage be not a *perfect* one, whether circumstances render a Refusal or a compliance most adviseable on the present occasion?

The Right of Dominion involves that of excluding (under the Restrictions imposed by Humanity) all Foreigners. This Right is very rigidly exercised by some States, particularly the Empire of China. European Nations consider this as a general Right or Rule, and as subject to Exceptions in favor not only of Nations at *Peace*, but also of Nations at *War*. The Exceptions which respect the *former* do not touch the present question. Those which relate to the *latter*, seem to be comprized within *two* Classes vizt. cases of *urgent necessity*, and Cases of *Convenience*. The present case belongs to the latter. Vattel, who well understood the subject, says in the 7th: chapter of his 3d. Book:

That an *innocent* Passage is due to all Nations with whom a State is at Peace, and that this comprehends Troops equally with Individuals—That the Sovereign of the country is to judge whether this Passage be *innocent*—That his Permission must be asked—and that an Entry into his Territories without his consent, is a violation of the Rights of Dominion—That if the neutral Sovereign has *good* Reasons for refusing a Passage, he is not bound to grant it; but that if his Refusal be evidently unjust (the Passage requested being *unquestionably innocent*) a nation may do itself Justice, and take by force, what it was unjustly denied; so that such Requests may be refused in all Cases, except in those rare Instances, where it may be most evidently shewn that the Passage required is absolutely without Danger or Inconvenience.

If the Passage in contemplation should appear to be of this Complection, a Refusal would generally be deemed improper, unless the united States should declare and make it an invariable maxim in their Policy, *never to permit the Troops of any nation to pass thro' their country.* Such a measure *might* be wise, in Case the U.S. were in capacity to act accordingly; but that not being as yet the Case, it would perhaps in the present moment be unseasonable.

I say "such a measure *might* be wise." Whether it would or not, is a question that involves others, both legal and political of great Magnitude. Nations have *perfect* Rights. Regard to mutual Convenience may and often does induce Relaxations in the Exercise of them; and those Relaxations, from Time and usage, gradually assume to a certain Degree the Nature of Rights. I think it would appear on a full Investigation of the Subject, that the United States, being a new nation, are not bound to yield the same Relaxations, which in Europe from long Practice and acquiescence amount almost to an implied Cession; and therefore, that they may justly exercise rigorously the Right of denying free Passage to foreign Troops. It is also to be observed, that if they deny this Priviledge to others, it will also be denied to them; but this leads to political consequences and Considerations not necessary now to develope or investigate.

If a Passage should be requested and insisted upon, on the Ground of its being perfectly *innocent*, and accompanied with such Terms and Precautions, as that a Refusal, altho justifiable, would not appear to be more than barely so; then it will be adviseable to calculate the Probability of their being restrained by such a Refusal.

If the Probability should be, that they would nevertheless proceed; then it would become important to consider whether it would not be better to grant Permission, than by a Refusal to hazard one of two enevitable Inconveniences vizt. that of opposing their Progress by Force of arms, and thereby risque being involved in the War; or of submitting to the Disgrace and Humiliation of permitting them to proceed with Impunity. In my opinion it would in such a Case be most prudent, considering the actual State of our affairs, to consent to the Passage. The answer therefore to be given to Lord Dorchester, in Case he should apply for Permission to march Troops thro' the Territory of the U.S. from Detroit to the Missisippi, will I think necessarily depend on the nature of the Propositions contained in the application, compared with the before mentioned Principles and Probabilities.

As to the notice proper to be taken of the Measure, if it should be under taken *without* Leave? There appears to me to be no choice. Such a Measure would then be so manifest a Departure from the Usage of civilized nations, so flagrant and wanton a Violation of the Rights of Sovereignty, and so strong and indecent a mark of Disrespect and Defiance, that their March (if after Prohibition persisted in) should I think be opposed and prevented at every Risque and Hazard.

But these Remarks in my Judgment retain but little Force, when applied to the leading of Troops from Posts in their actual Possession, thro' Territories under their actual Jurisdiction, altho' both the Posts and the Territories of right belong to the U.S. If therefore they should march their Troops from such posts, thro' such Territories, that measure would not appear to me to afford *particular* cause of complaint. On their arrival by such a Route at the Missisippi, they may in Virtue of the 8th article of the Treaty navigate it up to its source, or down to the ocean.

This subject naturally brings into View a Question both difficult and important vizt. whether as the Possession of the Floridas would afford G. Britain additional means and Facilities of annoying the U.S. the latter would for that Reason be justifiable in endeavouring to prevent it by direct and hostile opposition? The Danger of permitting any nation so to preponderate, as to endanger the Security of others, introduced into the Politics of Europe the Idea of preserving a Ballance of Power. How far the Principles which have thence been inferred, are applicable to the present Case, would merit serious Inquiry, if the U.S. had only to consider what might be right and just on the occasion. But as the State of their affairs strongly recommends Peace, and as there is much Reason to presume that it would be more prudent for them *at present* to permit Britain to conquer and hold the Floridas, than engage in a War to prevent it, such Inquiries would be premature.—With the most perfect Respect and Esteem I have the Honor to be Sir, Your most obt. & most humble Servant

JOHN JAY

RC (DLC: Washington Papers).

XIII. Opinion of the Vice-President

SIR   New York August 29[1] 1790

That New Orleans, and the Spanish Posts on the Missisippi, will be among the first attempts of the English, in case of a war with Spain, appears very probable: and that a combined operation from Detroit, would be convenient to that end cannot be doubted.

The Consequences, on the western Settlements, on the commerce with the West Indies, and on the general Security and tranquility of the American confederation, of having them in our rear, and on both our flanks, with their navy in front, are very obvious.

The interest of the United States duely weighed, and their Duty conscientiously considered, point out to them, in the Case of Such a War, a neutrality, as long as it may be practicable. The People of these States would not willingly Support a War, and the present government has not Strength to command, nor enough of the general Confidence of the nation to draw the men or money necessary, untill the Grounds, causes and Necessity of it Should become generally known, and universally approved. A pacific Character, in opposition to a warlike temper, a Spirit of Conquest, or a disposition to military Enterprize, is of great importance to us to preserve in Europe: and therefore We Should not engage even in defensive War, untill the Necessity of it, should become apparent, or at least untill We have it in our Power to make it manifest, in Europe as well as at home.

In order to preserve an honest Neutrality, or even the Reputation of a disposition to it, the United States must avoid as much as possible, every real Wrong, and even every appearance of Injury to either Party. To grant to Lord Dorchester in case he Should request it, permission to march troops through the territory of the United States, from Detroit to the Missisipi, would not only have an appearance offensive to the Spaniards, of partiality to the English, but would be a real Injury to Spain. The Answer therefore to his Lordship Should be a refusal, in terms clear and decided, but guarded and dignified, in a manner, which no Power has more at command than the President of the United States.

If a measure so daring offensive and hostile, as the march of Troops through our Territory to Attack a Friend, Should be hazarded by the English, without leave, or especially after a refusal, it is not so easy to answer the Question, what notice ought to be taken of it.

The Situation of our Country is not like that of most of the nations in Europe. They have generally large numbers of Inhabitants in narrow territories: We have Small numbers Scattered over vast regions. The Country through which the Brittons must pass from Detroit to the Missisipi, is, I Suppose, so thinly inhabited, and at such a distance from all the populous Settlements, that it would be impossible for the President of the United States to collect Militia or march troops Sufficient to resist the Enterprize. After the Step shall have been taken there are but two Ways for Us to proceed one is War and the other negotiations. Spain would probably remonstrate to the President of the United States but whether she should or not, the President of the United States should remonstrate to the King of Great Britain. It would not be expected I suppose by our Friends or Ennemies that the United States should declare War at once. Nations are not obliged to declare War for every Injury or even Hostility. A tacit Acquiescence under Such an Outrage, would be misinterpreted on all hands; by Spain as inimical to her and by Brittain, as the effect of Weakness, Disunion and Pusillanimity. Negotiation then is the only other Alternative.

Negotiation in the present State of Things is attended with peculiar difficulties. As the King of Great Britain, twice proposed to the United States, an Exchange of Ministers, once through Mr. Hartley and once through the Duke of Dorsett, and when the United States agreed to the Proposition, flew from it: to Send a Minister again to St James's till that Court explicitly promises to send one to America is an humiliation to which the United States ought never to Submit. A Remonstrance from Sovereign to Sovereign cannot be Sent, but by an Ambassador of some order or other: from Minister of State to Minister of State, it might be transmitted in many other Ways: A Remonstrance in the form of a Letter from the American Minister of State to the Duke of Leeds, or whoever may be Secretary of State for foreign affairs, might be transmitted, through an Envoy, Minister Plenipotentiary, or Ambassador of the President of the United States, at Paris, Madrid or the Hague and through the British Ambassador at either of those Courts. The Utmost length, that can be now gone, with Dignity would be to send a Minister to the Court of London, with Instructions to present his Credentials, demand an Audience, make his Remonstrance, but to make no Establishment and demand his audience of leave and quit the Kingdom in one, two or three Months if a Minister of equal degree were not appointed and actually sent to the President of the United States, from the King of Great Britain.

It is a Misfortune, that in these critical moments and Circumstances, the United States have not a Minister of large Views, mature Age Information and Judgment, and Strict Integrity, at the Court of France Spain London and the Hague. Early and authentick Intelligence from those Courts may be of more importance than the Expence: but as the Representatives of the People, as well as of the Legislatures, are of a different opinion they have made a very Scanty Provision for but a part of such a system. As it is, God knows where the Men are to be found who are qualified for such Missions and would undertake them. By an Experience of ten years which made me too unhappy at the time to be ever forgotten, I know, that every Artifice which can deceive, every temptation which can operate on hope or fear, Ambition or Avarice, Pride or Vanity, the Love of Society Pleasure or Amusement will be employed to divert and warp them from the true line of their Duty and the impartial honour and interest of their Country.

To the Superior Lights and Information derived from office; the more Serene temper and profound Judgment of the President of the United States, these crude and hasty thoughts concerning the Points proposed, are humbly Submitted, with every Sentiment of respect and Sincere Attachment, by his most obedient and most humble Servant   JOHN ADAMS

RC (DLC: Washington Papers); at foot of text: "The President of the United States."   1 Adams first wrote "28" and then altered it to read as above.

XIV. Opinion of the Secretary of War

SIR   War office 29th August 1790

In answer to your secret communication of the 27th instant, and the questions stated therein I humbly beg leave to observe,

That the United States, by not being under the obligation of any treaty, either with Spain or England, are in a situation, to grant, or deny, the passage of troops, through their territory, as they shall judge fit.

The granting or refusing therefore the expected demand of a free passage to the troops of England, through the territory of the United States, in order to attack the dominions of Spain upon the Mississippi, will depend upon a due estimation of the consequences arising from either alternative.

The United States are too well aware, of the great and permanent evils, which would result from Englands becoming possessed of the Mississippi and West Florida, to concur in any arrangements to facilitate that event.

The law of Nations establish the principle, that every neutral nation may, refuse the passage of troops through its territory, when such passage may tend to its injury.

In the present case, the passage of the British troops, would be to effect an object directly contrary to the interests and welfare of the United States. If therefore the demand should be made, it may be refused, consistently with the principles of self preservation, and the law of Nations.

But there are two modes of refusal—a denial, unaccompanied by any other act; and a denial accompanied by force to oppose the passage, if it should be attempted after having been refused.

The first mode is all that can with propriety be done under the present state of things. If after the denial, the british troops should proceed, they become the aggressors, and establish a just cause of War, whenever the interests of the United States shall dictate the measure. Although a denial, unaccompanied by any other act, might be unpleasant to great Britain, yet she would not probably think it, of itself, a sufficient cause for waging war against the United States. But if a force should be actually opposed to the passage of the troops, a war with great Britain would appear to be the inevitable and immediate consequence.

The true interests of the United States dictate a state of neutrality in the affair between Spain and England. Should the United States be dragged into the war in the present moment, the loss of their commerce might justly be expected; The Source of their revenue would be cut off, and the proposed system of public credit fatally postponed if not entirely blasted. These are serious evils and to be avoided if possible.

It is however to be remarked that it is highly improbable that Spain would enter into the War, unless she expected to be supported by France—Nor does there appear any solid objections to this expectation, but the present debilitated and convulsed state of France. The family compact and other treaties between the two Kingdoms will continue to exist, notwithstanding the situation of France, until formally renounced. This has not been the case. The probability therefore is that France will be combined with Spain.

If this should be the case, every effort on the part of France will be employed to associate America in the War. And it is a question of great moment whether the United States could strictly comply with the treaty of friendship and Commerce entered into with France on the 6th of February,[1] and observe an exact neutrality.

Although it would seem hardly possible that either England,

or France and Spain combined, would make such Offers to the United States as to counterbalance the advantages of Neutrality, yet the case may be otherwise, or the United States may be obliged to enter into the War in order to avert a greater evil.

These considerations with their several extensive relations unite in dictating an answer to Lord Dorchester in terms as little exceptionable as possible.

That the United States had recently manifested their sincere desires, not only to continue at peace with Great Britain but to cement the same by commercial arrangements which might be reciprocally beneficial.

But that the real causes of dispute between England and Spain were too little understood at present by the United States for the President to consent to a measure which would seem to be inconsistent with that strict neutrality the United States would desire to observe.

But if notwithstanding this answer, or if no request should be made for the purpose, and the troops march through the territory of the United States, to attack the dominions of Spain it might be proper for the President of the United States to convene immediately the legislature if the occasion should be so urgent as to require their meeting at an earlier day than the adjournment, and to lay the whole affair before them, with his opinion of the measures proper to be pursued. For the Congress are vested with the right of providing for the common defence, and of declaring war, and of consequence they should possess the information of all facts and circumstances thereunto appertaining.

In the mean time the dispositions and designs of the contending parties will unfold themselves, The terms of each side be known and estimated, and the United States better able than at present, to judge of the exact line of conduct they ought to pursue.—I have the honor with perfect Respect to be Sir Your humble Servant

H KNOX

RC (DLC: Washington Papers); at foot of text: "The President of the United States"; endorsed by Washington: "From The Secry. of War 29th. Augt. 1790."

Knox' allusion to the recent manifestation of a desire to effect COMMER-CIAL ARRANGEMENTS with Great Britain can only refer to the letter of credence given by Washington to Morris on 13 Oct. 1789; Washington, *Writings*, ed. Fitzpatrick, XXX, 439-40.

1 Thus in MS, the date 1778 being omitted.

XV. Opinion of the Secretary of the Treasury

New York September 15. 1790

Answers to Questions proposed by The President of the United States to the Secretary of the Treasury

Question the first

"What should be the answer of the Executive of the United States to Lord Dorchester, in case he should apply for permission to march troops through the territory of said States from Detroit to the Mississippi?

Answer

In order to a right judgment of what ought to be done in such case, it may be of use previously to consider the following points.

First, whether there be a right to *refuse* or *consent*, as shall be thought most for the interest of the United States.

Secondly, The consequences to be expected from *refusal* or *consent*.

Thirdly, The motives to the one or to the other.

As to the first point, if it were to be determined upon principle only, without regard to precedents, or opinions, there would seem to be no room for hesitation about the right to refuse. The exclusive jurisdiction, which every independent Nation has over its own territory appears to involve in it the right of prohibiting to all others the use of that territory in any way disagreeable to itself, and more especially for any purpose of war, which always implies a degree of danger and inconvenience: with the exception only of cases of necessity.

And if the United States were in a condition to do it, without material hazard, there would be strong inducements to their adopting it as a general rule never to grant a passage for a voluntary expedition of one power against another, unless obliged to it by treaty.

But the present situation of the United States is too little favourable to encountering hazards, to authorise attempts to establish rules, however eligible in themselves, which are repugnant to the received maxims or usages of Nations.

It is therefore necessary to inquire what those maxims or usages enjoin in the case suggested.

With regard to usage it has been far from uniform. There are various instances in ancient and modern times of similar permissions being demanded; many in which they have been granted;

[122]

others in which they have been refused and the refusal acquiesced in; but perhaps more in which, when refused, a passage has been forced, and the doing it has often been deemed justifiable.

Opinions are not more harmonious. Among those who may be considered as authorities on such subjects, Puffendorf and Barbeyrac confine within narrow limits *the right of passage* through neutral territories; while Grotius and Vatel, particularly the former, allow to it greater latitude. Puffendorff treats it not as a natural right but as derived from compact or concession; especially when the enemy of a neighbouring state desires leave to march troops through a neutral Country against its neighbour. For it seems (says he) to be a part of *the duty which we owe to our neighbours*, especially such as have been kind and friendly, not to suffer any hostile power to march through our Country to their prejudice; *provided we can hinder the design with no great inconvenience to ourselves*. And as it may have a tendency to make our own Country the theatre of the war, (since the power intended to be attacked may justifiably march within our limits to meet the approaching enemy) he concludes that it is the safest way of acting in such case, *if we can do it, without any considerable prejudice to our own affairs* to deny the enemy passage, and *actually to oppose him*, if he endeavour to force it without our consent. But if we are either too weak to hinder his progress or must on this score engage in a dangerous war, he admits, that the plea of necessity will fairly justify us to our neighbour.

Examples, he adds, have little force in the decision of this question. For, generally, as people have been stronger or weaker, they have required passage with modesty or with confidence, and have in like manner granted or refused it to others.*

Barbeyrac in his commentary on Grotius is still stronger against the right of passage.† He affirms that even though we have nothing to apprehend from those who desire a passage, we are not therefore obliged in rigour to grant it. It necessarily follows (says he) from the right of property, that the proprietor may refuse another the use of his goods. Humanity indeed requires that he should grant that use to those who stand in need of it, when it can be done without any considerable inconvenience to himself; but if he even then refuses it, though he transgresses his duty, he does them no wrong, properly so called; *except they are in extreme necessity*,

---

* Puffendorffs Law of Nature and Nations pages 239, 240.
† Note I on Book II Chapt II § xiii.

which is superior to all ordinary rules. Thus far and no further extends the reserve with which it is supposed the establishment of property is accompanied.

Grotius on the other hand, expresses himself thus:‡ A free passage ought to be granted to persons where *just occasion* shall require, over any lands or rivers, or such parts of the sea as belong to any nation; and after enumerating several examples in support of his position, he concludes that the *middle opinion* is left; to wit, that the liberty of passing ought first to be demanded, and if denied may be claimed by force. Neither (says he) can it be reasonably objected that there may be suspicion of danger from the passing of a multitude; for one man's right is not diminished by another man's fear. Nor is the fear of provoking that prince against whom he that desires to pass is engaged in a *just* war, a sufficient reason for refusing him passage. Nor is it any more an excuse that he may pass another way, for this is what every body may equally allege, and so this right of passing would be entirely destroyed. But 'tis enough that the passage be requested without any fraud or ill design, by the nearest and most convenient way. *If* indeed, he who desires to pass undertakes an *unjust* war, or *if* he brings people who are my enemies along with him, I *may* deny him a passage; *for in this case* I have a right to meet and oppose him, even in his own land, and to intercept his march. Thus it would seem to be the opinion of Grotius that a party engaged in a just war has a right, of course, to a passage through a neutral territory, which can scarcely, if at all, be denied him, even on the score of danger or inconvenience to the party required to grant it.

But Vatel, perhaps the most accurate and approved of the writers on the laws of Nations, preserves a mean between these different opinions. This is the sum of what he advances:* That an *innocent passage* is *due* to all nations, with whom a state is at peace, for troops equally with individuals, and to annoy as well as to avoid an enemy. That the party asking and the party asked are both, in different degrees, judges of the question *when innocent?* That where the party asked has *good reasons* for refusing, he is not under any obligation to grant, and in *doubtful* cases his judgment ought to be definitive; but in evident ones, or those in which the harmlessness of the passage is manifest, the party asking may, in the last resort, judge for himself, and after *demand* and *refusal* may force his way. That, nevertheless, as it

‡ Rights of War and Peace Book II Chap II § xiii No. 1.2.3.4.
* Book III Chap: VII § 119. 120. 121. 122. 123.

is very difficult for the passage of a powerful army to be absolutely innaocent, and still more difficult for its innocence to be apparent, a refusal ought to be submitted to, *except* in those *very rare* cases, when it can be shewn in the most palpable manner, that the passage required is absolutely without danger or inconvenience. And lastly that this right of passage is only *due* in a war *not manifestly unjust.*

Perhaps the only inference to be drawn from all this is, that there exists in the practice of nations and the dogmas of political writers a certain vague pretension to a right of passage in particular cases, and according to circumstances, which is sufficient to afford to the strong a pretext for claiming and exercising it, when it suits their interests, and to render it always dangerous to the weak to refuse, and, sometimes not less so, to grant it.

It is, nevertheless, a proper inquiry, whether a refusal could be placed on such ground as would give no reasonable cause of umbrage to the party refused, and as in the eye of the world would justify it.

Against the propriety of a refusal are the following circumstances; that there is no connection between us and Spain, which obliges us to it: That the passage asked will be down rivers, and for the most part through an uninhabited wilderness; whence no injury to our citizens or settlements will be to be apprehended: And that the number of troops to be marched, especially considering the route, will probably not be such as on their own account, to be a serious cause of alarm. These circumstances may give our refusal the complexion of partiality to Spain and of indisposition towards Britain, which may be represented as a deviation from the spirit of exact neutrality.

In support of the propriety of a refusal, the following is the only assignable reason: That it is safer for us, to have two powerful, but *rival* nations, bordering upon our two extremities, than to have one powerful nation pressing us on both sides and in capacity, hereafter, by posts and settlements, to invelop our whole interior frontier.

The good offices of Spain in the late war; the danger of the seduction of our Western inhabitants; the probable consequences to the trade of the Atlantic States; are considerations rather to be contemplated, as motives, than alleged, as reasons.

The first reason, however, is of a nature to satisfy the mind of the justice of a refusal; admitting the authority of the more moderate opinions, which have been cited. And the danger, too, upon the supposition of which it is founded, appears to be obvious enough to vindicate it in the opinion of the disinterested part of Mankind; little likely as it may be to engage the acquiescence of the party whose wishes would be thwarted by the refusal. It deserves notwithstanding to be noticed on this point, that the ground of dissent would not result from the thing itself, that is the *mere passage*, but from the nature of the *acquisition*, to which it would give facility. This circumstance may somewhat obscure the clearness of the conclusion that there is a perfect right to refuse.

But upon the whole there does not appear to be room enough for a scruple about the right, to deter from refusal, if upon examination it shall be found expedient.

Does the right of consenting to the passage stand upon ground equally unexceptionable?

This question *Vatel* answers in the following manner:* "When I have no reason to refuse the passage, the party against whom it is granted has *no room for complaint,* much less for making it a pretence for war; since I did no more than what the law of nations enjoins. Neither has he any right to require, that I should deny the passage, because he is not to hinder me from doing what I think is agreeable to my duty, and *even* on occasion *when I might with justice deny the passage,* it is *allowable* in me *not to make use of* my right; *especially when I should be obliged to support my refusal by my sword.* Who will take upon him to complain of my having permitted the war to be carried into his own country rather than draw it on myself? It cannot be expected, that I should take up arms in his favour, unless obliged to it by a Treaty." And Puffendorff admits, as has been before noted, that if we are either *too weak* to hinder his progress or must on that score engage in a *dangerous* war, the plea of necessity will fairly justify us to our neighbour.

Nothing need be added to reasoning so perspicuous and convincing. It does not admit of a moment's doubt as a general rule that a neutral state, unfettered by any stipulation, is not bound to expose itself to a war, merely to shelter a neighbor from the approaches of its enemy. It remains to examine, if there are any circumstances, in our particular case, capable of forming an exception to that rule.

It is not to be forgotten that we received from France, in our late revolution, essential succour, and from Spain valuable countenance and some direct aid. It is also to be remembered that France is the

---

* Vattel Book III Chap VII Section 127.

intimate ally of Spain, and that there subsists a connection by treaty between the former power and the United States.

It might thence be alleged that obligations of Gratitude towards those powers require that we should run some risk, rather than concur in a thing prejudicial to either of them, and particularly in favour of that very nation against which they assisted us. And the natural impulse of every good heart will second the proposition, 'till reason has taught it, that refinements of this kind are to be indulged with caution, in the affairs of Nations.

Gratitude is a word the very sound of which imposes something like respect. Where there is even an appearance upon which the claim to it can be founded, it can seldom be a pleasing task to dispute that claim. But where a word may become the basis of a political system, affecting the essential interests of the state, it is incumbent upon those who have any concern in the future administration, to appreciate its true import and application.

It is necessary then to reflect, however painful the reflection, that gratitude is a duty or sentiment which between nations can rarely have any solid foundation. Gratitude is only due to a kindness or service, the predominant object of which is the interest or benefit of the party to whom it is performed. Where the interest or benefit of the party performing is the predominant cause of it, however there may result a debt, in cases in which there is not an immediate adequate and reciprocal advantage, there can be no room for the sentiment of gratitude. Where there is such an advantage there is then not even a debt. If the motive to the act, instead of being the benefit of the party to whom it is done, should be a compound of the interest of the party doing it and of detriment to some other, of whom he is the enemy or the rival, there is still less room for so noble and refined a sentiment. This analysis will serve as a test of our true situation, in regard both to France and Spain.

It is not to be doubted that the part which the Courts of France and Spain took in our quarrel with Great Britain is to be attributed, not to an attachment to our independence or liberty, but to a desire of diminishing the power of Great Britain by severing the British empire. This they considered as an interest of very great magnitude to them. In this their calculations and their passions conspired. For this, they united their arms with ours and encountered the expences and perils of war. This has been accomplished; the advantages of it are mutual; and so far the account is ballanced.

In the progress of the war* they lent us money, as necessary to

---

* France has made us one loan since the peace.

its success, and during our inability to pay they have foreborn to press us for it. The money we ought to exert ourselves to repay with interest, and as well for the loan of it, as for the forbearance to urge the repayment of the sums, which have become due, we ought always to be ready to make proportionate acknowlegements, and, when opportunities shall offer, returns answerable to the nature of the service.

Let it be added to this, that the conduct of France in the manner affording her aid bore the marks of a liberal policy. She did not endeavour to extort from us, as the price of it, any disadvantageous or humiliating concessions. In this respect, however she may have been influenced by an enlightened view of her own interest, she intitled herself to our esteem and good will. These dispositions towards her ought to be cherished and cultivated but they are very distinct from a spirit of romantic gratitude calling for sacrifices of our substantial interests; preferences inconsistent with sound policy; or complaisances incompatible with our safety.

The conduct of Spain towards us presents a picture far less favourable. The direct aid we received from her during the war was inconsiderable in itself, and still more inconsiderable compared with her faculty of aiding us. She refrained from acknowleging our independence, has never acceded to the Treaty of Commerce made with France, though a right of doing it was reserved to her, nor made any other Treaty with us. She has maintained possessions within our acknowleged limits without our consent. She perseveringly obstructs our sharing in the navigation of the Mississippi; though it is a privilege essential to us, and to which we consider ourselves as having an indisputable title. And perhaps it might be added upon good ground that she has not scrupled to intrigue with leading individuals in the Western County to seduce them from our interests and to attach them to her own.

Spain therefore must be regarded, upon the whole, as having slender claims to peculiar good will from us. There is certainly nothing that authorises her to expect we should expose ourselves to any extraordinary jeopardy for her sake. And to conceive that any considerations relative to France ought to be extended to her would be to set up a doctrine altogether new in politics. The ally of our ally has no claim, as such, to our friendship. We may have substantial grounds of dissatisfaction against him, and act in consequence of them, even to open hostility, without derogating in any degree from what we owe to our ally.

This is so true, that if a war should really ensue between Great Britain and Spain, and if the latter should persist in excluding us from the Mississippi (taking it for granted our claim to share in its navigation is well founded) there can be no reasonable ground of doubt that we should be at liberty, if we thought it our interest, consistently with our present engagements with France, to join Britain against Spain.

How far it might be expedient to place ourselves in a situation, which in case France should eventually become a party in the war, might entangle us in opposite duties on the score of the stipulated guarantee of her West India possessions, or might have a tendency to embroil us with her would be a mere question of prudential and liberal calculation, which would have nothing to do with the right of taking side against Spain.

These are truths necessary to be contemplated with freedom, because it is impossible to foresee what events may spring up, or whither our interests may point; and it is very important to distinguish with accuracy, how far we are bound, and where we are free.

However vague the obligations of gratitude may be between Nations, those of good faith are precise and determinate. Within their true limits, they can hardly be held too sacred. But by exagerating them, or giving them a fanciful extension, they would be in danger of losing their just force. This would be converting them into fetters, which a nation would ere long become impatient to break, as consistent neither with its prosperity, nor its safety. Hence while it is desireable to maintain with fidelity our engagements to France, it is adviseable on all occasions to be aware, that they oblige us to nothing towards Spain.

From this view of the subject there does not appear any circumstance in our case capable of forming an exception to the general rule; and as it is certain that there can hardly be a situation less adapted to war than that in which we now find ourselves, we can with the greatest sincerity offer the most satisfactory excuse to Spain for not withholding our consent, if our own interests do not decide us to a contrary course. The conclusion from what has been said is that there is a right either to refuse or consent as shall be judged for the Interest of the United States; though the right to consent is less questionable than that to refuse.

The consequences to be expected from refusal or consent present themselves next to consideration. Those of consent shall be first examined.

An increase of the means of annoying us, in the same hands is a certain ill consequence of the acquisition of the Floridas and Louisiana by the British. This will result not only from contiguity to a greater part of our territory but from the increased facility of acquiring an undivided influence over all the Indian tribes inhabiting within the borders of the United States.

Additional danger of the dismemberment of the Western Country is another ill consequence to be apprehended from that acquisition. This will arise as well from the greater power of annoying us, as from the different policy, which it is likely would be pursued by that nation, if in possession of the key to the only outlet for the productions of that Country. Instead of shutting, they would probably open the door to its inhabitants and by conciliating their good will on the one hand, and making them sensible on the other of their dependence on them for the continuance of so essential an advantage they might hold out to them the most powerful temptation to a desertion of their connection with the rest of the United States. The avarice and ambition of individuals may be made to cooperate in favour of those views.

A third ill consequence of that acquisition would be material injury in time to come to the Commerce of the Atlantic states. By rendering New Orleans the emporium of the products of the Western Country, Britain would at a period, not *very* distant have little occasion for supplies of provisions for their Islands from the Atlantic States; and for their European Market they would derive from the same source copious supplies of Tobacco and other articles now furnished by the Southern States: whence a great diminution of the motives to establish liberal terms of Commercial Intercourse with the United States collectively.

These consequences are all expressed or implied in the form of the Question stated by the President. And as far as our consent can be supposed likely to have influence upon the event they constitute powerful objections to giving it.

If even it should be taken for granted that our consent or refusal would have no influence either way, it would not even then cease to be disagreeable to concur in a thing apparently so inauspicious to our interests. And it deserves attention, that our concurrency might expose us to the imputation either of want of foresight to discover a danger or of vigour to withstand it.

But there is almost always in such cases a comparison of evils; and the point of prudence is to make choice of that course which threatens the fewest or the least, or sometimes the least certain. The consequences of refusal are therefore to be weighted against those of consent.

It seems to be a matter taken for granted by the writers upon the subject, that a refusal ought to be accompanied with a resolution to support it if necessary by the sword; or in other words, to oppose the passage, if attempted to be forced, or to resent the injury, if circumstances should not permit an effectual opposition. This indeed is implied in the nature of the thing; for to what purpose refuse, unless it be intended to make good the refusal? Or how avoid disgrace, if our territories are suffered to be violated with impunity, after a formal and deliberate prohibition of passage?

These are cases in which a nation may without ignominy wink at infractions of its rights; but this does not appear to be one of them. After having been asked its permission and having refused it, the presumption will be that it has estimated the consequences, calculated its means, and is prepared to assert and uphold its rights. If the contrary of this should turn out to be its conduct, it must bring itself into contempt for inviting insult which it was unable to resist, and manifesting ill will towards a power whom it durst not resist. As on the one hand, there cannot be conceived to be a greater outrage than to pass through our country, in defiance of our *declared* disapprobation, so on the other there cannot be a greater humiliation than to submit to it.

The consequence therefore of refusal if not effectual must be absolute disgrace or immediate war. This *appears* at least to be the alternative.

Whether a refusal would have the desired effect is at best problematical. The presumption, perhaps, is, that Great Britain will have adverted to the possibility of it; and if under the uncertainty of what would be our conduct she should still have resolved on prosecuting the enterprise through our territory, that she will at the same time have resolved, either to ask no questions or to disregard our dissent. It is not unlikely, that the reasoning of the British Cabinet will have been to this effect. If the United States have no predilection for Spain, or if their views of their own interest are not opposed to the acquisition we meditate, they will not withold their consent; if either the one, or the other be the case, it ought to be determined before hand, whether their enmity be a greater evil, than the projected acquisition, a good; and if we do not choose to renounce the one, we must be prepared to meet the other.

A further ill-consequence of the refusal, if ineffectual, not *wholly* destitute of weight, is this, that Great Britain would then think herself under less obligation to keep measures with us and would feel herself more at liberty to employ every engine in her power to make her acquisition as prejudicial to us as possible; whereas, if no impediment should be thrown in the way by us, more good humour may beget greater moderation, and in the progress of things, concessions securing us, may be made, as the price of our future neutrality. An explicit recognition of our right to navigate the Mississippi to and from the Ocean, with the possession of New Orleans, would greatly mitigate the causes of apprehension from the conquest of the Floridas by the British.

The consequences of refusal or consent constitute leading motives to the one or to the other; which now claim a more particular discussion.

It has been seen that the ill effects to be apprehended from the conquest of the Spanish territories in our neighbourhood, are an increase of the means, whereby we may be hereafter annoyed, and of the danger of the separation of the Western Country from the rest of the Union, and a future interference with the trade of the Atlantic States, in a manner too not conducive to the general weal.

As far as there is a prospect that a refusal would be an impediment to the enterprize, the considerations which have been mentioned afford the strongest inducements to it. But if *that* effect of it be doubtful, the force of these inducements is proportionably diminished; if improbable, it nearly ceases. The prospect in this case, would be that a refusal would aggravate instead of preventing the evil, it was intended to obviate. And it must be acknowleged that the success of it is at least *very doubtful*.

The consideration that our assent may be construed into want of foresight or want of vigour, though not to be disregarded, would not be sufficient to justify our risking a war in our present situation. The cogent reasons we have to avoid a war are too obvious and intelligible; not to furnish an explanation of and an apology for our conduct in this respect.

Whatever may be the calculations with regard to the probable effect of a refusal, it ought to be predicated upon the supposition, that it may not be regarded, and accompanied with a determination to act as a proper attention to national dignity would in such an event dictate. This would be to make war.

For it is a *sound maxim*, that a state had better hazard any calamities than submit tamely to absolute disgrace.

Now it is manifest, that a Government scarcely ever had stronger motives to avoid war, than that of the United States, at the present juncture. They have much to dread from war; much to expect from peace; something to hope from negotiation, in case of a rupture between Britain and Spain.

We are but just recovering from the effects of a long arduous and exhausting war. The people but just begin to realise the sweets of repose. We are vulnerable both by water and land without either fleet or army. We have a considerable debt in proportion to the resources which the state of things permits the government to command. Measures have been recently entered upon for the restoration of Credit, which a war could hardly fail to disconcert, and which if disturbed would be fatal to the means of prosecuting it. Our national government is in its infancy. The habits and dispositions of our people are ill suited to those liberal contributions to the treasury, which a war would necessarily exact. There are causes which render war in this country more expensive, and consequently more difficult to be carried on than in any other. There is a general disinclination to it in all classes. The theories of the speculative and the feelings of all are opposed to it. The support of public opinion (perhaps more essential to our government than to any other) could only be looked for in a war evidently resulting from necessity.

These are general reasons against going into war. There are others of a more particular kind. To the people at large the quarrel would be apt to have the appearance of having originated in a desire of shielding Spain from the arms of Britain. There are several classes of men to whom this idea would not be agreeable, especially if the Dutch were understood to be in conjunction with the British. All those who were not friendly to our late revolution would certainly dislike it. Most of the descendants of the Dutch would be unfriendly to it. And let it not be overlooked, that there is still a considerable proportion of those who were firm friends to the Revolution who retain prepossessions in favour of Englishmen, and prejudices against Spaniards.

In a popular government especially, however prejudices like these may be regretted, they are not to be excluded from political calculations.

It ought also to be taken into the account, that by placing ourselves at this time in a situation to go to war against Great Britain we embark with the weakest party, with a total uncertainty what accession of strength may be gained, and without making any terms, with regard either to succour, indemnity or compensation.

France is the only weight which can be thrown into the scale capable of producing an equilibrium. But her accession however probable ought not to be deemed absolutely certain. The predominant party there may choose to avoid war as dangerous to their own power. And if even obstacles should not arise from that quarter, it cannot be foreseen to what extent France will be in condition to make efforts. The great body of malcontents comprehending a large proportion of the most wealthy and formerly the most influential class; the prodigious innovations which have been made, the general and excessive fermentation which has been excited in the minds of the people, the character of the Prince, or the nature of the government likely to be instituted, as far as can be judged prior to an experiment, does not prognosticate much order or vigour in the affairs of that country for a considerable period to come.

It is possible indeed that the enthusiasm which the transition from Slavery to Liberty may inspire, may be a substitute for the energy of a good administration, and the spring of great exertions. But the ebullitions of enthusiasm must ever be a precarious reliance. And it is quite as possible that the greatness, and perhaps immaturity, of that transition may prolong licentiousness and disorder. Calculations of what may happen in France must be unusually fallible; not merely from the yet unsettled state of things in that kingdom, but from the extreme violence of the change which has been wrought in the situation of the people.

These considerations are additional admonitions to avoid as far as possible any step that may embroil us with Great Britain. It seems evidently our true policy to cultivate neutrality. This at least is the ground on which we ought to stand, until we can see more of the scene, and can have secured the means of changing it with advantage.

We have objects which in such a conjuncture are not to be neglected. The Western posts, on one side, and the navigation of the Mississippi, on the other, call for a vigilant attention to what is going on. They are both of importance. The securing of the latter may be regarded in its consequences as essential to the unity of the Empire.

But it is not impossible if war takes place, that by a judicious attention to favourable moments we may accomplish both, by negotiation. The moment however we became committed on either side the advantages of our position for negotiation would be gone. They would even be gone in respect to the party, with whom we were in cooperation; for being once in the war we could not make terms as the condition of entering into it.

Though it may be uncertain how long we shall be permitted to preserve our neutrality; that is not a sufficient reason for departing from it voluntarily. It is possible we may be permitted to persist in it throughout. And if we must renounce it, it is better it should be from necessity than choice; at least till we see a prospect of renouncing, with safety and profit. If the government is forced into a war the chearful support of the people may be counted upon. If it brings it upon itself, it will have to struggle with their displeasure and reluctance. This difference alone is immense.

The desire of manifesting amity to Spain, from the supposition, that our permanent interest is concerned in cementing an intimate connection with France and Spain ought to have no influence in the case. Admitting the existence of such an interest, it ought not to hurry us into premature hazards. If it should finally induce us to become a party, it will be time enough, when France has become such and after we shall have adjusted the conditions, upon which we are to engage.

But the reality of such an interest is a thing about which the best and the ablest men of this country are far from being agreed. There are of this number, who, if the United States were at perfect liberty, would prefer an intimate connection between them and Great Britain as most conducive to their security and advantage; and who are of opinion, that it will be wise to cultivate friendship between that country and this, to the utmost extent which is reconcileable with the faith of existing engagements: While the most general opinion is, that it is our true policy, to steer as clear as possible of all foreign connection, other than commercial, and in this respect to cultivate intercourse with all the world on the broadest bases of reciprocal privilege.

An attentive consideration of the vicissitudes which have attended the friendships of nations, except in a very few instances, from very peculiar circumstances, gives little countenance to systems which proceed on the supposition of a permanent interest to prefer a particular connection. The position of the United States, detached as they are from Europe admonishes them to unusual circumspection on that point. The same position, as far as it has relation to the possessions of European powers in their Vicinity, strengthens the admonition.

Let it be supposed that Spain retains her possessions on our right and persists in the policy she has hitherto pursued without the slightest symptom of relaxation of barring the Mississippi against us, where must this end, and at a period not very distant? Infallibly in a War with Spain, or separation of the Western Country. This Country must have an outlet for its commodities. This is essential to its prosperity, and if not procured to it by the United States must be had at the expence of the Connection with them. A war with Spain, when our affairs will have acquired greater consistency and order, will certainly be preferred to such an alternative. In an event of this sort we should naturally seek aid from Great Britain. This would probably involve France on the opposite side, and effect a revolution in the state of our foreign politics.

In regard to the possessions of Great Britain on our left, it is at least problematical, whether the acquisition of them will ever be desireable to the United States. It is certain that they are in no shape essential to our prosperity. Except therefore the detention of our Western posts (an object too of far less consequence than the navigation of the Mississippi) there appears no necessary source of future collission with that power.

This view of the subject manifests, that we may have a more urgent interest to differ with Spain, than with Britain. And that conclusion will become the stronger, if it be admitted, that when we are able to make good our pretensions, we ought not to leave in the possession of any foreign power, the *territories* at the mouth of the Mississippi, which are to be regarded as the key to it.

While considerations of this nature ought not to weaken the sense, which our Government ought to have of any obligations which good faith shall fairly impose, they ought to inspire caution in adopting a system, which may approximate us too nearly to certain powers, and place us at too great a distance from others. Indeed every system of this kind is liable to the objection, that it has a tendency to give a wrong biass to the councils of a Nation, and sometimes to make its own interest subservient to that of another.

If the immediate cause of the impending war between Britain and Spain be considered, there cannot be drawn from thence any inducements for our favouring Spain. It is difficult to admit the reasonableness or justice of the pretensions on her part, which occasioned the transaction complained of by Great Britain, and certainly the monopoly, at which those pretensions aim, is intitled to no partiality from any maritime or trading people. Hence considerations, neither of justice nor policy, as they respect the immediate cause of the quarrel, incline us towards Spain.

Putting therefore all considerations of peculiar good will to Spain or of predilection to any particular connection out of the Question, the argument respecting refusal or consent, in the case supposed, seems to stand thus.

The acquisition of the Spanish territories, bordering upon the U States, by Britain would be dangerous to us. And if there were a good prospect, that our refusal would prevent it, without exposing us to a greater evil, we ought to refuse. But if there be a considerable probability that our refusal would be ineffectual, and if being so, it would involve us in war or disgrace, and if positive disgrace is worse than war, and war, in our present situation, worse, than the chances of the evils, which may befal us, from that acquisition, then the conclusion would be that we ought not to refuse. And this appears to be the true conclusion to be drawn from a comprehensive and accurate view of the subject; though first impressions are on the other side.

These reflections also may be allowed to come in aid of it. Good or evil is seldom as great, in the reality, as in the prospect. The mischiefs we apprehend may not take place. The enterprise, notwithstanding our consent, may fail. The acquisition, if made, may in the progress of things be wrested from its possessors. These if pressed hereafter (and we are willing to accept it) may deem it evident to purchase our neutrality by a cession to us of that part of the territory in question, which borders on the Mississippi accompanied with a guarantee of the navigation of that river. If nothing of this sort should happen, still the war will necessarily have added millions to the debt of Britain, while we shall be recruiting and increasing our resources and our strength. In such a situation, she will have motives of no inconsiderable force for not provoking our resentment. And a reasonable confidence ought to be reposed in the fidelity of the inhabitants of the Western County; in their attachment to the Union; in their real interest to remain a part of it, and in their sense of danger from the attempt to separate, which *at every hazard* ought to be resisted by the United States.

It is also to be kept in view, that the *same* danger, if not to the *same* extent, will exist, should the territories in question *remain in the hands of Spain.*

Besides all this, if a war should ever be deemed a less evil than the neighbourhood of the British in the quarter meditated, good policy would still seem to require as before intimated, that we should avoid putting ourselves in a situation to enter into it, till we had stipulated adequate indemnities and considerations for doing so; that we should see a little further into the unravellment of the plot, and be able to estimate what prospect there would be by our interference of obviating the evil. It deserves a reflection, that if those territories have been once wrested from Spain, she will be more tractable to our wishes, and more disposed to make the concessions, which our interests require, than if they never passed into other hands.

A question occurs here whether there be not a middle course between refusal and consent; to wit, the waving an answer by referring the matter to further consideration. But to this there appear to be decisive objections. An evasive conduct in similar cases is never dignified, seldom politic. It would be likely to give satisfaction to neither party, to effect no good, to prevent no ill. By Great Britain, it would probably be considered as equivalent to a refusal, as amounting to connivance by Spain, as an indication of timidity by all the world.

It happens that we have a post on the Wabash, down which River the expedition, it is presumeable, must go. If the Commanding Officer at that post has no orders to the contrary, it will be his duty to interrupt the passage of the British troops; if he does, it would seem necessary for them in order to the safe passage of their boats, with their artillery stores, provisions and baggage to take that post. Here then would be a passage through our territory, not only without our permission, but with the capture of a post of ours; which would be in effect making war upon us. And thus silence, with less dignity, would produce the same ill consequence, as refusal.

If to avoid this private orders were to be sent to the commanding officer of that post not to interrupt the passage, his not being punished for his delinquency would betray the fact and afford proof of connivance.

The true alternative seems to be to refuse or consent: And if the first be preferred, to accompany it with an intimation, in terms as free from offense as possible, that dispositions will be made to oppose the passage if attempted to be forced; and, accordingly, as far as practicable to make and execute such dispositions.

If on the contrary consent should be given it may deserve consideration whether it would not be expedient to accompany it with a candid intimation that the expedition is not agreeable to us, but that thinking it expedient to avoid an occasion of controversy, it has been concluded not to withold assent. There are however objections to this mode. In case of consent an early and frank *explanation should be given* to Spain.

Question the *Second*.

What notice ought to be taken of the measure, if it should be undertaken without leave, which is the most probable proceeding of the two?

If *leave* should be *asked* and *refused* and the enterprise should be prosecuted without it, the manner of treating it has been antici-pated, that is the passage if practicable should be opposed, and if not practicable, the outrage should be resented by recourse to arms.

But if the enterprise should be undertaken without *asking* leave, which is presumed to be the import of the question, then the proper conduct to be observed will depend on the circumstances.

As the passage contemplated would be by water, and almost wholly through an uninhabited part of the Country, over which we have no *actual* jurisdiction, if it were unaccompanied with any violence to our citizens or posts, it would seem sufficient to be con-tent with remonstrating against it, but in a tone that would not commit us to the necessity of going to war: the objections to which apply with full force here.

But, if as is to be feared will necessarily be the case, our post on the Wabash should be *forced*, to make good their passage, there seems to be no alternative but to go to war with them; unwelcome as it may be. It seems to be this, or absolute and unqualified humilia-tion: which, as has been already noticed, is in almost every situation a greater evil than war.

In such an event, it would appear advisable immediately to con-vene the Legislature; to take the most vigorous measures for war; to make a formal demand of satisfaction; to commence negotiations for alliances; and if satisfaction should be refused to endeavour to punish the aggression by the sword.

ALEXANDER HAMILTON
Secretary of the Treasury

MS (DLC: Washington Papers).
Hamilton enclosed the above opinion in his letter to Washington of 15 Sep. 1790 and explained its delay as fol-lows: "The urgent avocations, in which

I have been engaged, towards putting, in a train of execution, the laws of the last session, affecting my department, and a desire of reflecting, maturely, and giving the reasons for the result of my reflections, fully, have caused me to delay, longer than I wished, the answers to the questions . . . and I hope will excuse the delay.—The judgments formed, in particular cases, are almost always connected with a general train of ideas, in respect to some more comprehensive principles or relations; and I have thought it adviseable to lay that train before you, for the better explanation of the grounds of the opinion, I now give, or may hereafter have occasion to give on the like subjects, in obedience to your commands" (DLC: Washington Papers; full text in Syrett, *Hamilton*, VII, 36-7). Neither the delay nor the substance of the opinion, however, can be separated from the context of the discussions that Hamilton was engaged in with Beckwith and Humphreys at the time this document was being prepared.

On the arguments urged by Hamilton for a position of neutrality, of negotiation, and of seeking commercial "intercourse with all the world on the broadest bases of reciprocal privilege," Hamilton seemed to stand with TJ. So, too, on the matter of a realistic assessment of the national interest. But the whole drift of the argument, like that of Hamilton's negotiations with Beckwith, was calculated to lead to another position—that of some of the "best and the ablest men" who were of opinion that it would be wise to cultivate friendship between the United States and Great Britain "to the utmost extent which is reconcileable with the faith of existing engagements." These were almost the exact words that Hamilton had spoken to Beckwith. In neither case could he reveal to the President that this, in a peculiar sense, was his own view of policy, not just that of some of the best and the ablest men. The discourse on the irrelevance of a sentiment such as gratitude in the conduct of foreign policy was itself irrelevant, for the realities affecting the national interest were assumed in all of the other opinions to be determinative. But the irrelevancy served two purposes. It laid the foundation for such opinions as Hamilton might thereafter "have to give on the like subjects" and it concealed the predilections—whether arising from a comparable sentiment or from a regard for the national interest—that led Hamilton away from the position of neutrality and of commercial reciprocity that he professed. The true nature of Hamilton's position cannot be found in the convolutions of this involved and belated opinion, but must be sought in the clear tendency of his actions and his communications to Beckwith during the preceding year.

---

i. William Wyndam Grenville to Lord Dorchester

MY LORD   Whitehall, 6th May 1790

In addition to what I have said in my letter No. 22 of this date relative to the possible inducements which Spain may hold out to the United States to prevail upon them to take a part against Great Britain in case of war, I think it right to transmit to Your Lordship the enclosed copies of a communication made by Mr. Morris to His Grace the Duke of Leeds and of the answer given to it by his Grace.

This communication coming from Genl. Washington however vague and inexplicit it is, seems however to indicate some disposition on the part of the United States to cultivate a closer connection with this country than has hitherto subsisted since their separation from Great Britain. Although it was necessary in the first instance in answer to Mr. Morris's Letter to hold a language of firmness, which should point out the nonexecution of the Treaty on the part of America, and the inadequate return made for the liberal manner in which they have been treated in point of Commerce, it will certainly be our object to establish, if possible, a greater degree of interest than we have hitherto had in that country. Your lordship will of course endeavour to find the means of sending proper persons who may, though not authorized by any public commission, forward this object, and at the same time be able to give to your Lordship the earliest information of hostile designs, if any such should be meditated against the forts or against Canada itself.

I conceive that it would by no means be impossible to turn the tide of the opinion and wishes of America in our favor in case of a Contest with Spain on the business now in question. The right which Spain has asserted is exclusive against all the world, against the United States as well as against any European powers: And the Fur trade from the North West Coast of America may become a valuable accessary and assistant to the China trade in which the Americans have already embarked extensively. The object which we might hold out to them, particularly to the Kentucke and other Settlers at the back of the old colonies, of opening the Navigation of the Mississippi to them, is one at least as important as the possession of the Forts, and perhaps it would not be difficult to shew, that the former is much more easily attainable with the assistance of Great Britain against Spain, than the latter is by their joining Spain in offensive operations against this Country. I throw out these ideas to Your Lordship fully persuaded that you will omit no opportunity of improving them as far as circumstances will admit. It will be very material with a view of future arrangements that I should be apprized as early as possible of what appears to be the disposition prevalent in America on this subject. I am &c.

W. W. GRENVILLE

P.S. I send your Lordship the Copy of a Letter from Mr. Morris to the Duke of Leeds which has just been communicated to me.

Dft (PRO: CO 42/67, f. 93-7); at head of text: "*No. 24. Secret*"; postscript not printed by Brymner, *Report*, p. 133. Enclosures: (1) Washington to Morris, 13 Oct. 1789. (2) Leeds to Morris, 28 Apr. 1790. (3) Morris to Leeds, 30 Apr. 1790. Texts of all enclosures are to be found in same, f. 98-102, and are printed in Brymner, *Report*, p. 129-31.

In his LETTER NO. 22, Grenville announced augmentation of the armed forces and expressed the fear that, if war should occur, the United States might demand surrender of the forts and that possibly Spain might support the demand as an inducement to active participation against England. "As this is a point of the utmost importance to the British interests," Grenville added,

"I am persuaded that Your Lordship will feel how necessary it is that His Majesty should have in that part of His Dominions a person to whose experience, talents and character He may look with confidence for such a line of conduct as may be necessary to protect the whole of the remaining British Empire in America, and that Your Lordship will therefore readily be induced to relinquish Your wish of returning to Great Britain this season" (Brymner, *Report*, p. 131-2). In his third dispatch of this date to Dorchester, Grenville emphasized that the "Friendship of the Inhabitants of Vermont would under the circumstances of any alarm from the side of the United States, be of the greatest importance." He mentioned the discussions with Levi Allen who had for some time been in England "with authority to treat on their behalf for commercial arrangements" and added: "I am strongly inclined to think that if this concession [to export flour from Vermont into Quebec] could be the means of attaching the people of Vermont sincerely to the British interest, it would, under the present circumstances, be expedient to make it. I am . . . fully persuaded that Your Lordship will give to this subject the attention which it deserves, and that you will neglect no proper steps for ensuring so considerable an accession of strength as that which we should derive from the friendship of Vermont. Such encouragement has been given to Mr. Allen as will I hope dispose him to exert any influence which he or his connexions may possess in whatever manner Your Lordship may think proper to direct it" (same, p. 132, "No. 23, Secret"). Shortly after dispatching Beckwith to New York, Dorchester turned his attention to this subject, urging that permission be given for produce of all kinds to enter the ports of Quebec from the United States by land or by inland navigation. He argued this policy on the ground that Canada would profit by such a source of supplies, Great Britain by the increase of her carrying trade, "and both by interesting our neighbours to preserve in the hands of Great Britain, this outlet to the sea." This would lay the foundation for stronger connections. "It appears to me highly proper," Grenville concluded, "to form alliances with our neighbours, as soon as all things are well matured for that purpose, but their own interest alone can render them zealously at-

tached to us, and give duration to any of their engagements" (Dorchester to Grenville, 21 July 1790, PRO: CO 42/68, f. 276-7; endorsed as received 3 Sep. 1790).

The policy that Dorchester here urged upon the ministry was quite the opposite of that Hamilton represented him as proposing to the federal government. This was not a policy of alliance with the United States as a sovereign state but a policy of disruption and dismemberment. It related only to the states lying on the borders of Canada that had access to Quebec by land or by inland navigation. The Allens had been pressing for something like this from the time of Dorchester's arrival in Canada. In the summer of 1788 Ethan Allen gave the Governor General assurances that "Vermont . . . is not, and will not be, confederated" with the United States. He pictured the new national government as bent upon the "subjugation" of Vermont, declared that the state could bring 15,000 men into the field to defend themselves against aggression, and indeed hinted that Vermonters allied with Anti-Federalists "might form so strong a junction as to crush the promised federal government." Vermont might be small, but it was possible she could turn the scale and therefore be well worth the attention of Great Britain: "For besides her own natural population, she has a constant immigration from the United States, and whether whig or tory it alters not the case, as they remove to Vermont to obtain a landed interest, and to rid themselves and their posterity, from exorbitant taxation, very cordially unite in the policy of the state, in rejecting every idea of a confederation with the United States; for property not liberty is their main object." What Allen recommended was a return to the understanding that had prevailed in the last three years of the war which "answered all the purposes of an alliance of neutrality, and at the same time prevented the United States from taking any advantage of it." He therefore opposed at that time the adoption of any plan for a "formal and public alliance." The leading men of Vermont, he declared "are not sentimentally attached to a republican form of government, yet from political principles, are determined to maintain their present mode of it, till they can have a better . . . or till they can on principles of mutual interest and advantage, return to the British government without war or annoyance from the United States" (Ethan Allen to Dorchester, 16 July 1788, enclosed in Dorchester to Sydney, 16 July 1788, PRO: CO 42/60, f. 231-9).

At the time Grenville wrote the above dispatch, Levi Allen was in London, having arrived there early in 1789 on private business (negotiation of a contract with the admiralty to supply the British navy with masts and stores) and on his "Commission . . . to Assure the British Court, that Vermont was truly from local situation as well as inclination firmly attached to them, and that whenever Vermont should find it necessary to join Great Britain or Congress, they would Positively join the former." After two years of frustrating experiences Allen was still able, so he thought, to give assurances Vermont would not join the union (Levi Allen to Henry Dundas, Ranelagh, 9 Aug. 1791, PRO: CO 42/85, f. 371-2, endorsed as received 10 Aug. 1791). After arranging for transmission of funds and a secret channel of communication as suggested by Colonel John Graves Simcoe, Allen landed at Boston, identified himself to Dr. A. A. Peters as "Lewis Alden," drew on the Rev. Samuel Peters for £100 according to the arrangement, and then departed for Vermont. Three days later he learned to his "great mortification" that the state had become a part of the United States (Samuel Peters to Grenville, 19 Nov. 1791, PRO: CO 42/88, f. 161; Peters' copy of the letter from "Lewis Alden" dated at Boston, 15 Oct. 1791, endorsed as received 20 Nov. 1791, demonstrates the manner in which disaffected persons in the United States could communicate with the British ministry promptly and in almost perfect security; see also Levi Allen to [Henry Dundas], 27 Nov. 1791, same, f. 383).

ii. Lord Dorchester
to Major George Beckwith

SIR   Quebec, 27th June, 1790

An appearance of a War with Spain rendering it improbable that I shall obtain leave of absence from my government this season, I wish to take the earliest opportunity, after the receipt of this information, to return thanks for the polite and very obliging manner, in which the approbation of my passing through the United States in my way to Europe has been intimated.

You will therefore proceed to New York for this purpose.

You will at the same time express my hope, that neither the appearance of a war with Spain, nor its actually taking place, will make any alteration in the good disposition of the United States to establish a firm friendship and Alliance with Great Britain to the Mutual advantage of both Countries; I am persuaded it can make none on the part of Great Britain, whose liberal treatment of the United States in point of Commerce sufficiently evinces her friendly disposition, notwithstanding the non execution of the Treaty on their part, which, and various misrepresentations I have always attributed to an unsettled state of their government, and of the minds of the multitude, influenced perhaps by a power not very cordial even to the United States.

I hear with satisfaction that some steps towards an amicable

System have been commenced at home, through the Agency of Mr. Morris, though not yet so explicit and formal as the case may require.

The rights asserted by Spain being to the exclusion of all the world, as well the United States, as all the European Powers, I think the interests of the United States, in case of a war, may be more effectually served by a junction with Great Britain, than otherwise.

I have heard with concern of hostilities committed on the Ohio, by some Indians of that District, at the instigation of some Southern tribes, supposed to be under the influence of Spain.

I have from my arrival in this Country endeavoured to preserve peace, and to extend it to friends and neighbours, though no stranger to the language held in the North Western Territory, nor that of Captain Hart on Lake Erie, and the schemes thrown out by Hendrick Wemple to the Six Nations, which, and all such discourses, I consider as the effusions of sanguine minds, ill digested and without authority.

You may communicate these sentiments, as occasion may require, and your discretion direct. I am with regard,

DORCHESTER

Tr (PRO: CO 42/68, f. 255); at foot of text: "Copy." This text was enclosed in Dorchester to Grenville, 7 July 1790 (same, f. 252-3). In this letter Dorchester explained why he had given Beckwith two sets of instructions: "He is furnished with Instructions which may clothe him with consequence, and authorize him to speak generally on certain public topics [A]; he has a second set of Instructions for his private guidance only [B]." The instructions designated "A" are those in the above text, which Beckwith showed to Hamilton on the morning of 8 July 1790; those designated "B" and labelled *"Secret"* are set forth in the following document.

iii. Lord Dorchester
to Major George Beckwith

SIR   Quebec, 27th June, 1790.

Besides the objects of your Instructions of this day of a less secret nature, you will also, while in the States, take all opportunities of learning the disposition of their Government, and people, towards peace or war, separately, and unconnected with the affairs of Spain, what difference a war with Spain is likely to produce, whether the States are likely to join with that power, what may be the extent of their views, and whether they expect any assistance from France in her present situation.

There being an appearance of cordiality between the Governor of the Northwestern Territory, and the Spaniards, who are supposed to have appointed a joint conference with the Indians on the Wabash (which is rather extraordinary, seeing what grounds there are to think the Southern Tribes are set on by that power) you will endeavor to find out the nature and object of these supposed negotiations, whether a Spanish Officer or Agent has actually been present at any conference of Mr. St. Clair with those Indians, of what nations and numbers it has been composed, and what has been the result.

A subject of France of the name of de Bon, after making some stay among the Indians on the Missouri having lately passed from Saint Louis des Illinois to Detroit, and thence to Niagara and into the States, you will endeavour to find out what may have been the object of his journey, where he now is, and how he is connected and employed.

You will pay particular attention to the characters of military men, likely to be employed, to all military arrangements, to the increase of their troops, their position and movements, the number and magnitude of deposits of military stores, and provisions, and the arming of any ships for War, to act under Spanish Commissions or otherwise.

Should you find them disposed to be more friendly, you will endeavour to discover what might induce them to unite with us in the event of a war with Spain.

As there may be a difference of opinion concerning the Western Country, and the navigation of the Mississippi, you will be cautious in advancing anything specific on that head, but rather lead them to explain the different lines of policy, each party may have in view, endeavouring to ascertain the extent and importance of the adherents of each particular system. In general you may assert it as your own opinion, that in case of a War with Spain you see no reason why we should not assist in forwarding whatever their interests may require.

You will give me as full and accurate a report as you can on these and all other points, which you may think interesting to the King's American Dominions, or to His service in general.

You will give direct information to His Majesty's Secretary of State of all matters, in which the delay incident to the communication through this province may be prejudicial.

You will remain at New York or in the States as long as you find your presence there may be of advantage to the King's service.

You will inform yourself of the progress made by the Commissioners for settling the affairs of Vermont and on your return you will make it your business to see as many of the leading men of that district as you can, in order to learn their views and dispositions, and what effect the opening their commerce does, or is likely to, produce, on the face of their Country, and on the minds of that people, in case of a War. I am with regard,

DORCHESTER

Tr (PRO: CO 42/68, f. 258-60); at head of text: "*Copy Secret.*" See note to preceding document.

iv. Memorandum from the Secretary of the Treasury to the President

[New York, 8 July 1790]

Memorandum of the Substance of a Communication made on Thursday the Eighth of July 1790 to the Subscriber by Major Beckwith as by direction of Lord Dorchester

Major Beckwith began by stating that Lord Dorchester had directed him to make his acknowlegements for the politeness which had been shewn in respect to the desire he had intimated to pass by New York in his way to England;[1] adding that the prospect of a War between Great Britain and Spain would prevent or defer the execution of his intention in that particular. He next proceeded to observe that Lord Dorchester had been informed of a negotiation commenced on the other side of the water through the Agency of Mr. Morris;[1] mentioning as the Subscriber understood principally by way of proof of Ld. Dorchesters knowlege of the transaction that Mr. Morris had not produced any regular credentials, but merely a letter from the President directed to himself, that some delays had intervened partly on account of Mr. Morris's absence on a trip to Holland as was understood and that it was not improbable those delays and some other circumstances may have impressed Mr. Morris with an idea of backwardness on the part of the British Ministry. That his Lordship however had directed him to say that an inference of this sort would not in his opinion be well founded as he had reason to believe that the Cabinet of Great Britain entertained a disposition not only towards a friendly intercourse but towards an alliance with the United States. Major Beckwith then proceeded to speak of the particular cause of the expected rupture between Spain and Britain observing that it was one in which all Commercial nations must be supposed to favour the views of G. Britain. That it was therefore presumed, should a war take place, that the U States would find it to be their interest to take part with Great Britain rather than with Spain.[1]

Major Beckwith afterwards mentioned that Lord Dorchester had heared with great concern of some depredations committed by some Indians on our Western frontier.[1] That he wished it to be believed that nothing of this kind had received the least countenance from him. That on the contrary he had taken every proper opportunity of inculcating upon the Indians a pacific disposition towards us; and that as soon as he had heared of the outrages lately committed he had sent a message to endeavour to prevent them. That his Lordship had understood that the Indians alluded to were a banditti composed chiefly or in great part of Creeks or Cherokees over whom he had no influence; intimating at the same time that these tribes were supposed to be in connection with the Spaniards.

He stated in the next place that his Lordship had been informed that a Captain Hart in our service and a Mr. Wemble and indeed some persons in the Treaty at Fort Harmar had thrown out[1] menaces with regard to the Posts on the Frontier and had otherwise held very intemperate language; which however his Lordship considered rather as effusions of individual feelings than as the effects of any instructions from authority.

Major Beckwith concluded with producing a letter signed Dorchester; which letter contained ideas similar to those he had expressed though in more guarded terms and without any allusion to instructions from the British Cabinet. This letter it is now recollected hints at the non execution of the treaty of peace on our part.[1]

On the Subscriber remarking the circumstance that this letter seemed to speak only the sentiments of his Lordship Major Beckwith replied that whatever reasons there might be for that course of proceeding in the present stage of the business, it was to be presumed that his Lordship knew too well the consequence of such a step to have taken it without a previous knowlege of the intentions of the Cabinet.

MS (DLC: Washington Papers); undated and unsigned (possibly through haste or oversight since Hamilton, in whose hand it is written, refers to himself as the "Subscriber"), but written before or soon after Hamilton's consultation with the President on 8 July 1790.

The fact that Beckwith, contrary to habit, made no report to Dorchester of this conversation suggests that in showing the letter of instructions to Hamilton he may have expected—as he did on a later occasion—that the letter itself would be shown to the President. Comparison of this text with that of Dorchester to Beckwith of 27 June 1790 indicates a parallel in the sequence of topics and occasionally in phraseology, one of these striking similarities occurring in the allusion to the letter. In this passage Hamilton almost casually "recollected" what had been said about the treaty. Dorchester's blunt reference to "the non execution of the Treaty on their part" was scarcely the hint that Hamilton called it, but it seems strange that the Secretary of the Treasury should have been so vague in recollection about the substantive fact when his own allusion to this passage matches Dorchester's words almost exactly. The parallels between the two texts—except for the obviously contrived distortions—would seem to remove all doubt that Hamilton had Dorchester's letter before him when he prepared his own memorandum.

[1] Compare phraseology with that in Dorchester's less secret letter of instructions of 27 June 1790.

v. Report by the Secretary of the Treasury to the President

[New York, 15 July 1790]

In my second interview with Major Beckwith which was on Thursday the 22d.[1] instant I spoke to him nearly as follows

I have made the proper use of what you said to me at our last interview.

As to what regards the objects of a general nature mentioned by you, though your authority for the purpose from Lord Dorchester is out of question, and though I presume from his Lordship's station and character and the knowlege he appears to have of what is passing on the other side of the water with regard to Mr. Morris, that the Step he has taken through you is conformable to the views of your Cabinet and not without its sanction; yet you are no doubt sensible that the business presents itself in a shape, which does not give the proper authenticity to that fact, and is wholly without formality. You must also be sensible that there is a material difference between your situation and that of Mr. Morris. His Credentials though not formal proceed from the proper source. Your's are neither formal nor authoritative.

This state of things will of course operate in what I am going to say on the subject.

As to what relates to friendship between Great Britain and the United States, I conceive myself warranted in declaring that there is in this country a sincere disposition to concur in obviating with candor and fairness all ground of misunderstanding which may now exist, in reference to the execution of the late Treaty of Peace and in laying the foundation of future good understanding by establishing liberal terms of commercial intercourse.

As to alliance; this opens a wide field. The thing is susceptible of a vast variety of forms. 'Tis not possible to judge what would be proper or what could be done unless points were brought into view. If you are in a condition to mention particulars, it may afford better ground of conversation.

I stopped here for an answer.

Major Beckwith replied that he could say nothing more particular than he had already done.

That being the case (continued I) I can only say that the thing is in too general a form to admit of a judgment of what may be eventually admissible or practicable. If the subject shall hereafter present itself to discussion in an authentic and proper shape, I have no doubt we shall be ready to converse freely upon it: And you will naturally conclude that we shall be disposed to pursue whatever shall appear under all circumstances to be our interest as far as may consist with our honor. At present I would not mean either to raise or repress expectation.

Major Beckwith seemed to admit that as things were circumstanced nothing explicit could be expected and went on to make some observations which I understood as having for object to sound whether there existed any connection between Spain and us and whether the questions with regard to the Mississippi were settled.

Perceiving this I thought it better in a matter which was no secret to avoid an appearance of Mystery and to declare without hesitation, as I did—

"That there was no particular connection between Spain and the U States within my knowlege, and that it was a matter of public notoriety that the questions alluded to were still unadjusted."

The rest of our conversation consisted chiefly of assurances on my part that the menaces which had been mentioned by him as having been thrown out by some individuals with regard to the Western posts were unauthorised, proceeding probably from a degree of irritation, which the detention of the posts had produced in the minds of many—and of a repetition on his part of the assurances which he had before given of Lord Dorchesters disposition to discourage Indian Outrages.

Something was said respecting the probable course of military operations in case of war between Britain and Spain which Major Beckwith supposed would be directed towards South America alleging however that this was mere conjecture on his part. I hinted cautiously our dislike of an enterprise on New Orleans.

MS (DLC: Washington Papers); undated (see note 1) and quite likely the report was made on another day than that on which the interview took place; in Hamilton's hand. Dft (DLC: Hamilton Papers); on verso of final leaf, Hamilton appended the note which is quoted and discussed above (see p. 52, note 104).

1 On the date given here (which may indicate that Hamilton's memorandum was written on or after 22 July), see p. 50-51, notes 101-103, also note to the following document.

vi. Report by Major George Beckwith to Lord Dorchester on Conversations with the Secretary of the Treasury

[New York, 15 July 1790]

[1]

Supposed 7 [Alexander Hamilton].—I have communicated to the President, the subjects, on which we have conversed; however authoritative they may be on your part, in so far as respects Lord Dorchester, and however evident it is to me that His Lordship is apprized by your Cabinet of Mr. Morris's Agency, yet you must be sensible, that official formality is wanting, but it is conceived that His Lordship would not have gone the length he has, without being acquainted with the general views of your administration, as they respect this Country.

Having premised this, I feel warranted to assure you that there is the most sincere good disposition on the part of the Government here to go into the consideration of all matters unsettled between us and Great Britain, in order to effect a perfect understanding between the two countries, and to lay the foundation for future amity; this, particularly as it respects commercial objects, we view as conducive to our interest.

In the present stage of this business, it is difficult to say much on the subject of a Treaty of Alliance; Your rupture with Spain, if it takes place, opens a very wide political field; thus much I can say, we are perfectly unconnected with Spain, have even some points unadjusted with that Court, and are prepared to go into the consideration of the subject.

The Speeches or declarations of any person whatever in the Indian Country, or to the Westward, suggesting hostile ideas respecting the forts, are not authorized by this government.

Lord Dorchester's conduct with respect to the Indians is held by us to be a strong proof of His Lordship's dispositions to promote harmony and friendship.

It appears to me that, from the nature of our Government, it would be mutually advantageous, if this negotiation could be carried on at our seat of Government, as it would produce dispatch and obviate misconception. . . .¹

[2]

Secret

Supposed 7.—There is one thing more I wish to mention to you; I do it altogether as from one gentleman to another, and I trust it will be so considered.

I have decided on doing it at this time from the possibility of my not having it in my power to come to such an explanation hereafter.

If it shall be judged proper to proceed on this business by the sending or appointing a proper person to come to this country to negotiate on the spot, whoever shall then be our Secretary of State, will be the person in whose department such negotiation must originate, and he will be the channel of communication with the President; in the turn of such affairs the most minute circumstances, mere trifles, give a favorable bias or otherwise to the whole. The President's mind I can declare to be perfectly dispassionate on this subject. Mr. Jefferson our present Secretary of State is I am persuaded a gentleman of honor, and zealously desirous of promoting those objects, which the nature of his duty call for, and the interests of his country may require, but from some opinions which he has given respecting Your government, and possible predilections elsewhere, there may be difficulties which may possibly frustrate the whole, and which might be readily explained away. I shall certainly know the progress of the negotiation from the president from day to day, but what I come to the present explanation for is this, that in case any such difficulties should occur, I should wish to know them, in order that I may be sure they are clearly understood, and candidly examined; if none take place the business will of course go on in the regular official channel.

———————

[George Beckwith:] "I cannot form any opinion upon the Manner, in which our administration may proceed in the business you mention, I shall make proper use you may depend on it of what you have said, nor shall it ever be brought by me in a way to convey an impression different from the causes which occasioned it."²

[Alexander Hamilton:] "I am persuaded it will not, it is not necessary for me to say, that in this I am steadily following up, what I have long considered to be the essential interest of this country; on this point I have already so fully explained my ideas, that a repetition is needless."[2]

Tr (PRO: CO 42/69, f. 16-25); undated, but beyond doubt the conversation took place on 15 July 1790. This is indicated both by Beckwith's allusion to the date in a subsequent interview with Hamilton and by his affixing the date to the extract discussed below. The two numbered parts of the above report were enclosures No. 1 and No. 2 in Dorchester's dispatch No. 48 to Grenville of 25 Sep. 1790, in which the Governor General said that Beckwith's report had been received on 5 Aug. 1790 (PRO: CO 42/69, f.14, endorsed as received 4 Nov. 1790). The two enclosures reported a single conversation between Beckwith and Hamilton on the date given. Reasons of delicacy respecting the appropriate channel for making such an extraordinary communication as that contained in enclosure No. 2 and also the special requirement of secrecy caused the report of the conversation to be separated into two parts. As indicated above, p. 52-4, that part of the conversation in the second enclosure and indeed some remarks of that in the first were not reported by Hamilton to the President.

On 5 Aug. 1790 Beckwith wrote directly to Grenville transmitting several enclosures, of which the first was an extract identified by the agent as follows: "No. 1. contains communications made to me by the Gentleman high in office, with whom I am in the regular habits of intercourse." This extract contains no allusion to that part of the conversation in enclosure No. 2 discussed above and omits the first and concluding paragraphs of enclosure No. 1. The text as sent to Grenville reads:

"Extract   New York July 15th. 1790

I have communicated to the President the subjects on which we have conversed, and feel warranted to assure you that there is the most sincere good disposition on the part of the Government here, to go into the consideration of all matters unsettled between Great Britain

and us, in order to effect a perfect understanding between the Two Countries, and to lay the foundation for future amity; this, particularly as it respects commercial objects, we view as conducive to our interests.

In the present stage of this business, it is difficult to say much on the subject of a treaty of Alliance; your rupture with Spain (if it shall take place) opens a very wide political field; thus much I can say, we are perfectly unconnected with Spain, have even some points unadjusted with that Court, and are prepared to go into the consideration of the question. The speeches or declarations of any persons whatever, in the Indian Country or to the Westward, suggesting hostile ideas respecting the Forts, are not authorised by this Government.

Lord Dorchester's conduct with respect to the Indians, is held by us to be a strong proof of his Lordship's dispositions to promote harmony and friendship" (PRO: FO 4/12, f. 9-12; endorsed as received 14 Sep. 1790).

Clearly Beckwith intended to let his immediate superior, Lord Dorchester, transmit Hamilton's remarkable suggestion about the manner and place of conducting negotiations.

[1] Following this point in enclosure No. 1, Beckwith reported upon his conversations with William Samuel Johnson, Thomas Scott, and a merchant of New York identified as "Mr. McCormick."

[2] Quotation marks in MS. The first of these two concluding paragraphs is set off by lines in the MS; although unidentified, it is clearly Beckwith's assurance to Hamilton. It is equally obvious that the final paragraph, also unidentified, is Hamilton's response. In reporting a dialogue Beckwith normally identified his own questions or remarks by putting them in quotation marks. In this case he inadvertently did the same for Hamilton's answer.

vii. Secretary of the Treasury to the President

Sir   New York Sepr. 30. 1790

I had lately a visit from a *certain Gentleman* the sole object of which was to make some observations of a delicate nature, concerning *another Gentleman* employed on a *particular errand*; which, as they were doubtless intended for your ear, and (such as they are) ought to be known to you, it is of course my duty to communicate.

He began (in a manner somewhat embarrassed which betrayed rather more than he seemed to intend to discover) by telling me that in *different companies* where he had happened to be, *in this City* (a circumstance by the way very unlikely) he had heared it mentioned that that *other Gentleman* was upon terms of very great intimacy with the representative of a certain Court at the one where *he* was employed and with the head of the party opposed to the Minister; and he proceeded to say, that if there were any symptoms of backwardness or coolness in the Minister, it had occurred to him that they might possibly be occasioned by such *an intimacy*; that he had no intimation however of this being the case, and that the idea suggested by him was mere matter of conjecture; that he did not even know it as a fact that the intimacy subsisted. But if this should be the case (said he) you will readily imagine that it cannot be calculated to inspire confidence or facilitate free communication. It would not be surprising, if a very close connection with the representative of another power should beget doubts and reserves; or if a very familiar intercourse with the head of the opposition should occasion prejudice and distance. Man, after all, is but man; and though the Minister has a great mind, and is as little likely as most men to entertain illiberal distrusts or jealousies; yet there is no saying what might be the effect of such conduct upon him. It is hardly possible not to have some diffidence of those, who seem to be very closely united with our political or personal enemies or rivals. At any rate, such an intimacy, if it exists, can do no good, may do some harm.

This, as far as I recollect was the substance of what he said. My answer was nearly as follows—

I have never heared a syllable Sir, about the matter you mention. It appears to me however very possible that an intimacy with both the persons you mention may exist: With the first, because the situation of the parties had naturally produced such an intimacy, while both were in this Country; and to have dropped and avoided it there would not have been without difficulty, on the score of politeness, and would have worn an extraordinary and mysterious aspect: With the last, from the patronage of American affairs, which is understood to have been uniformly the part of that Gentleman, and in some degree, from a similarity of dispositions and characters; both brilliant men, men of wit and genius; both fond of the pleasures of society. It is to be hoped that appearances, which admit of so easy a solution will not prove an obstacle to any thing which mutual interest dictates. It is impossible that there can be any thing wrong.

He replied that he certainly had no idea that there could be any thing wrong; but that as trifles often mar great affairs he thought it best to impart to me his conjecture, that such use might be made of it as should be thought adviseable.

I have the honor to be with the most perfect respect & truest attachment Sir Your Most Obedt & humble servt,

A HAMILTON

PS The letters herewith were through hurry omitted in my dispatch of yesterday.

RC (DLC: Washington Papers); MS slightly mutilated, affecting a few words and parts of words, which have been supplied from Tr (DLC: Hamilton Papers).

The assertion that A CERTAIN GENTLEMAN (Major George Beckwith) sought the interview described above for the sole object of making delicate observations about ANOTHER GENTLEMAN (Gouverneur Morris) is flatly contradicted by Beckwith's account of the conversation and of another that followed shortly thereafter, in both of which other topics not disclosed to Washington were discussed (see following document and its note). When Washington accepted this letter at face value but discounted its allegations, Hamilton replied in words that seem a tacit admission of frustration in the attempt to discredit Morris: "It is certainly very possible," he wrote to the President, "that motives different from the one avowed, may have produced a certain communication; and in matters of such a nature, it is not only allowable, but the dictate of prudence, to receive suggestions with peculiar caution." In the same letter Hamilton went on to say: "A certain Gentleman [Beckwith], who called on me to day, informed me, that a Packet had sailed the 16 of August for Quebec, in which went passenger General Clarke. He added that the rumour in England was that Sir Guy Carleton was to return in her. *He made no other communication*" (Hamilton to Washington, 17 Oct. 1790, Syrett, *Hamilton*, VII, 118-19; italics supplied). The rumor of Dorchester's return seems incredible. No other documentary evidence of the existence of such a rumor has been found. Dorchester had received specific orders not to return because of the war crisis, and this fact had been reported to Washington by Hamilton in July. Beckwith in his account of the conversation makes no mention of such a rumor. And both Beckwith and Hamilton thought war likely; as Beckwith said in their interview that day: "We have now a probability of a Spanish War, and a possibility of a French one." The reasons for Dorchester's remaining in Canada must, therefore, have appeared to Beckwith even more compelling and urgent in mid-October than in mid-July. It is difficult to believe that he would have given credit to such a dubious report himself, much more so that he would have passed it on as the principal communication to be made to a high officer in government. Hamilton's statement about the rumor can be given little if any credence, a fact unimportant in itself save as it reflects a persistent pattern.

But in asserting that Beckwith made no other communication and in leading Washington to suppose that nothing else was discussed, Hamilton did indubitable violence to the truth. The conversation with Beckwith on that day was, in fact, a very important one in which matters of policy of the highest importance were canvassed. Beckwith reported it both to Dorchester and to Grenville, and in the dispatch to the former he gave evidence that his visit to Hamilton was prompted by the arrival of the English packet the day before with news causing "Things [to] wear the appearance of war." To the Secretary for Home Affairs, who became Baron Grenville before the letter arrived, Beckwith wrote: "Upon the present occasion when the direct navigation from Quebec is nearly closed for this season, I have the honor to transmit to you the substance of a late conversation with the gentleman in high office in this country, to whom I am in the usual habits of addressing myself; it will shew in a narrow compass some of the leading objects wished for by the States, and give an insight into the sentiments of their administration as they regard their political connection with France." In this interview Hamilton again urged that the British West Indies be opened to Americans "under certain limitations at the commencement of a war." He told Beckwith that, despite some exceptions, there was on the whole no foundation for the idea that Indian hostility in the Northwest was receiving British encouragement—an idea that others in the administration did not reject so emphatically. However, Hamilton went on, "in the critical state of the two countries, if I may be permitted to say it, prudence would dictate the most pointed instructions to your Officers at Detroit." Returning to his old theme, he argued that the friendship of the United States was not unimportant to Great Britain even then and that it would "become infinitely more so" in future. In response to Beckwith's question about American possession of New Orleans, he declared that the rapid increase of population in the West rendered it certain that this outlet would have to be acquired "in a very short space of time, whatever individual interests may be opposed to it." On the

crucial subject of relations with France Hamilton's views, carefully expressed as "merely the opinions of an individual," were unequivocal: "it does not appear to me from the present condition of things, that we shall consider it to be encumbent upon us, to take any part with France in a contest in which she is altogether an auxiliary, it will be for our consideration whether we ought not to avail ourselves of the period in which Spain shall be involved in a war, to secure those points which are in contest between us and that power; things may change, but as they are circumstanced at present, we are in my opinion perfectly at liberty to follow up our own interest, and certain matters have occurred since the peace, which leave us altogether free with respect to France *even if she should go to war as a principal*: I think it proper also on this occasion to declare positively and directly, that no treaty, stipulation, or agreement of any sort subsists between us and France, excepting the public printed treaty universally known" (italicized passage is underscored in MS). Hamilton went on to assure Beckwith that the federal courts could be relied upon to uphold treaty provisions as against state laws that placed obstacles between British creditors and their American debtors—that indeed "nothing but an insurrection in opposition to their decisions can in future prevent the regular and usual course of justice." He declared it as his opinion that the government gained "daily strength and consistence in the public mind," that the census would show a population of at least three millions and a half, and finally that, looking forward to what the United States would become in a few years time, "it would be an act of wisdom in the Minister of Great Britain to attach and connect the States upon political as well as commercial considerations."

In a literal sense most of the "communication" in this conversation was that of Hamilton, though Beckwith did suggest that it would "be greatly for the benefit of your Western territory if you were to conclude a just and honorable peace with the savages within your limits." He also expressed the hope —repeating Dorchester's instructions— that the probability of war would not interrupt tranquil relations between the two countries. And it was he who asked the pointed questions. The interview, held on the eve of the removal of the national government from New York to Philadelphia, seemed intended in its forthright questions and candid answers to place "in a narrow compass some of the leading objects" toward which Hamilton had been so urgently and consistently pressing. As proved by one of the three texts of Beckwith's report of it, the conversation took place at "New York October 17th. 1790"—the very day the Secretary of the Treasury reported to the President that the "certain Gentleman" had communicated nothing more than, as it seems now, an idle and incredible rumor.

Beckwith's final question in the exchange that Hamilton thus untruthfully concealed from Washington was this: "You are going to remove in a few days to Philadelphia; if any thing should happen that I might wish to communicate to you, can you point out a mode of my doing it by letter?" The invitation to engage in the sort of clandestine correspondence that Beckwith had carried on with informers, double agents, and traitors during the war involved a risk that Hamilton dared not take. His answer symbolizes the whole enterprise in duplicity: "That," declared Hamil-

ton, "would be precarious, there seems a necessity for my seeing you." There was nothing for Beckwith to do but follow the government and take up residence in Philadelphia, where the pattern of deception would continue to manifest its indubitable characteristics.

The three texts of Beckwith's report of this conversation are the following: (1) Beckwith to Grenville, 3 Nov. 1790, enclosing the undated report, PRO: FO 4/12, f. 17-22, endorsed as received 6 Dec. 1790. (2) Duplicate of Beckwith to Grenville, 3 Nov. 1790, enclosing report bearing date "New York October 17th. 1790," PRO: CO 42/21, f. 299-303. (3) Copy of Beckwith's report as enclosed in Dorchester to Grenville, 20 Nov. 1790, PRO: CO 42/72, f. 147 (the covering letter, indicating that Dorchester received the report on 17 Nov. 1790), f. 149-54, with endorsement showing receipt of the report at Whitehall on 30 Dec. 1790. Only the second of these texts gives the date of the conversation between Hamilton and Beckwith and only the third identifies Hamilton with the figure 7. The third also contains some matter not in the other two.

viii. Extract of Report by Major George Beckwith on Conversation with the Secretary of the Treasury

[New York, before 30 Sep. 1790]

. . . 7. [Alexander Hamilton] 23. [Gouverneur Morris] is a man of capacity, but apt at particular times to give himself up too much to the impressions of his own mind.

From the Duke of Leeds's reply to 23.'s first application I confess I did not think favorably of the prospect, although it was far from being conclusive. The June packet brought us accounts of his interviews with Mr. Pitt, and from 23.'s own detail of what passed, there was a something in his conduct on that occasion, which I confess I do not altogether approve.

[Beckwith] "It strikes me as possible that 23. has been occasionally out of England, has he been in France?"

[Hamilton] Not that I know of, and if 23. has cultivated an intimacy with the Ministers of any other power in Europe, or has caused suspicion on that ground with respect to France, or elsewhere, he has had no authority, for so doing; it occurs to me, that he was very intimate with Monsr. de La Luzerne the Ambassador of France now in London, when he was Minister in this country, possibly from that circumstance he may have been more frequently there, than prudence ought to have dictated, and the knowledge of this circumstance may have produced a greater reserve on the part of Your administration; these ideas strike me, although I have no grounds to go upon.

[Beckwith] "Do you wish to have a West India Island?"

[Hamilton] I answer without hesitation No, we do not, it is not in our contemplation. We wish the liberty of trading in that quarter, at least this is decidedly my own opinion, we should consider the Sovereignty of a West India island as a burthen. Our territories are already very extensive, and I can assure you, the idea of having possessions further to the northward than our present boundaries would be esteemed an incumbrance, *with an exception to the Forts*. On that score therefore I cannot foresee any solid grounds for a national difference with you; to the southward the case is very different. *We look forward to procuring the means of an export for our western country, and we must have it.* We cannot suffer the navigation of the Mississippi to remain long in its present state. That country is at this moment ready to open it if they met with the smallest encouragement, and undoubtedly we look forward to the possession of New Orleans.

[Beckwith] "Since my arrival here I have made it a point to preserve the strictest silence with respect to (23) yet I have more than once had occasion to hear his name mentioned by his relations and their acquaintances; it came out in their conversations that 23 is greatly liked in London, that he is frequently with the French Ambassador Monsieur de la Luzerne, and with Mr. Fox, who had expressed himself to be greatly pleased with his character and company."

[Hamilton] Yes, it is so reported; I believe it in some measure to be true; I am the more inclined to be of this way of thinking from extracts of letters, which I have seen of 23., in which he throws out, that such and such were Mr. Fox's opinions on particular subjects, and from the former intimacy, which subsisted here between 23 and Monsieur de la Luzerne, as well as from Mr. Fox's line of politics during the war, his general character, and from my knowledge of 23 himself.

I do not question this gentleman's sincerity in following up those objects committed to his charge, but to deal frankly with you, I have some doubts of his prudence; this is the point in which he is deficient, for in other respects he is a man of great genius, liable however to be occasionally influenced by his fancy, which sometimes outruns his discretion.

[Beckwith] "Mr. Fox is a very able man, very generally respected, and his character as a statesman is known in the world; but professing every possible respect for Mr. Fox, and for Mr. de la Luzerne likewise, it is for your consideration, how far a gentleman in 23. situation ought to form intimacies with persons in public political situations, excepting they are in administration."

[Hamilton] I am quite of your opinion, and this amongst other causes led me to remark, that it is greatly desirable, that this negotiation should be transferred to our seat of Government. However we have no reason on the whole to question Mr. Pitt's good dispositions towards us, on the contrary he seemed personally disposed to grant us more, than other members of your Cabinet thought advisable for your general commercial interests.

Tr (PRO: CO 42/72, f. 61-8); this was enclosure A in Dorchester to Grenville, 10 Nov. 1790, which the Governor General had received on 27 Oct. 1790; enclosure B was another conversation between Beckwith and Hamilton, among others, received on 30 Nov. 1790 (f. 59-60, 69-72; endorsed as received at Whitehall, 30 Dec. 1790). Both conversations with Hamilton evidently took place before 30 Sep. 1790—the first certainly did—when Hamilton reported to Washington that Beckwith had sought the interview for the sole purpose of commenting on Gouverneur Morris. See preceding document; that part of the interview with Hamilton in enclosure B is printed in Syrett, *Hamilton*, VII, 73-4, under the conjectural date 26-30 Sep. 1790. In this second conversation, which of course was not reported to Washington, Hamilton set forth his views of the interests of England and of the United States, discussed the party divisions existing in the country according to pro-English or pro-French sympathies, and concluded: "We consider ourselves perfectly at liberty to act with respect to Spain in any way most conducive to our interests, even to the going to war with that power, if we shall think it advisable to join you."

Symbols and Abbreviations

The editorial apparatus in this volume is identical with that of *The Papers of Thomas Jefferson*. Citations unaccompanied by title to volume numbers and to letters written to or received by Jefferson (here alluded to in notes as TJ) are to be understood as referring to the series in which the present work originated. The symbols for archival and library repositories mentioned in the notes to this volume are as follows:

DLC: The Library of Congress
DNA: The National Archives
   RG 59: Records of the Department of State
      DD: Diplomatic Dispatches
      MLR: Miscellaneous Letters Received
      PCC: Papers of the Continental Congress
      SDC: State Department Correspondence
MHi: Massachusetts Historical Society
NN: New York Public Library
NNC: Columbia University Library
NjP: Princeton University Library
PRO: The Public Record Office, London
      CO: Records of the Colonial Office
      FO: Records of the Foreign Office
      AO: Records of the Audit Office
      PMG: Records of the Paymaster General

The following symbols describe various kinds of original manuscripts:

Dft: Draft
RC: Recipient's copy
PrC: Press copy
FC: Retained file copy
Tr: Transcript or contemporary copy

All save the last two types of documents are to be understood as being in the hand of the author—the last two as in the hand of someone other than the author—unless otherwise stated.

Abbreviated titles employed in this volume are the following:

Bemis, *Jay's Treaty*: Samuel Flagg Bemis, *Jay's Treaty A Study in Commerce and Diplomacy* (revised edition, New Haven, 1962)

Brymner's *Report*: Douglas Brymner, *Report on Canadian Archives ... 1890* (Ottawa, 1891)

Malone, *Jefferson*: Dumas Malone, *Jefferson and his Time*, 3 vols. (Boston, 1948-1962)

Miller, *Hamilton*: John C. Miller, *Alexander Hamilton Portrait in Paradox* (New York, 1959)

Syrett, *Hamilton*: Harold C. Syrett, Editor, and Jacob E. Cooke, Associate Editor, *The Papers of Alexander Hamilton* (New York, 1961—)

Other abbreviations:

AHR: *American Historical Review*
MAH: *Magazine of American History*
PMHB: *Pennsylvania Magazine of History and Biography*
WMQ: *William and Mary Quarterly*

SJL and SJPL refer respectively to Thomas Jefferson's Summary Journal of Letters and Summary Journal of Public Letters.

Index

14.95